Changing Perspectives in
Latin American Studies:
Insights from Six Disciplines

Contributors LOURDES ARIZPE S.
ALBERT FISHLOW
TULIO HALPERÍN DONGHI
ALEJANDRO PORTES
SAÚL SOSNOWSKI
ARTURO VALENZUELA

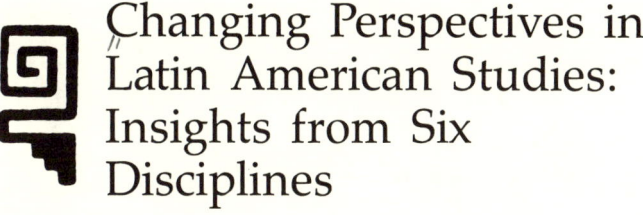
Changing Perspectives in Latin American Studies: Insights from Six Disciplines

Edited by CHRISTOPHER MITCHELL

WITHDRAWN

Stanford University Press
Stanford, California ▪ 1988

Stanford University Press
Stanford, California
© 1988 by the Board of Trustees of the
Leland Stanford Junior University
Printed in the United States of America

CIP data appear at the end of the book

In memory of
Kalman H. Silvert
1921–1976

Preface

This book sets out to review the present state of Latin American studies, a field covering segments of many scholarly disciplines. Our essays grew from the work of the 2,000-member Latin American Studies Association (LASA), which includes individuals from forty-eight nations and more than fifty fields of study. Since its founding in 1966, LASA has sought to advance inter-American scholarship combining the highest quality with broad social awareness. As we prepared for the association's 12th International Congress, held in April 1985 in Albuquerque, New Mexico, the Congress Program Committee hoped to design synthesizing sessions that would address widely shared scholarly concerns. With this goal in mind, the committee requested original papers from six outstanding scholars, evaluating the current situation and future prospects of key disciplines in Latin American research. At each of the near-plenary Congress sessions where these papers were presented, several discussants helped to shape the disciplinary debate.

As the Albuquerque LASA meeting progressed, it became clear that the "State-of-the-Disciplines" papers might afford, with modest editorial changes, a well-integrated, up-to-date overview of hemispheric studies. The six disciplinary critiques, we reasoned, might make both a broader and more lasting scholarly contribution if they were published together as a book. Contributors were energetic in responding to editorial suggestions, in a process of revision that concluded in April 1987. We are grateful to several LASA colleagues, including Werner Baer, Abraham F. Lowenthal, and Kenneth Maxwell, who especially encouraged this editorial project, and to Jan Hanvik and Sueann Caulfield of New York University, who assisted in preparing the manuscript. Helene Anderson and Katherine Pettus skillfully translated Saúl Sosnowski's complex Spanish text, conveying faithfully its author's intertwining of content and form.

In addition to the six contributors of essays, many people helped the disciplinary review project in important ways. The 1985 LASA Program Committee worked long, patiently, and expertly, with special concern for the overview panels. Committee members included Werner Baer (economics), Eliana Rivero (literature), Ina Rosenthal-Urey (anthropology), and Joseph Tulchin (history); I chaired the committee and focused on issues in political science. Four of the review panels were chaired by the Program Committee member from the discipline concerned.

Discussants on the six panels helped our authors to refine the arguments presented here, not all of which (of course) they would agree with. These commentators were: Heraclio Bonilla and Thomas Skidmore (history); Richard Fagen, Daniel H. Levine, and Barbara Stallings (political science); Shane Hunt and Rosemary Thorp (economics); Susan Eckstein, Louis Wolf Goodman, and J. Samuel Valenzuela (sociology); Richard N. Adams, Susan C. Bourque, María Patricia Fernández-Kelly, Emilio F. Morán, and Helen I. Safa (anthropology); and Efraín Barradas, Elizabeth Garrels, René Jara, and Nils Larsson (literature).

The Latin American Studies Association's officers and staff afforded assistance and backing to the Program Committee, which made these panels and nearly 150 additional meetings possible in Albuquerque. The committee enjoyed the colleagueship and vigorous support of three LASA presidents: Jorge Domínguez, Helen Safa, and Wayne Cornelius. LASA Executive Director Richard Sinkin and his assistant Jana Greenlief dealt cheerfully with problems both substantive and procedural. Our host institution, the University of New Mexico, was both hospitable and efficient; most particularly, the collaboration of Theo Crevenna, Gilbert Merkx, and UNM President Tom Farer aided our efforts greatly.

The Program Committee's work was based at New York University's Center for Latin American and Caribbean Studies, and both NYU and its staff have our gratitude. The NYU Faculty of Arts and Science provided funding for staff and supplies; Center Research Assistants Teresa Bell and Claire Johnston helped keep correspondence straight; George Sharrard was a tireless adviser in the use of computers. Most particularly, Deborah Truhan coordinated the entire program preparation with patience, good humor, and a mature understanding of our hemisphere and its scholarship.

C.M.

Contents

Introduction   1
    CHRISTOPHER MITCHELL

1 The State of Latin American History   13
    TULIO HALPERÍN DONGHI

2 Political Science and the Study of Latin America   63
    ARTURO VALENZUELA

3 The State of Latin American Economics   87
    ALBERT FISHLOW

4 Latin American Sociology in the Mid-1980's: Learning from Hard Experience   121
    ALEJANDRO PORTES

5 Anthropology in Latin America: Old Boundaries, New Contexts   143
    LOURDES ARIZPE S.

6 Spanish-American Literary Criticism: The State of the Art   163
    SAÚL SOSNOWSKI

    Notes   185   Index   229

The Authors

LOURDES ARIZPE S. is Director of Mexico's Museo Nacional de Culturas Populares and a researcher at El Colegio de México.

ALBERT FISHLOW is Professor of Economics at the University of California at Berkeley.

TULIO HALPERÍN DONGHI is Professor of History at the University of California at Berkeley.

CHRISTOPHER MITCHELL is Associate Professor of Politics at New York University.

ALEJANDRO PORTES is Professor of Sociology at the Johns Hopkins University.

SAÚL SOSNOWSKI is Professor of Spanish and Portuguese at the University of Maryland, College Park.

ARTURO VALENZUELA is Professor of Government at Georgetown University.

Changing Perspectives in Latin American Studies: Insights from Six Disciplines

Introduction

CHRISTOPHER MITCHELL

The conclusion of the 1980's is an appropriate moment for scholars of Latin American societies to stand back and assess their work, reviewing what they and fellow researchers have attempted and accomplished during the past two-and-one-half decades. Since the contemporary period in Latin American studies began during the 1960's, half a dozen major disciplines have had opportunities to sharpen their concepts and broaden their coverage of hemispheric affairs. Two and sometimes three scholarly "generations" have matured during this period; links between Latin American and North American social scientists have been created and (with difficulty) maintained; experience has built up in using varied forms of organization and finance for the gathering of new knowledge. As many Latin American societies "reopen" under civilian democratic rule, hemispheric scholarship may now face a constructive challenge as profound as the wrenching political and economic strains it bore throughout the past two decades.

This book undertakes just such a review and evaluation of contemporary Latin American studies. Accomplished scholars in anthropology, economics, history, literary criticism, political science, and sociology analyze here the current state of their disciplines. They have not tried to prepare an exhaustive catalogue of recent hemispheric scholarship, though a great deal of research is cited and many references furnished. Instead, their approach has been that of the constructive critic. Each author assesses the advances made in the field of study concerned; sometimes these discussions focus on the development of new analytic concepts, and sometimes on distinguished works that have conveyed new data, new insights, or both. The mutual influences among "schools" within several disciplines are explored. The essays point out, as well, those directions of research that have been little traveled, abandoned, or incorporated into new investigative routes during the past two decades. Most contributors, finally, consider which important issues have been slighted or ignored by their disciplines since the mid-1960's.

Other overviews of Latin American studies have, of course, preceded ours since the mid-1960's, and some of those critiques helped to shape Latin American studies even as they assessed the progress of the field. Two of those earlier scholarly compendia, one edited by Charles Wagley (1964) and the other compiled by Manuel Diégues Júnior and Bryce Wood (1967), undertook surveys as broad as we essay in this volume, reviewing multiple analytic streams in at least six disciplines.[1] The inter-American scholarly dialogue outlined in those two works encounters, as I will assert shortly, an interesting juncture, though not a resolution, in the present volume.

Other examinations of the progress of Latin American studies have taken more limited or specialized approaches. Historians possess the most extensive record: Howard Cline edited major writings in English on Latin American historiography in 1967,[2] while Roberto Esquenazi-Mayo and Michael C. Meyer devoted half of their 1971 *tour d'horizon* to historical material, in addition to assessing political science and literature.[3] Wide employment of specialized analytic techniques (in five or six disciplines) was reviewed and advocated by the contributors to Robert S. Byars and Joseph L. Love's co-edited *Quantitative Social Science Research on Latin America* (1973).[4] While these works have lost much direct applicability with the passage of time, they provide a record of how the central tradition and distinct branches of Latin American studies have arrived at their present state.

I will not try in this essay to summarize the reflections of six diverse and subtle analysts on developments within each scholarly specialty. Readers will no doubt enjoy encountering those perceptions firsthand. My discussion centers, rather, on themes that (necessarily) appear only as fragments in the individual essays. What common traits and experiences have been shared by the social sciences dealing with the Western Hemisphere, and how have these six branches of learning influenced one another? What links have existed between research traditions and Latin America's social reality during the past twenty years? In the light of this record, how should we approach setting future priorities for Latin American studies?

Developing Research Traditions in Latin American Studies

Three major common characteristics may be discerned in the recent record of the social sciences focusing on Latin America: marked increases in analytic power and empirical reach; expansion of interdisciplinary links; and development of inter-American connections. Let us consider these one at a time.

Analytic power and empirical reach. The past two decades have witnessed, on balance, a remarkable strengthening of the hemispheric social sciences. Though some of our essayists have moments of pessimism, their consensus is that the analytic lenses through which we view Latin America are notably sharper now, and permit us to survey a wider horizon. A handful of major analytic breakthroughs have placed powerful tools in scholars' hands. The concept of dependency probably leads this short and distinguished list; it provides a set of insights that have reordered many scholars' images of what had seemed familiar social terrain, often introducing completely new priorities for research. The notions of clientelism, the "bureaucratic-authoritarian" state, and internal colonialism have made related and only slightly less significant alterations in many scholars' perceptions of how hemispheric societies work.[5]

Sweeping conceptual revisions must, at the same time, share the stage with empirical achievements in the study of key conjunctures in hemispheric affairs. As Tulio Halperín Donghi notes in this volume, the historical literature on the Mexican revolution has now reached a state of "critical mass," incidentally providing important background to current studies on Mexican politics and public policy. A diverse array of scholars has taken part in the burgeoning of Brazilian studies since the early 1960's, exploring the coalitions and cleavages among social forces that lay behind Brazil's authoritarian government. Original and insightful research also focused on the origins and distortions in Brazil's pattern of economic growth after 1964.[6] Literary critics have shed light on the forces (social and aesthetic) shaping Latin America's post–World War II novelistic "boom." The roots and impact of Peru's post-1968 "Revolutionary Government of the Armed Forces" have been explored in a literature that, for precision and scholarly authority, surpasses the coverage of politics and society in any other mid-sized nation of Latin America.[7]

It would be fatuous to claim that during the past twenty years Latin American studies have moved serenely from strength to strength, without faltering or falling. Recent hemispheric research has had its share of errors and omissions. In political science, key concepts such as dependency and bureaucratic authoritarianism may not have been adequately tested empirically, nor findings duly compared. Institutional factors and the evolution of public policies have received less attention than they deserved, in part because the former were often viewed as the chosen focus of "old-fashioned" research. Historians' explorations of both the Spanish Colonial system and of post-independence politics may provide only the beginnings of understanding; the needed density of historical coverage has only been achieved in relation to a few eras and societies. Literary scholars, in Saúl Sosnowski's view, have often been unproductively divided between social and stylistic critical traditions, and have often put exaggerated stress on the work of a few "superstar" narrators. One might note, at the same time, that hemispheric social science has generally made its own mistakes. It has not, with very few exceptions, served unique, static, or intolerant social interests.

Through our authors' discussions of the net gains made by hemispheric studies, the reader may see—as in a David Hockney photographic collage—the outlines of some of Latin America's principal social structures and problems. Conditions including poverty, class rivalry, political oppression, lack of margin for maneuver in international life, and the struggle for cultural identity become well-recognized features in the Latin

American landscape as one explores the critical essays in this volume. Recent social science literature also affords new insights into the *interconnectedness* of these key hemispheric problems. There are scant grounds for retaining any impression that hemispheric dilemmas have a single cause, a simple resolution, or a social texture that is less than complex.

Interdisciplinary links. A principal source of the growing clarity and sophistication shown by the disciplines of Latin American studies has been their mutual influence and, at times, collaboration. Some of the key paths of interaction among specialties are described in this volume's essays. Concepts from economics and from economic history have helped to shape every other hemispheric research tradition. The dependency approach has been the vehicle for a good deal of this influence; the breadth of its propositions made it both a tool within disciplines and a communications channel among them. The central tenets of *dependencia* have indeed been so widely accepted in some disciplines—especially in sociology and political science—that the leading edge of research has moved on to issues of social organization and policy implied by dependency's logic. Other economic concepts have played more specific roles in related fields of study. Much of the record of Latin American politics since World War II would be unintelligible without a grasp of the theory and experience of economic development and planning. The theories of trade and international finance (as well as those emphasizing development) shed crucial light on the growth of multinational manufacturing in Latin America, a trend with effects ranging from social migration to cultural alienation.

Hemispheric anthropology and political science have influenced each other deeply during the past two decades. Numerous political scientists have adopted anthropological research methods, especially in the study of urbanization and agrarian change.[8] Anthropologists' horizons, in turn, have broadened to include national and even international patterns and sources of culture.

Both of these areas of study have profoundly affected the documentation and understanding of Latin America's past. While political history as such has languished during recent decades, political scientists' current concern with social forces has suggested many issues for clarification by historians. Anthropology's traditional grass-roots focus helped to move hemispheric historiography away from its more traditional focus on social and political elites.

One of the two important streams in the study of Latin American literature has focused on the social contexts of creative writing. To accomplish this analysis, critics have drawn on the core concepts of sociology and political science, as well as on the historical record. Historians, reversing this flow of intellectual influence, have perceived new facets of their subject through the prism of novelists' and poets' special vision.

Interdisciplinary studies have indeed become so much a hallmark of research on Latin America that our primary focus on the traditional disciplines might be seen as inappropriate. Certainly, a variety of cross-field research efforts—stressing, for example, inter-American relations, women's roles in the hemisphere, and many aspects of development and rural change—deserve more extensive analysis than our essays can give them. Stress on basic disciplines, however, helps to structure a potentially sprawling task of criticism and clarifies lines of intellectual development over time.[9]

In Latin America, cross-disciplinary research styles are generally more congruent with intellectual traditions and institutional structures than in the United States where they must contend with narrower disciplinary ladders of professional advancement. Cross-field undertakings, stemming from North America, have often needed to be fostered by regional-studies centers within universities and by the aggregative efforts of the Latin American Studies Association, its regional groupings, and similar organizations. It is true, as Arturo Valenzuela notes, that comparative theories stemming from Latin American studies now enjoy marked prestige within U.S. political science, but that is an isolated circumstance. Hemispheric studies are much more often (as in sociology) isolated within each U.S. specialty.

Inter-American connections. Twenty years have passed since an essay by the Brazilian sociologist Florestan Fernandes challenged the assumptions and approaches of many Latin Americanists in the United States:

These scholars lack both information and understanding about the Latin American scene, and they are excessively preoccupied with the academic status of Latin American studies in United States university circles. . . . The intellectual effort exerted by Latin American countries to develop the teaching and application of the social sciences, as well as research in this field, is usually not fully or thoroughly described, as if this effort were a marginal activity of no great value or major importance. . . . The margin between this and an active kind of "scientific colonialism" is a narrow one.[10]

During the two intervening decades, remarkably fruitful efforts have been made to close the gap that Fernandes perceived, or at least to establish and maintain communication across it. *Contact* has been maintained through periodic research conferences, joint study projects, new norms of collegial contact for field investigators, and the work of a few hemispheric "star scholars" who now divide their time between the United States and Latin America. *Collaboration* has been made easier by the emergence of analytic models shared among specific research groups, including dependency, corporatism, the authoritarian state, and the myriad influences of social class; these paradigms have often made the inter-American journey from South to North. The inter-American scholarly encounter has been rendered more diffuse by the advent of strong Latin American studies programs in Europe (especially in the field of graduate training) and in Japan.[11] The network of inter-American scholarly contacts has relied primarily on private sources of organization and support, including the Social Science Research Council, the Wilson Center's Latin American Program, LASA, and the Ford, Tinker, and Doherty foundations. Among public providers of support, the Fulbright program and the Inter-American Foundation have distinguished themselves.[12]

In spite of these multiple advances, scholarly ties between the Americas are still fragile and intermittent, subject to fiscal, political, and ideological hazards. Researchers and institutions in both cultures are still far from defining their goals and efforts in a consistent transnational framework, and the essays in this collection demonstrate the spectrum of strengths enjoyed by inter-American connections in different disciplines. Nationalistic orientations within scholarship have proven most durable, in the views of Tulio Halperín Donghi and Saúl Sosnowski, in the fields of history and literary criticism.[13] Inter-American cooperation may well be strongest, conversely, in sociology and political science.

Social Science and Social Forces in Latin America

A second image is conveyed, as by a mosaic, through the essays in this volume: an outline of Latin American studies as a participant in hemispheric social change. In heterogeneous roles—as investigators, chroniclers, critics, planners, teachers, victims—social researchers in Latin America have taken active parts in the past two decades' hemispheric drama. This involvement, diverse in form, has brought with it a good deal of discord and debate.

Along with the growing quality, transnationalism, and breadth of scholarship on Latin American issues has come a widespread commitment to focus on what are taken to be hemispheric peoples' most urgent needs. Sociologists and political scientists, to cite an illustration, have given a high research priority to the grim situation and constructive strategies of the urban poor; an influential strand in economic research examines trends in income distribution, permitting a more critical perception of what constitutes "development"; social psychologists are exploring the crippling "culture of fear" that is often fostered by bureaucratic-authoritarian regimes.

These investigations of well-defined problems are supplemented by a more diffuse but still influential trend toward emphasizing the common people's experience of Latin American life. In the field of history, the growing literature on indigenous peoples' reactions to colonial rule accords with this tendency, as does the present current in literary analysis that explores popular culture. Of course, scholarly curiosity, disciplinary tradition, and other motivations continue to play roles in defining research questions. However, the relevance of research to the needs of broad segments of Latin American societies is more consciously weighed now than in earlier decades.

A variation on this theme of social science's social integration is the development of applied social analysis in Latin America. Economic theory has frequently been brought to bear on practical questions, and diverse economists have recommended and/or sought to implement public policies for governments of contrasting ideologies. Much smaller-scale efforts have been mounted by anthropologists as well.

The insertion of Latin American social science into the hemisphere's urgent concerns exists alongside reciprocal ties that are chronicled in most of the essays in this book: a set of linkages through which social pressures influence or assail social research. To begin with, overall social circumstances and values have helped to condition undertakings in social science. Such factors obviously contributed to the populist research efforts and problem-centered conceptual advances of the past two decades. Some boundaries have also been set by social structures and traditions. Tulio Halperín Donghi points out the reluctance of many historians to undermine cherished national symbols such as Bolívar's reputation, and the agenda of literary studies has sometimes been distorted by disproportionate attention to limited national authors and themes. Forms of organization *within* scholarship have also affected its scope and agenda; Arturo Valenzuela traces some of the omissions in recent hemispheric political research to the system of research conferences that, in his view, leaves too little opportunity for new investigation.

Second, applied social science in Latin America has been subject to revision in the light of practical experience. This positive trend is most apparent in the study and practice of economic development and in such fields as agrarian reform and urban planning. Less directly constructive—if no less enlightening—has been the backwash of political pressures on applied macroeconomic theory. Such models have been subject to political fashions that have sometimes shifted radically, leaving scholars to try to discern—along with their compatriots—the painful lessons learned.

Both of these social influences could be found, perhaps in more muted form, in many nations and eras. A third pressure felt by Latin American scholars during the past two decades has been of a very different order: researchers have been censored, attacked economically and physically, killed, and driven into exile. Such assaults have been most publicized in the Southern Cone and in Central America, but social scientists have also been persecuted in Bolivia, Colombia, Cuba, Paraguay, Peru, and elsewhere. These policies have attenuated research considered subversive by the state or by powerful social groups, have closed off access to some methodologies, and have at various times distorted research access along lines of nationality. In the Southern Cone, for example, political research by Latin American scholars became almost impossible in the early 1970's, and large-scale surveys in sociology virtually ended. U.S.-based political scientists, however, might have pursued inquiries much more freely, while smaller-scale anthropological and sociological studies remained feasible. Nor can any scholar, in the repressive atmosphere that continues unabated in Central America, be sure that a "prudent" research agenda will afford shelter or safety. As was true earlier in Argentina, Chile, and surrounding nations, social inquiry or even learning itself is frequently assumed to contradict state values and goals.

One of the concepts undergirding many authoritarian governments' profound antagonism toward scholars has been the positivistic ideal of research isolated from current social issues. Hemispheric scholars, by contrast, have tended to view their social involvement as inescapable, affording a choice among fidelities rather than the option of detachment. Alejandro Portes describes "the pursuit of scientific inquiries in isolation from the current social and political situation" as "a bad form of escapism" in Latin American societies, constituting (one might add) implicit backing for the social and political status quo. That Latin American specialists have consistently shown great autonomy from the programs of party or sect in engaging key social issues does little to reduce the radical opposition of repressive governments.

What of the relationship between Latin American studies and the government of the United States? The pluralism and stability of U.S. politics have served to protect and even, in some respects, advance hemispheric studies since the mid-1960's. The Title VI program of federal aid to regional-studies centers has been a major long-term success, and the federally financed Inter-American Foundation has played a constructive role in sponsoring research as well as projects in grass-roots development.

At the same time, there have been many politicized points of friction between Washington and Latin Americanists during the past twenty years. Hemispheric scholars have criticized a wide array of U.S. policies, especially those toward Cuba, multinational corporations, Brazil, and Central America. Probably the

Introduction 11

most traumatic scholarly outcry was produced by Washington's active opposition to the Allende government in Chile, followed by U.S. support for the totalitarian Pinochet regime. A few channels of direct communication with the makers of U.S. hemispheric policy have remained open, but these are limited in visibility and influence.[14] U.S. decision-makers have more often shown—particularly since 1981—a blend of indifference and hostility toward Latin American studies.

The building of barricades between Latin Americanist academics and the U.S. administration logically extended the more ideological style of hemispheric politics into the U.S. domestic debate. A special North American twist could, however, be discerned in this process. Few participants in the debate saw themselves—as in the past—as contributing to a national consensus on hemispheric issues. But the *appearance* of representing a popular consensus (or long-standing American political values) remained an important stake in the contention between policy alternatives.

Only a relatively few Latin Americanists have usually given high priority to communicating with a broad policy-interested public audience, and efforts at public suasion have shown few immediate results.[15] The debate over Central America and other contemporary issues may display a change in this pattern, however. Several groups of concerned Latin American specialists have oriented policy recommendations toward the ampler audience reachable through press reports and newspapers' op-ed pages.[16]

Looking to the Future: Agendas or Processes?

As one reads over the six essays in this collection, one encounters the manifold efforts, dilemmas, achievements, and setbacks of the fields of study included. The reader may explore (at one remove) such diverse subjects as the nineteenth-century roots of Mexico's delayed development, the impact of international migration on households in the Dominican Republic, the much-debated sources of inflationary pressures in Latin America, and the links between Spanish Colonial philosophy and Latin American regimes' search for legitimacy.[17] One may note, as well, the decline into which studies of Latin American education, political parties, and (especially surprising) the military have fallen. With this background, what may we expect and plan for in the future development of hemispheric social science?

Varied and pressing research themes in Western Hemisphere affairs quickly suggest themselves. These subjects would include: the social and political consequences of what Albert Fishlow terms "the Great Latin American Depression of the early 1980's"; crucial aspects of Central American political economy, international relations, and (especially) history; and the problematic evolution of Latin American cultures pounded by modernization, migration, and urban growth. Much remains to be learned about Latin American political conservatism, the nexus between religion and society, and rural history in general. Policy-oriented studies beckon in the fields of economic restructuring and development, urban improvement on a human scale, and the growth of assertive workers' organizations. Yet, with the exception of Arturo Valenzuela, the contributors to this volume present no highly specified research agendas for their fields of study.

This does not betoken, however, pessimism about the future course of Latin American studies. On the contrary, the essays that review anthropology, economics, and sociology are explicit in describing the current era as a positive period for constructive social research. In all three disciplines, the claims made for competing models have become less sweeping in recent years, and more common ground among such approaches is perceived. Most of our contributors are optimistic, in other words, that the present juncture favors the *methods of work* established in Latin American studies over the past twenty-five years and more. These inter-American, interdisciplinary, socially aware lines of action have kept scholarship tested, shaken up, stretched, and stimulated; they emphatically do not represent the easy route. These unsettled and unsettling qualities are nascent traditions in our area of study. They prepare us to undertake—with integrity and independence—research that will in part be specified by the needs of societies and cultures in which we live.

ONE

The State of Latin American History

TULIO HALPERÍN DONGHI

Discussing the state of Latin American historiography has never been an easy task; today it is probably even less easy than a quarter-century ago, and the growing difficulty has less to do with changes in the Latin American field than with the erosion of the certainties that underlay the impressive overall expansion of the discipline in the fifties and early sixties. While there was then as little agreement on ideological or theoretical issues as is always the case among historians, their views on research priorities, which of course reflected implicit agreements on which themes and problems were really important, were remarkably coincident: economic and social change, its geographic, demographic, social, and (among the most venturesome) even social-psychological preconditions and consequences, was very much at the core of the agenda that dominated a period of exceptional growth in the discipline.

These certainties, shared even (albeit not always consciously) by historians from the two worlds engaged in mortal ideological battle in that most frigid period of the Cold War, lost much of their grip on the discipline in the late sixties; by then it was not so much the agenda itself (this was to come only later) as the deeply unhistorical character of the approaches developed to tackle it that inspired among many historians a rebellious mood against what were now seen as simplistic explanations that did not do justice to the diversity of the processes they pretended to explain. But this readiness to explore new interpretive (and soon also thematic) avenues, better able to reflect the complexity, and even ambiguity, inherent in historical development, born in the climate of unqualified optimism that had also inspired the all-encompassing explanations against which it rebelled, survives now mostly as a weary search for new interpretive keys to replace those repudiated perhaps too hastily under the mood of reckless euphoria present at its inception.

The erosion of disciplinary certainties is not particularly helpful in our specific area of studies, which had depended for so long on inspirations coming from those that were more established. Only yesterday, Enrique Florescano provided us with a new, rich, and subtle image of the silver age in Bourbon Mexico by applying to it the lessons of the *Annales* school. What the likely result would be of fledgling Latin American scholars seeking a similar lesson from Emmanuel Leroy Ladurie's youthful readiness to explore a new way of writing history in each of his books is anybody's guess. There is no denying that Leroy Ladurie can achieve very attractive results by renouncing all magisterial *gravitas* to engage in extremely inventive *ballets* of ideas, but surely our comparatively young field cannot as yet dispense with masters who aim at teaching rather than at dazzling.

Latin American history needs such teaching mentors not only because it is a young field but even more because unity and coherence are not inherent in its subject of study: these qualities can only be imposed by the conceptual framework introduced by the historian. The student of U.S. history may ponder on how to define what is specifically "American" about it; this will not bring him to wonder whether the United States exists as a reasonably self-contained object of study. As for Latin America, while disputing its existence as a well-defined unit fit for historical study is now out of fashion, it is a fact that its global history can only exceptionally be cultivated—except in the most superficial way—in Latin America itself. People at the Colegio de México proudly and truthfully describe their Latin American history collection as the best in Spanish America; yet, their collection is not as good as those which we are invited to visit on U.S.

campuses new in the field, by librarians who, rather than exalting their riches, prefer to dwell on their plans for future acquisitions.

Under these conditions, it is not surprising that Latin American historians preferred for more than a century to concentrate on their national histories, leaving the task of dealing with the region as a whole to colleagues who did not belong to it. Or was it rather the other way around? Was the persistent lack of a scholarly infrastructure covering the whole of Latin America a product of the fact that these historians defined their task as one of building a national history, on the prestigious model of their liberal-nationalist European mentors, and were not interested in what the new countries had in common—namely, a colonial past of backwardness and oppression, and its dark heritage, better consigned to oblivion?

This perhaps regrettable—but at least clear-cut—division of labor has been almost completely abandoned, although the resources to do work on the history of Latin America in Latin America itself are not much richer than a century ago. Liberal-nationalist historiography gradually evolved into an empty cult of the national past. The result is that, in the last half-century or so, Latin American historians have gradually discarded the framework created by the founders of their national historiographies. These historians have chosen to explore, still mostly within the national boundaries that their available sources seldom allowed them to transcend, the very same issues that were gradually attracting the attention of foreign Latin Americanists.

For the non-Latin Americans, the shifting of thematic and problematic emphasis has progressed less dramatically and is evidenced by a slow but steady movement from the history of the conquest to that of colonization in two central dimensions: the creation of a colonial society and that of an imperial political and administrative system. Only in the last quarter-century is the expansion of the Latin American field in schools of history in the United States and—to a more limited degree—in Europe reflected by the emergence of a new generation of foreign scholars eager to conduct research on the post-independence history of the new nations. At the same time, a new breed of Latin American national historians—schooled in the United States and even more frequently in Europe (and including, after some time, also their students)—approached the study of their national history armed with the insights and methods they had learned from their overseas mentors. On the other hand, and notwithstanding all the difficulties in achieving an informed global view of Latin America from Latin America, some Latin American scholars (who, not accidentally, happen to have easy access to scholarly centers in the developed world and, hence, to their resources) have also proven ready to articulate their own views on the course of Latin American history. In recent decades, this trend has developed a counterpoint evidenced in the publications of André Gunder Frank, Fernando Henrique Cardoso and Enzo Faletto, Stanley and Barbara Stein, Marcello Carmagnani, Richard Morse, and Claudio Véliz (to mention only some that achieved a significant impact on the scholarly community and beyond its boundaries). Their work revealingly reflects the complex ways in which roots in a distinctive national experience can influence an author's perspective on the Latin American past (and his or her speculative view about the Latin American future).

While all this makes the task of anyone trying to make sense of the current state of the discipline even more difficult, it does not necessarily mean that these are not exciting times to work in this field of study. Where Latin American historiography is going may be anybody's guess; the current general pattern of the field is perhaps as enigmatic as its future course. But the most recent trend is only partly attributable to the loss of faith in the inherited directions that had guided its progress until comparatively recent times. It is to an equal degree the consequence of the discovery of new problems and issues (or, more frequently, of new dimensions in these) that lends them a much vaster interest than recognized in the past. The result is that while the observer would find some of the royal routes of Latin American historiography almost deserted, many previously obscure corners are buzzing with frantic explorations and lively discussions.

I will not try here to impose on the field a unity that it lacks. Rather, I would like to convey the multiplicity of directions in which progress is currently being made by concentrating on works that I find representative of the most promising trends in today's Latin American historiography. Here a disclaimer is in order: my purpose is *not* to offer a dean's list of worthy books and worthy historians; nor is it to provide a complete inventory of the fields, subfields, and themes in which work is currently being done. The view I have to offer is supported by some implicit assumptions on the promise of areas and themes available for exploration in the Latin American past, and the historiographical landscape sketched on these assumptions will necessarily look wrong to anyone who finds the assumptions themselves to be wrongheaded. I am, of course, well aware of the arbitrary dimension of this exercise. I am not ready, however, to apologize for this possible shortcoming, because to allow oneself the luxury of engaging in—one hopes—constructively provocative arbitrariness is mostly the point of this kind of effort. Surely its purpose cannot be to offer the contents of the relevant sections in recent volumes of the *Handbook of Latin American Studies* reorganized into longer paragraphs.

My presentation will proceed in the time-honored manner that divides the field into sub-areas (Caribbean, Brazilian, Spanish American) and, especially in the last one, stresses also the division between the colonial and the post-independence eras. In starting with the Caribbean, and continuing with the Brazilian area, I am aware that I am treading on what is for me almost foreign territory. Therefore, I intend to be necessarily more sketchy on these topics; and I apologize for being less decisive and more eclectic than when I feel on more secure ground. Even so, I am not sure that I shall be able to avoid pitfalls that, hidden to me, are probably obvious to more seasoned observers.

The Caribbean

The Caribbean as a unified field of history is—let us belabor the obvious—an extremely problematic one. This area of first Spanish settlement soon became an imperial backwater that only slowly abandoned its somnolence after Spanish dominance started to be eroded by the encroachments of Spain's European rivals. The most traditional approach, organized upon imperial history and the history of imperial rivalries in politics, war, and trade, made these conflicts the very substance of Caribbean history (a viewpoint fallen into such disfavor in the profession that not even the obvious impact of twentieth-century imperialism on the region has brought about a return of interest for the insights it might provide for the present). More recently, the history of the Caribbean is becoming more and more organized around the common theme of plantation slavery, its impetuous expansion, its quick demise, and the kind of segmented and badly integrated society that it left behind. Is it possible to structure a coherent history of the area centered on this theme? Perhaps it is. But it is enough to peruse Franklin Knight's gallant attempt to do just this in *The Genesis of a Fragmented Nationalism*[1] to be persuaded that the moment for this synthesis has not yet arrived.

While keeping in mind the existence of a Caribbean history field (albeit more as a common aspiration reflected in an agenda for future work than an integrated historical framework), I shall restrict my comments to the Spanish Caribbean. Here, of course, the most important contribution comes from Cuba, while only recently the history of nineteenth-century Puerto Rico is starting to be reshaped by historians who are aware of the issues and problems the island shares with the whole area.[2] Old Cuba had a vigorous and complex historiographical tradition, and its late start into independence made for a much shorter and less complete sway of the debased patriotic version of national-liberal historiography so influential on the Spanish-American mainland. The glaringly incomplete character of the independence Cuba had won lent even its patriotic historiography a more militant and less emptily celebratory tone than usual in the rest of Spanish America.

The fact that the national state and its history were comparatively new—and comparatively less influential—aspects of Cuban life, while not necessarily favoring the precocious emergence of a Cuban historiography more alert to the nonpolitical dimensions of history, lent an exceptional historical significance to studies that approached Cuban problems from perspectives other than that of history. Examples of this work are the studies of Fernando Ortiz as well as Ramiro Guerra y Sánchez's eloquent tract for the times,[3] from which historians and nonhistorians alike were to acquire some of their basic notions on the course of Cuban history.

The radical change brought about by Cuba's socialist revolu-

History 19

tion had a more complex and ambiguous impact on its historiography than could have been expected. Some historians left, including Levi Marrero, who, after completing the herculean task of retracing the history of the "empty centuries" before the expansion of the sugar plantations, is now ready to approach this big subject.[4] Some stayed (or returned from exile or semi-exile) and ensured some continuity with a far from undistinguished historiographical past. Thus, Guerra y Sánchez was to die in Havana in 1971; but his admirable handbook on the history of Cuba to 1868[5] is still in use as a college text. Julio Le Riverend developed a very successful career in the Academy and the National Library. The photostatic reproduction of the chapters on the economic history of Cuba that he had contributed to the multi-volume history of Cuba edited by the pre-revolutionary Academy[6]—reunited in a thick volume—is still the standard textbook on Cuban economic history assigned at the national universities.

The most important historiographic product of the new Cuba, Manuel Moreno Fraginals's *El ingenio*,[7] also has its roots in pre-revolutionary Cuban historiography but is far from its mainstream. This masterly reconstruction of a slave society for once fulfills the ambitious promise of Marxian historiography by developing its lines of explanation starting from the relations of production and reaching in a subtle and meandering line the apparently remotest aspects of ideological and cultural history. The work achieves this exceptional triumph by grounding in a detailed study of the economics and technology of sugar production the analysis of nineteenth-century social and political ideas and their links to Cuban realities that were developed with ruthless intellectual honesty by Raúl Cepero Bonilla in his pioneering *Azúcar y abolición*.[8]

Cepero Bonilla's approach was never popular in the old Cuba. In an effort to address what other historians preferred to dismiss quickly and with proper reticence, Cepero Bonilla attempted to focus on the roots of the Cuban patriotic elite in plantation society. This approach was badly received by a public that desperately needed to find in the past the reasons for unqualified national pride that would compensate for the humiliating acquiescence of Republican Cuba to the fake independence brought about by the end of Spanish rule. Perhaps not surprisingly, these viewpoints were also not immediately popular in the new Cuba. What now made them inopportune was the need (deeply felt by the new rulers) to safeguard the historical continuity of Cuba's revolutionary traditions, from (at the latest) 1868 to their belated fulfillment in 1959. Juan Pérez de la Riva, whose viewpoints were very close to those of Moreno Fraginals, was to discover that his uncompromising views on José Antonio Saco, his martyrdom (in circumstances of affluent and comfortable ease that make it difficult for scholars raised in the twentieth century to react with the compassion and awe expected from them), and his extremely qualified abolitionism were not received much more enthusiastically in revolutionary Cuba than before 1959.[9]

The lack of immediate popularity of these viewpoints helps to explain what a perusal of current Cuban historiographical production easily confirms: namely, that Moreno Fraginals's example does not carry there an authority commensurate with the unmatched excellence of his work. Another factor also accounts for the limited influence in Cuba of Moreno Fraginals's work: this sincere revolutionary cannot help belonging to the old Cuba. Between it and the new—and even in the absence of ideological discrepancies—a no-man's-land has been created as a result of too many hollow generations, of a radical change in the texture of national life, from its day-to-day rhythms to its cultural style, and—closer to historiography itself—of the difficult integration of Cuba's scientific and academic life into a different international system with its own style and routines, as well as its specific ideological assumptions and constraints. The results of this long travail are still not visible in a specific new shape for Cuban historiography and depend to a considerable extent upon the future evolution of historiographical currents less static in their approaches than the monotony of their politico-ideological professions of faith would suggest.

The constraints created for outside scholars by their limited access to Cuban sources cannot help being reflected in their work; Knight's study on slavery,[10] while offering a vigorous and judicious synthesis supported by considerable research based on primary sources, does not really break new ground. Only in very specific topics such as those studied by Louis A. Pérez[11] do the abundance of outside sources (and the paucity of earlier scholarly contributions) allow the historian to dare a more independent stance vis-à-vis previous scholars. But, even here, the contrast cannot be eliminated between the rich reconstruction of U.S. reactions and the necessarily more sketchy treatment of Cuban developments. While the future of Cuban historiography in Cuba depends on the future development of Cuban life in the new political and international framework that was introduced by the revolution, the future of Cuban historical studies abroad is still the hostage of imperial politics.

All of this helps to maintain Cuban historiography close to that of other Caribbean areas that have developed a less rich and well-established tradition of historical studies. For Cuba, it is easier to find perceptive analyses of this or that feature of its past than to achieve a more general new sense of this history. The exception is the bold and successful, but isolated, work of Moreno Fraginals. Yet, even this admirably spare masterwork necessarily leaves some important tracks and some significant connections unexplored.

Brazil

Brazil offers a very different historiographical landscape. The abundance of loose ends here is not so much due to an unavoidably fragmentary approach to an only partially unified object of study as to the abundance of new lines of exploration that, while answering old questions, impose the formulation of new ones. One consequence of this progress is the growing awareness of the strong peculiarities of the Brazilian colonial experience within the Iberian mold. Brazil's colonial history required the development of a separate field of study because its connection with the history of Portugal and the Portuguese empire attracted to its study scholars with a different background from those who undertook the study of the Spanish colonial experience. The vast consequences of Brazil's peculiar mode of integration in its own imperial system were therefore only gradually to be discovered and are not yet assessed with the desirable precision. It is already clear, however, that the slow development of Brazil as a colony of settlement (to use here the old-fashioned expression) not only differed greatly from the model dominant until the eighteenth century in Spanish America, where the conquerors strove to reorganize to their advantage the highly developed societies they now ruled, but also differed from the Portuguese empire in the Old World, then built as a network of mercantile emporia supported by a minimal territorial base. These differences pose historical problems different in very important ways from those central to Spanish American colonial historiography.

The history of colonial Brazil remained closely integrated within the framework of the Portuguese empire for a longer period than was the case of Spanish America with the Spanish colonial system. There are several compelling reasons for this integration: the comparative homogeneity of the gigantic Portuguese colony, its late blooming (reflected even at the end of the colonial era in its considerably smaller population, half of that of Mexico), its complex integration into a more heterogeneous imperial system, and—no less important—its dependence on slavery and the slave trade, which brought about a less self-contained development of the colonial economy and society than was the case in the other Iberian empire. It is not surprising, then, that the great works of Charles Boxer retained after World War II an allegiance to the Imperial framework that decades earlier had lost its sway on Spanish American colonial historiography. Also, there is no Spanish American equivalent for Kenneth Maxwell's more recent *Conflicts and Conspiracies*,[12] although even within its own Portuguese-Brazilian context this powerful work is exceptional in its ability to weave together the threads of local and imperial history, and move with graceful ease from Minas Gerais to Lisbon and back.

The historians of colonial Brazil seem now to be more inclined to join those of the post-independence era in an exploration of the specific trajectory of Brazilian history. This new approach is beginning to reshape the image of the pre-national period by bringing to the fore some issues that were to win pride of place in the national era.

Few attempts have been made to explore the colonial prehistory of these issues in an imperial perspective, and this is perhaps as well. Even the highly intelligent and sophisticated discussions contributed by Fernando Novais[13] are not entirely convincing, in that the connections between the changes in imperial models (themselves reconstructed by Novais from a rather limited base of facts and contemporary statements), those in actual administrative practices, and finally the concrete course of Brazilian colonial history are far from clear. Whatever may be the case, the colonial period clearly requires a lot of future attention. Much has still to be done to reach for the whole span of Brazilian colonial history the mastery of general process and significant detail achieved by Dauril Alden[14] for a short, although admittedly crucial, stage in the development of imperial institutions.

From this institutional perspective, the history of imperial administration lends itself to a treatment not substantially dissimilar from the one that dominates Spanish American historiography. Revealingly, Stuart B. Schwartz's work on the Bahia magistrates[15] applies its Weberian sources of inspiration following the example of J. L. Phelan's studies on Spanish colonial administration. Admittedly, Schwartz's conclusions stress again—implicitly even more than explicitly—the divergence between the administrative styles of both Iberian empires; but this result is achieved by exploring a conceptual landscape common to both areas.

There is yet another crucial difference between the two neo-Iberian sections of the American continent. The role of slavery is much more dominant in Brazil, while the Brazilian equivalents of the alternative legal sources of non-free labor found in Spanish America are comparatively unimportant. In this, colonial Brazil is sharply different from the neighboring Spanish areas. Because of this difference, an additional thread of continuity (missing in Spanish America) is maintained between its history and that of the post-independence era. The discussion of slavery as an historiographic subject demands the adoption of a common perspective and a unified treatment for the colonial and independent eras.

In Brazil, the closer politico-institutional continuity between colonial and independent times is due not exclusively (or even mainly) to the repercussions of slavery and its long and vigorous survival in early independent Brazil. The complexity and sophistication of imperial political institutions offered a flattering contrast with the rudimentary institutional life developing in early independent Spanish America. Their peculiarities were to be explored at length, and proudly stressed as unique, by students of the political history of the Brazilian empire. This is perhaps a pity. The role of the Crown in Brazilian imperial politics (and the emergence of its *poder moderador*) looks less exquisitely Brazilian than admiring contemporary observers and later historians assume. (Close equivalents can be found among constitutional monarchies in the less developed areas of Europe, from Restoration Spain to late nineteenth-century Italy and the Balkans—everywhere, indeed, that for lack of an organized and vigorous system of electoral parties parliamentary elections were routinely won by the factions that were granted by the Sovereign the opportunity to call for them.)

Even in their Brazilian context, imperial political institutions would perhaps be better understood against the colonial background. The tactics employed by the Emperor in his arbitral role are more than a little reminiscent of the Crown's administrative-political style in the context of the Iberian empires, as described, for instance, in J. L. Phelan's well-known seminal article.[16]

The view of the Brazilian empire as a political system is being modified by a growing awareness of what that system has in common with that of the Old Republic rather than by the introduction of a comparative approach. Half a century after the 1930 revolution, Empire and Old Republic appear integrated into a century-long Ancien Régime, towards which—continuing a venerable tradition—men active in public life or otherwise concerned about the current course of Brazilian public life turn for interpretive clues. Yesterday, Joaquim Nabuco, a first-rank politician of the Old Republic, took time to write a massive biography of his father, a first-rank politician of the Empire. This work included a masterful collective presentation of the imperial political class and a shrewd description of the political mechanisms that underlay the regime. Today, Raimundo Faoro, also drawn to public life by a strong calling, contributes an opinionated, shrewd, intellectually ambitious, and elegant argument about the issues that Nabuco kept in the background.[17]

Faoro is not the only one to redefine the old issues posed by the political history of nineteenth-century Brazil in a new context of ideas. While in his case it is above all the shadow of more recent political experiences that modifies the contours of the past, one sees mostly the influence of newly prestigious historiographical models at work in more strictly professional (but not necessarily less politically committed) historians. This is very much the case with Carlos Guilherme Mota's influential *Nordeste 1817*,[18] admirable for its thorough research and subtle analysis, but still slightly disquieting in its conclusions, at least for this reader. The reason for this feeling is perhaps worth mentioning, because it is present to a variable extent in a reading of more than a few of the most innovative works of recent Brazilian historiography (it can be detected also in Fernando Novaes's pathbreaking study on the transformations of the imperial link with Portugal). Mota builds a very ambitious interpretation of the social background and dominant social views in the Pernambuco uprising of 1817 on the very narrow base of the revolutionaries' use of the term "class" (in contexts which, as he hastens to add with admirable intellectual honesty, exclude even the possibility of finding here anything like its later meaning in the Marxian tradition or empirical sociology). For all the author's diligence, obvious talent, and hermeneutic sophistication, the doubt lingers that this is too little upon which to build so much. What makes the situation even more puzzling is that while historians who are indifferent to the factual relevance of their constructs are usually also less than exhaustive in their factual research, Mota (and his Brazilian contemporaries) could not be more painstaking and thorough in collecting his facts. As a result of this peculiar approach, we have works that are admirable for their solid and sophisticated craftsmanship but not always wholly persuasive in their conclusions.

On the political history of the Empire, Brazilian historians have proven less innovative than for earlier and later periods; but the contributions of foreign scholars and those in other social sciences make up to a certain extent for this relative neglect. Revealingly, the most recent authoritative studies on the phasing out of the slave trade and then of slavery have both been authored by non-Brazilian historians.[19] Their Brazilian colleagues' comparative neglect of the protracted agony of Brazil's peculiar institution suggests that they do not find in it anymore, as they did in the past, the thematic and problematic core for the history of the Empire. Both they and some of their foreign colleagues are instead more interested in making sense of the coexistence of a complex centralized state administration and a society that had achieved very limited integration (and, on several levels, was far behind the degree of development that would make these institutions workable). The traditional assumption that in the central state there was less than met the eye, that Brazil was run by sturdier and cruder institutional arrangements, while the formal state apparatus was so completely irrelevant to the real process of governance that there was no reason to challenge it (thus, its very longevity could be used to prove its intrinsic weakness), is not tenable without basic qualifications. Simon Schwartzman, a political scientist, proposed to replace this traditional assumption with an opposite one—namely, that both under the Empire and the First Republic, Brazil had been ruled by a strong and effective central administration. Unfortunately, he also brought to extremes the tendency also present in Mota's much more thoroughly researched study, and his radically innovative conclusions are apparently based mostly on his conviction of being in the right against practically everyone else. Less radically, other studies try to explore through specific institutions how the compatibility of state institutions with social forces was actually achieved. Examples of this approach include the work of historian Thomas Flory on the judiciary[20] and that of sociologist Fernando Uricochea on the National Guard.[21]

The Old Republic lends itself, perhaps even better than the Empire, to the exploration of the core issues of state and society relations. The end of the Crown's *poder moderador* brought these issues to the fore, and hence their consequences become more conspicuous, if not necessarily easier to decipher. One of the ways of reaching them is through the avenue of regional politics. Joseph Love pioneered the subject with his *Rio Grande do Sul and Brazilian Regionalism*,[22] a study that offered even more than the ambitious title promised. In order to place the southern state in the republican system, he needed to make sense of the system itself and met this challenge with a spare sketch that, while doing full justice to the baffling complexity of political life under the Old Republic, vigorously underlines its unstable integration of military tutelage and parliamentary brokerage. This book inaugurated a whole line of studies in state politics and has given us some admirably competent monographs (one by Love himself on São Paulo), which cannot, however, retain the flavor of daring intellectual discovery that makes the reading of Love's first book such a joyful experience. Among these, the one de-

History 27

voted to Bahia by Eul Soo Pang squarely faces the issues around *coronelismo*, already far from absent in the others.[23] The author's attempt to establish a typology of *coroneis*, while plausible enough as far as it goes, does not achieve significant explanatory value. More suggestive insights on these baffling political figures can be found in Ralph Della Cava's book on a rather atypical *coronel*, Father Cicero,[24] a study that offers more to the line of studies on state politics than to religious history. This reluctant exile from his church who led a vigorous local cult based on the memory of a problematic miracle was apparently a charismatic personality mostly in the Weberian sense. Della Cava's insistent and extremely intelligent attempts to delve into the religious context of the episode suffer from this, although what he has to say about the tension between nativistic impulses and institutional loyalties in late nineteenth-century Brazilian Catholicism is shrewd and sounds right. But surely Linda Lewin's much-awaited study on Paraiba, a state where *coronelismo* developed with exceptional luxuriance, will do a lot to place the institution in not only its political context but also the even more complex one afforded by the peculiar role of the family in a society where too many formal institutions are latecomers comparatively devoid of autonomous vitality.

Of course, she will not be the first to discover the need to integrate the threads of historical and sociocultural explanation. Historians and nonhistorians alike owe many of their notions on both *coronelismo* and messianism to contributions from other social sciences. While one would not like to impose the label of any specific discipline on *Os sertões*, its approach is clearly nonhistorical, and the same is true of *Eleições, enxada e voto*, the work of a jurist with a keen and perceptive eye for observing the interplay between institutions and society. More recent works fashioned in the matrix of specific social sciences—such as Maria Isaura Pereira de Queiroz's studies on Brazilian messianism and its sociopolitical functions—have also acquired widespread influence.[25]

The Second Republic and its authoritarian outcome are currently in the process of being incorporated into the territory of political history. Thomas Skidmore offered the first systematic historical exploration of the period. The years that have passed since the publication of his book[26] have been kind to it: it still sounds basically right (although, with time, some lines of inquiry that he did not follow, in part because they did not have a place in a general presentation, in part because the climate of ideas then dominant made them look less attractive than now, have won the attention of scholars and public opinion alike). Partly as a consequence of the book's lasting success and partly as a consequence of the growing awareness of the complex nature of the process of change during these feverish decades, it is unlikely that a serious attempt will be made to replace Skidmore's work. On the revolution that started the Second Republic, another book[27] was less well served by its even more complete success. Boris Fausto sounds so right so frequently that with equal frequency he may appear to belabor the obvious. It is easy to forget that what now looks obvious was then extremely controversial; and the fact that it now may look otherwise is due partly to Fausto's extremely convincing presentation of his viewpoint. The rightness of Fausto's diagnosis was also to be vindicated by later history, with a persuasiveness that could not be matched by the most cogent of historical arguments. The subtle influence of the post-populist experience on the retrospective view of the Vargas era is indeed pervasive. But, rather than helping to achieve a new line of interpretation, this influence has introduced unsolved ambivalences and ambiguities in those interpretations that were dominant up to the late sixties. Simply put, it has imposed the need for a new look at the *Estado Novo*, which now could not just be considered a perhaps unsavory but necessary stage in the pre-history of populism but could be recognized as a political experiment with obvious affinities (and less obvious but very real genetic connections) with "bureaucratic-authoritarianism."

With these perspectives, I am not sure that the thin line has not been transgressed that separates the history of the present from the systematic exploration of its problems under the sign of other disciplines. The assimilation of their insights into an historical perspective, always one of the chief dynamic forces in the development of Brazilian political history, is just beginning.

Other historiographical fields are even more dependent than political history on the images of the Brazilian national experience that have been developed in the framework of other disciplines. These, even more than those born in the matrix of more traditional historiography, bear the stamp of a very Brazilian *ufania*, both reflected and sustained in the unshakable conviction that the national history has never lost (indeed, cannot lose) its direction. Thus, when students of other disciplines explore the past and future course of Brazilian history, they very seldom share the brooding mood so frequent in Spanish America. Instead of deploring unshakable fatalities, they prefer to celebrate the development in time of a creative national experience, frequently translating into the language of twentieth-century ideas the affirmative mood of the liberal-nationalist historiography of the past. Thus, Antônio Cândido's admirable work, while totally immersed in the ideological world of our time, dares to do what not many literary historians consider feasible anymore. His anachronistic courage has been vindicated by a masterpiece that is indeed as fully a history of a nation through its literature as the one written a century ago by Francesco de Sanctis for Italy.[28]

But the influence of literary history on historiography pales in comparison with the massive contributions of the social sciences. Anthropology guided the first attempts to cope with the African background of Brazil and the impact of slavery. After the first courageous attempts to apply anthropological insights developed under the influence of racist assumptions to combat these very assumptions, Gilberto Freyre was to reshape the field by reformulating its basic issues in the language of cultural anthropology. But what makes his work both more fascinating and more open to controversy is that with him cultural anthropology, although offering a more substantial and systematic theoretical underpinning than Euclydes's scientific naturalism, had essentially the same role: it lent a vocabulary of ideas to a view of Brazilian realities that belonged to the scion of an enlightened patrician *nordestino* lineage rather than that of the former student of Franz Boas. Not surprisingly, while abroad his massive and affectionate reconstruction of the "patriarchal society" was to gain durable popularity as the book to read as a first introduction to Brazilian realities, in Brazil itself its memory is kept alive mostly by the need everyone apparently feels to dismiss the seductive but misleading keys it offers to Brazilian history.

Other more conventional anthropological works were to win

an influence less pervasive, but also more specific, than that of Freyre's saga of the rise and fall of the patrician sugar belt. While the historical significance of the African presence cannot be separated from that of slavery, it is in the aspects in which slavery conditions this presence least that the lessons of anthropology (and later of anthropological sociology) attain their maximum relevance. But only gradually are attempts being started to make historical sense of an African presence as lively today, almost a century after abolition, as in the plantation era.

When looking at these necessarily fragmentary and in part tentative explorations, the distance between the viewpoint of the historian and that of the social scientist should not be overstressed. Between Florestan Fernandes's study of Blacks in urban society after abolition[29] and Emilia Viotti da Costa's *Da senzala a colonia*[30] the degree of emphasis on historical detail establishes, of course, a difference, but both authors share many analytical perspectives and general assumptions on the direction and meaning of the historical process that they both explore from complementary vantage points. And Fernandes, who exerted a powerful influence on the course of these disciplines in contemporary Brazil, refused to recognize an impassable barrier in the boundary between history and the social sciences. Thus, when he was fortunate enough to have Fernando Henrique Cardoso *and* Octavio Ianni among his students, he encouraged the first to write an historical dissertation on slavery in Rio Grande do Sul and the second to approach race relations in contemporary Santa Catarina with the tools of sociology.

More recently, the study of both slavery and the Black condition has been affected by the development of these fields in U.S. historiography. Thus, Carl Degler's stress on the "mulatto escape-hatch,"[31] while not persuading all his Brazilian readers, has helped them to define more precisely and to recognize more fully the significance of the issues they need to address to make sense of the Black role in twentieth-century Brazil.

Slavery is, of course, one of the central themes of Brazilian history. From what can be seen, active work is being done on issues such as the coexistence of a slave and an expanding free Black population, the roads that brought individual Blacks from one to the other, and—more generally—the influence that the massive presence of slavery exerted on the relations among social groups in the free sector of Brazilian society. Examples of this work range from Stuart Schwartz's pioneering explorations of the colonial era to Maria Sylvia de Carvalho Franco's brilliant *Homens livres na ordem escravista*.[32] Franco deftly weaves into the argument the impact of the new constitutional order, which introduced a more egalitarian ideology that was to ensure the loyalty of the free poor to their landowning political leaders (but, here again, the interpretations the author offers of her painstakingly explored sources are not always persuasive).

Perhaps the most obvious area in which to explore the impact of slavery is agricultural history. Here Stanley Stein's *Vassouras*[33] has not been matched for its unerring lucidity in the exploration of the ecological and economic imperatives that fashioned a whole way of life and for its understated elegance in the reconstruction of that way of life itself. Stein's study has pride of place not only in the field of slave history but also in that of rural history. The transition to free labor in the coffee belt has been studied, as already mentioned, by Emilia Viotti da Costa. In more recent times, two U.S. historians, Warren Dean and Thomas Holloway, offer diametrically opposed interpretations. Dean follows the whole historical span of coffee agriculture in Rio Claro[34] and stresses the continuities between slavery and post-abolition solutions. In his presentation, the landowning elite has total control of the process and uses it in a self-serving and not particularly innovative manner. While the reader may find the sometimes shrill tone of Dean's denunciations an unwelcome consequence of his proclaimed conversion to "populist history," his argument is on the whole more persuasive than that of Holloway,[35] who posits that the rhythm of coffee expansion was dictated by the pressure of new immigrants on the land (a curious argument to make for a system that in its crucial formative stage relied on subsidized and controlled immigration).

While Holloway's position is overstressed beyond verisimilitude, it shrewdly underscores some aspects in the history of Brazilian agriculture that have been neglected as a consequence of the almost total concentration on the study of the plantation. The general thrust of Holloway's argument had indeed been anticipated by a prodigal son of the Paulista planter class, who was to become the dean of Marxist historiography in

Brazil. Caio Prado, Jr.,[36] had long been aware that—while Marxists and non-Marxists alike went on discussing the feudal nature of Brazilian large agricultural exploitations—in the most dynamic sectors of Brazilian agriculture, plantations were losing their earlier dominant position, never as complete as imagined, and that an accurate social history of Brazilian agriculture would require the introduction of a larger and more complex cast of characters than usually believed.

While Caio Prado's robust Marxist convictions were enriched by his keen eye for Brazilian realities, this was more evident in his analysis of concrete developments than in his theoretical and methodological views, which, when compared with the sometimes precious refinements cultivated by later Brazilian Marxists, now sound deceptively simple. This is mostly a misleading impression; and, furthermore, whatever is lacking in subtlety is compensated for by the creation of a sturdy conceptual base for Prado's powerful reconstruction of the course of Brazilian economic history, seen (in Marxist fashion) as part and parcel of the conflictive development of Brazilian society.

Generationally, Caio Prado still belonged to the times when students of the Brazilian past did not feel constrained by the boundaries of a specific discipline. The planter turned revolutionary had this in common with another Paulista, Roberto Simonsen,[37] a leading businessman influential in political and policy matters, who was to offer an alternative view of his country's colonial economic history. With Celso Furtado's *Formaçao economica do Brasil*,[38] we have instead the marriage of history and economics as scholarly disciplines, along lines that looked promising in the sixties and under theoretical inspirations that are not as distant as could be expected from those that underlay the most famous product of those years of perhaps foolish expectations: W. W. Rostow's non-Communist manifesto. In Furtado's eloquent book, the *Zeitgeist* of that ephemeral moment was reflected in an eager readiness to explore the whole sweep of Brazilian economic history from the vantage point afforded by its future development, the main lines of which were as clear to Furtado as the past economic course of Brazil.

While this prospective (or prophetic) dimension has not aged particularly well, Furtado's work had also more solid virtues that set it apart from what Professor Gerschenkron once described as

"Professor Rostow's delightful *pressappochismo*," so frequently taken over by his imitators. What makes the work of this professional economist still so valid as history is his constant effort to specify as much as possible the historical context of every economic phenomenon that comes to his attention. This allowed him, for instance, to anticipate by twenty years the parallel conclusions reached by John Coatsworth for Mexico by suggesting that it was in the quarter-century closed in 1850 that the lag of the Brazilian economy behind those of the new industrial nations became so extreme that not even its better than respectable performance since then was ever able to overcome its effects.

More recently, Brazilian economic history, especially that of the current century, has become even more the province of the professional economist-historian, while the issues under the now fashionable heading of political economy are mostly explored in a self-contained way by historians and political scientists alike. The situation (for which parallels can easily be found in Spanish America) is not without its dangers. Only the best historiographic works manage to incorporate into their framework a proper awareness of the economic conditionings and constraints in the process they study. This awareness contributed, no doubt, to ensure the persistent youth of Stanley Stein's study on the textile industry,[39] otherwise a link with a perhaps happier past in which so much in the "theoretical frameworks" used to death in later studies was not as yet explicitly defined.

The field of social history—in a culture so open to innovation and so eager for it as the Brazilian—cannot help being influenced by the general state of flux it experiences in Europe and the United States. Classic themes in this field (defined by Marxists and non-Marxists alike on the assumption that the core issues were rather directly linked with the at least partially conflictive relations among social groups whose place in society was defined using economic criteria) are now less cultivated than twenty years ago. Warren Dean's admirable *Industrialization of São Paulo*[40] has not been easily matched by later efforts in the same direction. It is perhaps symptomatic that, after a long interest in the history of labor, Boris Fausto is taking, in his *Crime e cotidiano*,[41] a new approach that, while still more interested in historical facts than in their collective representations (and, in this respect, impervious to what trendiness demands today from social historians), implicitly recognizes the at least partial dissolution of the old thematic core of the discipline.

It is not only social history that has today less precise boundaries than twenty years ago. The same is true with the history of ideas. This is due not only to the fact that this field has become, more than ever before, a history of people having ideas, rather than of the ideas themselves. It is also the result of the fact that work in this area offers just a starting point for a more radical metamorphosis in which the emphasis shifts to the connections between intellectual activity and society at large, as the concrete background against which that activity develops and also as the by no means passive recipient of such ideas. It would probably be better to stop here. The current historiographical trends grant historians a new freedom to define their fields. Assigning the name of a new discipline to each of these often strictly individual approaches would be a pointless exercise. For instance, in order to gauge the distance between Sergio Miceli's studies of Brazilian intellectuals and the interaction between their career patterns, their self-images, and their intellectual productions,[42] on the one hand, and the history of ideas as practiced only yesterday by, say, João Cruz Costa, on the other, we do not need to place Miceli's explorations under the heading of any specific historiographic discipline with a hyphenated composite name.

Colonial Spanish America

The current trends in Spanish American colonial history are, at least to this observer, comparatively easier to follow. Here, while the two main avenues of exploration (the imperial system and the creation of a colonial society) retain their position as the twin foci of that history, both have been affected (albeit unequally) by a gradual redefinition of their core problems and issues.

As a paradoxical result of a quarter-century of advances in our knowledge of the Spanish imperial system, our views have become progressively more blurred. The most important contribution of this work has been to prove that the assumptions on the nature and vicissitudes of the imperial link that were part of our conventional wisdom are mostly guesses of very dubious validity. To mention just one of the largest question marks: what happened to that link in the seventeenth century? Was it just weakened, or perhaps redefined in ways that are still not clear? And if the link was weakened, was this mostly due to the crisis in the metropolitan economy or rather to stagnation on the colonial side? It is now almost twenty years since John Lynch offered a series of brilliant hypotheses on these issues. They are still not much more than hypotheses; but, in the meantime, their postulation has influenced in complex ways the historians' view of that enigmatic century. Not that we do not know what should be done to provide less hypothetical answers to the questions addressed by Lynch, nor can it be said that nothing is done in that direction. But, in this area more than in any other, progress is reflected in a growing awareness of how much is still unknown.

Usually this awareness arises because new questions are born from the old ones. In this case, it is rather due to the fact that, in the process of trying to answer the old questions, historians are constantly discovering new difficulties relating to methodology and sources. As for transportation of goods and treasure in the Spanish Atlantic, historians today look at the Chaunus's historiographical monument from the pre-computer era with the awe that modern architects reserve for those built by Incas without the help of modern technology. This awe discourages them from a systematic revision of the Chaunus's data, but does not inspire in them unreserved confidence. As for the financial aspect of the imperial connection, even before historians can start assimilating the riches of TePaske and Klein's collection, methodological doubts and reservations have been raised against the whole enterprise (and also against not a few others in the same field). These reservations seldom coalesce in a global challenge to their conclusions, and it would be ungrateful not to remember, for instance, what the recent contribution of García Baquero-González did to lend new accuracy to our assessment of the impact of the free trade reforms of the 1780's[43] and, in general, to our views of imperial trade in the Bourbon era. But much more needs to be done to achieve a reasonably precise and accurate image of the changing metropolis-colony relation. In the meantime, most of the studies in the imperial system concentrate on its bureaucratic dimension.

The name of John Phelan has already been mentioned in connection with his influential presentation on the art of governance under the Spanish colonial administration, which, in his opinion, achieved the triumph of using its very weaknesses to ensure its survival. Phelan also contributed a model monograph on a career bureaucrat that is unmatched for the constant shrewdness of its analysis of the most disparate issues with which the royal administration had to deal, but that, even so, cannot completely avoid the eclectic and—to a certain extent—inconclusive progress that comes from studying administrative issues as they are faced by an individual bureaucrat in the course of his career. When Phelan wrote his study on Murga, the history of imperial administration had not yet been disaggregated into a system of more manageable topics. In part thanks to his own contribution, but also under the influence of work done in Europe on the administrative history of absolute monarchies, this situation was to change very quickly, as attempts were made to apply to Spanish America perspectives developed for early modern Europe, while modifying them to take into account the colonial dimension. A theme almost new to Spanish American history (except for John Parry's elegant but cursory general overview[44]) was the venality of offices. This theme was to be integrated with a very traditional one (the rivalry of Creole and peninsular in the conquest of bureaucratic positions) in a unifying perspective that stresses their link to two different stages in the Crown's lengthy effort to put the colonial bureaucratic machine under its effective control. This effort could only be successful if enough financial resources were available to create a salaried career bureaucracy. On this issue, the contribution of quantitative history was to prove particularly illuminating. Burkholder's studies, first of Lima and then of the colonial judiciary,[45] duly confirm the presence of the expected correlations between financial ease, the phasing out of the sale of offices, and the progressive invasion of the colonial courts by metropolitan magistrates. On the precise impact of this gradual shift upon the concrete experience of those serving in the ranks of the bureaucracy, the contribution of quantitative history can only be modest and indirect. Burkholder himself complemented it with a shrewd portrait of a Creole careerist—José de Baquíjano y

Carrillo—and his efforts to find advancement under these not very promising auspices.[46]

Another corner of the Spanish administration that attracted special attention from historians was the military. Lyle McAlister's educated guess that the military reforms introduced under Charles III launched Spanish America on the road toward post-independence militarism, by creating a privileged body of militia officers, stimulated a systematic exploration of these reforms and their impact, in part inspired by McAlister himself. While the results did not wholly confirm his assumptions, these regional studies were to offer new insights on the complex interplay between an expanding and more ambitious imperial administration and the society it was determined to protect and control but also to exploit more effectively than in the past.[47]

No systematic attempt has been made up to now to gauge the global impact of the Bourbon administrative reforms on colonial society. Even regional studies, such as those of John Lynch and John Fisher for the viceroyalties of Buenos Aires and Lima,[48] do not focus on the issue as fully as might be expected. There are perhaps good reasons for this shortcoming. Colonial reactions to the reforms reflected the baffling heterogeneity of Spanish America in the sunset of empire and do not lend themselves to global consideration. It is not easy to add up oligarchic-bureaucratic *frondes* (to be found everywhere), pro-Jesuit (and perhaps pro-Indian) riots in provincial towns of New Spain, anti-taxation protests in New Granada, and the largest Andean Indian rebellion and then make a coherent whole out of all this. As for the separate episodes themselves, some of them have attracted the interest of historians in connection with issues that only indirectly touch on administrative history. Again for excellent reasons, this is very much the case with the Peruvian and Upper Peruvian rebellions. Only for the *comunero* episode, J. L. Phelan left us a study (published posthumously in what was obviously not intended to be its final form) that did look at the rebellion from the perspective of imperial history.[49] While, as always, he had much to offer, his interpretations are not always convincing. Such is the case with his attempt to attribute Caballero y Góngora's unscrupulous and successful tactics to achieve a smooth "normalization" after the *comunero* rebellion (tactics that have so much in common with those currently used by General Jaruzelski to face similar problems) to the influence that Suarez's doctrines had won on the mind of that worldly prelate.

While imperial history has entered a transition the direction of which is as yet not completely clear, more substantial changes have happened and are happening in our views of Spanish-America as a colonial society that focus on the gradual forcing of the Indian into new roles as provider of labor in different contexts, but mainly in agriculture. In the process, a radical (and at the beginning not wholly conscious) change in perspective was to emerge, which—to use the felicitous expression borrowed by Nathan Wachtel from Miguel León Portilla—strove to identify with "*la visión de los vencidos.*" Of course, this shift in perspective was only possible because, during the last half-century, a more precise historiographical image of the experience of the vanquished gradually emerged; but the shift was also inspired by a change in the historian's sensibility, which has less to do with the quantitative progress in our historical knowledge than with the influence that the concerns of the post-industrial society exert on that historian.

Thus, while Woodrow Borah's recent *Justice by Insurance: The General Indian Court of Colonial Mexico and the Legal Aides of The Half-Real*[50] builds on the more precise view of the Indian colonial experience developed in the last decades and further enriches it, Borah uncompromisingly places his admirably successful reconstruction of an important and badly known administrative instrument in the framework of the colonizer's experience. Borah's terms of reference are the British and Dutch approaches to similar problems in Southern Asia and South Africa. The reason is obvious: this work is the result of a promise of youth fulfilled in maturity. After a much longer tour of duty in the field of demographic history than he had originally bargained for, he is finally free to complete the projects he had planned in the very different intellectual and ideological climate of the 1940's. The result is a work that is clearly on the cutting edge of historical scholarship and one that equally clearly advances against the stream of this scholarship. The situation is not new for Borah; and he is sustained in his defiance of the dominant trend by a strong vision of Mexican history, reflected in the image of the

Indian delegations he saw waiting in the central court of the Palacio Nacional for an audience with President Cárdenas, just as they had been doing since the times of Viceroy Mendoza. He is probably right in his conviction that his view of the Spanish American past is that of tomorrow as much as of yesterday; unarguably, it is not that of today.

The shift in perspectives, which Borah refused to join in his recent book, can be fully gauged by comparing two works separated by half a century of studies: Robert Ricard's *Conquête spirituelle du Mexique*[51] and Nancy Farriss's *Maya Society Under Colonial Rule*.[52] The problems Ricard intended to study were those posed to the missionaries by the Indians' limited comprehension of their new faith (and limited interest in it). The problems with which Farriss identifies are those of the Maya trying to keep a distinctive identity fashioned in the framework of their old beliefs while offering unavoidable obeisance to those forced on them by their conquerors.

To define her historiographical enterprise, Farriss offered as her main point of reference Charles Gibson's *The Aztecs Under Spanish Rule*. This "History of the Indians of the Valley of Mexico, 1519–1810"[53] did indeed mark the starting point for the transition toward a history of the whole colonial society and not just of its governance from the top, and it accomplished this feat in two ways. On the one hand, Gibson's treatment decisively closed the debate on many of the issues that had dominated the previous period. On the other, it offered a very precise view of what had happened to the subordinate Indian sector in the core area of colonial Mexico. On both accounts, Gibson provided explicit answers only after having built an overwhelming case on an equally firm foundation of carefully selected historical data, which made the offering of any explicit answers almost superfluous.

In this way, Gibson was able to lend a quiet and unobtrusive authority to his carefully understated conclusions. Thus, when he tells us that the main point about the Black Legend is that it is basically true, we are inclined to listen and trust. But, here again, this apparently blunt and uncomplicated support of what, after all, is a pretty conventional view of the Spanish imperial experience hides a carefully crafted new view of the impact of Spanish dominance on the native populations. Many of the crimes on which the Black Legend liked to dwell are real enough; but these are not as decisive for these populations as the relentless effort at "flattening" Indian society to change it into the peasant sector of a seigneurial neo-European society. The mills of the new lords, like those of the Lord, ground slowly, but they ground well; and the result is apparently the worst crime in the Spanish imperial record.

It is enough to state Gibson's viewpoint in terms that would have been too explicit for his own taste to become aware of how much in it was sustained by the strength of his historical convictions on the Spanish colonial experience rather than by the eloquence of facts. Of course, the "worst crime" made possible the gradual emergence of a unified *mestizo* nation (which for Justo Sierra was the secret redeeming grace for the bloody mess that was the history of Mexico). By looking at it as a crime, Gibson was already placing himself on the side of the great divide within the field of colonial social history that stressed a newly developed approach of looking at colonial society from the viewpoint of the subordinate sectors. This perspective looked away from the one that focused on the problems posed by colonial society for the colonial power and the dominant ethnic group or alternatively saw in it the pre-history of the creole-mestizo nations that were to emerge in the nineteenth and twentieth centuries.

This effort was to be sustained mostly by non–Spanish American scholars, a fact that is again understandable. The new approach runs very much against the grain of a cultural tradition in which aristocratic values struggle against egalitarian aspirations; but neither viewpoint is particularly interested in fostering cultural or ideological pluralism. Thus, in his *La patria del criollo*,[54] Severo Martínez Peláez keeps faith with these ingrained traditions when he closes his lengthy and eloquent indictment against the indignities lavished on the Guatemalan Indians by Spaniards and Creoles alike by announcing a revolutionary future in which Indians will become really and fully Guatemalan (which means, of course, that they will not be Indian anymore). On this issue, the view of the Spanish American Leninist scholar continues that of the nineteenth-century Liberal-progressive, which continued that of the preachers of the gospel of Enlightenment, which in its turn continued that of the missionaries of the *conquista espiritual*.

The approach inaugurated by Gibson has been developed mostly outside the area of Aztec Mexico; and this development is also not surprising. In that area, the "flattening" process was comparatively successful; and the transition "from Indian to peasant," to quote the felicitous title that Karen Spalding gave to one of her books, was achieved to such an extent that scholars pretty soon found themselves discussing the issues of peasant, rather than Indian, history. This becomes particularly evident when the sociocultural dimensions of this change are emphasized, as in William Taylor's *Drinking, Homicide and Rebellion in Colonial Mexican Villages*.[55] Even for Oaxaca, where the Indian influence was much stronger than in the valley of Mexico, the reader may wonder whether peasant life was different in kind from that of, say, contemporary Calabrian peasants under absentee landlords.

There can be no doubt that for the Yucatan Maya there was indeed a difference in kind. As already mentioned, Nancy Farriss tried to make sense of this difference in one of the most ambitious recent attempts at reconstructing not only the *"visión"* but also the active reaction of the vanquished to their defeat. Her reconstruction is also perhaps the most distant from the assimilationist views that explicitly or secretly dominate the Spanish American understanding of the colonial experience. Farriss has no doubt that the survival of their pre-Hispanic worldview is indeed a goal worth all the sacrifices the Mayan peoples were ready to offer to maintain it during their post-conquest history. This identification with a defined cultural peculiarity is at the core of her strong affective identification with her subject and explains her ready acceptance of some of these costs, which include the permanent control of Mayan life by a very superficially renovated pre-Hispanic elite, a development toward which scholars who write history "from the bottom up" usually develop more ambivalent reactions. This is, of course, very much her prerogative and does not detract from her remarkable historiographical achievement. But, even so, one wonders whether her approach, by prizing continuity above everything else, does not run the danger of overstressing its actual success.

This seems to be particularly the case in her final chapters. After two centuries of successful—if passive—resistance, the structures that sustained that continuity suddenly crumbled. Continuity, she tells us, was again saved within a new structural framework in which the creole landlords took over in part the role of the Indian elite they had finally crushed. Yet, again, one wonders whether this impression of continuity is not due partly to her stressing those aspects in which it is indeed maintained, to the detriment of those for which it is irretrievably broken.

The strength of Farriss's massive historiographical achievement is due in part to the almost perfect pertinence of her assumptions to Mayan realities. This pertinence (as she makes clear in her admirable first chapters) is in turn due to what is most atypical about the Mayan post-conquest experience, when examined in a Spanish American framework. The overwhelming demographic superiority of the conquered is just one of the consequences of the extremely tenuous Spanish presence, which, in turn, can be explained by the lack of attractions the area offered to conquerors or immigrants on the make. The Andean areas can only be explored by scholars whose work rests on assumptions at least partially different from those of Farriss. Rather than examining the collision of two mutually incompatible cultural blocs, what these historians try to understand is the complex articulation of a new society composed of victors and vanquished, which resulted from the self-serving modifications introduced by the Spaniards on the already immensely complex and remarkably unequal society fashioned by the still recent Inca conquest.

In the process of making sense of this new society, these scholars were to discover that they were laboring under the sway of not one "white legend" but two. They learned that Garcilaso Inca is not an authentic representative of the vanquished but of the earlier victors who could not reconcile themselves with the subordinate—but still privileged—position their successors were ready to grant them. This should have been pretty obvious (after all, it is equally obvious that translating Neoplatonic dialogues in Seville could not be the fate reserved by the conquerors for many Indians in their charge). Less obvious is what to do with this insight. Thus, it is not surprising that it was to be incorporated only slowly into the basic assumptions held by these historians about post-conquest Indian Peru. It is revealing, for instance, that Nathan Wachtel—who, in his *La vision des vaincus*,[56] clearly anticipated this new historiographic trend—could at the same time offer a subtle and convincing parallel between Garcilaso, the man between two worlds, and Guaman Poma, unequivocally Indian under a thin Spanish and Christian veneer, and still yield to the influence of the first's stylized rendering of the effects of the Inca conquest on the vanquished Andean peoples.

How much ground has been gained since can be measured from the subtitle of Karen Spalding's much awaited book, *Huarochirí: An Andean Society Under Inca and Spanish Rule*.[57] Not only because of the absence of a satisfactory general framework, but because of the irregularity of local sources, this work goes beyond local history to offer a vigorous overview of the transformations in Andean society through the long centuries of colonial rule. At some crucial junctures, not even Spalding's heuristic skills and creative historical mind allow her to offer much more than admittedly extremely convincing sketches. This suggests indeed that, for reasons that have to do with the course of colonial Andean history and, not unrelatedly, with what is available as its documentary base, this area does not lend itself as well as Mexico to studies that span whole epochs or cover comparatively large areas. This seems to be confirmed by the comparatively easier task Steve Stern has found in portraying that crucial transition in the emergence of the mature colonial order—the reforms introduced by Viceroy Toledo—through the vantage point of Huamanga. This impressive first book's theme is the transformation of the Huamanga Indians from being part of a subjugated people into their becoming members of a potential class, potentially ready for new struggles, which no longer aimed at breaking away from post-conquest society, but, even in their more revolutionary moments, at improving their place in it.[58]

Can this new place for Indian groups be defined as that of a peasant? Or, more generally, is it essentially defined just by the position of its members in the sphere of production? This does not seem to be the case. When compared to that of Meso-America, the pre-Hispanic legacy included in the Andean area a much heavier element of politically or administratively regulated economic activities. These activities were treasured not only by the conquerors for the opportunities they offered to graft on them their own instruments of exploitation, but also by the conquered, who learned to redirect them to the needs created by their new circumstances. (Hence, the sturdy survival of a pre-Hispanic institutional framework for the organization of production and surplus extraction explains the vast influence John Murra's powerful reconstruction of pre-Hispanic social arrangements has exerted on historians who fully recognize its relevance to post-conquest Peru.) There is no denying, however, that—at least since a comparatively early date—it is possible to look at these issues from the perspective of peasant history for some areas. In a seminal article,[59] Brooke Larson did just this for Cochabamba. While not too many Andean equivalents for that fertile valley come immediately to mind, her approach can be at least partially replicated for other areas.

Revealingly, the most significant Spanish American contributions to these new perspectives deal less with the Indian peoples than with the structure of domination that held them in thrall. I have already mentioned Severo Martínez Peláez's *La patria del criollo*. As the title itself informs us, this masterly reconstruction of colonial Guatemala looks at the society from a vantage point that is not that of the Indian and is especially admirable for the extremely subtle and perceptive reconstruction of the Creole worldview. Thus, in his brilliant pages on the Creole's view of the Indian and of the land, this true believer in the most relentlessly reductionist version of orthodox Marxism puts to shame his trendy colleagues who, while knowing all the new bywords of hermeneutics, find themselves at a loss as soon as they try to go through the motions they are able to describe and justify with pedantic precision. However, he has much less to say about the Indian mind.

Carlos Sempat Assadourian, the Argentine historian now working in Mexico, has contributed a view of the Andean colonial economy as a system[60] that incorporates these new perspectives into a theoretical framework that owes as much to François Perroux as it owes to the Marx of *Capital*. (Assadourian much prefers quaintness to trendiness and does not share in the cult of any of the "new Marx's" periodically rediscovered by focusing on previously dark corners of his writings.) This general preference is again reflected in Assadourian's belligerent defense of the views on the colonial economic order held by contemporary observers, on whose authority he depends to sustain some of his own conclusions.

The view that Assadourian proposes is as distant from that of the "dependentistas" (for whom the colonial link was a hindrance to Spanish American development) as from the neoclassic perspectives that dominate, for instance, Murdo McLeod's socioeconomic history of colonial Central America. Assadourian finds the colonial observers' stress on mining substantially justified. All other economic activities indeed existed for the sake of mining, in service not only of the intentions of the Royal administrators who defined the basic parameters of the colonial system but also of the colonial reality itself. It does not follow, however, that in terms of manpower needs, volume and value of production, or even actual control or influence exerted by the miners on other economic sectors, mining towered on the colonial economy. But this key sector did hold that economy together. Any stagnation or crisis in mining (an activity essential to the accumulation of the surplus taken away from the colony by the metropolitan interest) was not followed by any expansion in other sectors (as assumed by the dependentistas) but rather by their own stagnation and crisis. Assadourian's insights are grounded on a much more precise view of the colonial trade network—and especially its regional aspects—than previously achieved, acquired thanks to his systematic use of notary records (a source frequently neglected by Spanish American historians, and used by U.S. scholars mostly in the context of social—rather than economic—history; thus, James Lockhart, in his admirable *Spanish Peru*,[61] offers a brilliant example of what a strictly descriptive approach can achieve utilizing these sources). While Assadourian's insights on the colonial economy offer a logical complement to the view of Andean colonial society that is slowly emerging from recent research, the connection between both has still to be made.

The history of the incorporation of the Andean populations into the colonial system offers, then, a set of extremely promising themes that are only starting to be developed. From this viewpoint, what we have now for the area may be roughly compared with what was available for Mexico twenty years ago.

The advance of Mexican historiography on these issues is even more clearly reflected in the progress made in the study of the Bourbon silver age and its impact on society, and especially rural society. Here, David Brading's deservedly influential *Miners and Merchants in Bourbon Mexico*[62] not only offered a powerful set of interpretive lines for the period but also set an implicit agenda for future work. While the rural dimension was kept here very much in the background, Brading's interpretation of the silver age was sustained by a precise view of agriculture's role in it. This view is in substantial agreement with the conclusions of Enrique Florescano's study on the price of corn,[63] which reflected the impact on Mexican society of an agriculture that was stretching its resources to keep production up with the quickening pace of population growth. Through this approach, the notion that demography is destiny, implicit in the work of the Berkeley school of demographic history and made explicit for a crucial period of the Mexican past in the brilliant and daring hypotheses of Woodrow Borah's *New Spain's Century of Depression*,[64] was starting to be refashioned under the sign of Ricardo rather than Malthus.

The relationship of agriculture to population growth offered the focus for Brading's *Haciendas and Ranchos in the Mexican Bajío*,[65] a short book almost crushed by the wealth of ideas and insights the author strives to develop simultaneously. The underlying interpretive line is, however, not difficult to fathom; it follows the quick changes in agriculture that develop when demographic growth first reaches and then outdistances that of the economy. Recently, John Coatsworth applied the perspective of quantitative economic history to the same issues. The results are, as is always the case with him, extremely exciting, although the layman finds it sometimes difficult to agree with his conclusions. For instance, it is surprising to see Coatsworth stress the growing importance of agricultural production based upon the strength of its growing weight in the gross national product (GNP), a strength due, in turn, almost exclusively to the rise in the comparative prices of grain caused by the rural producers' inability to expand production as quickly as demanded by the rapid growth in population. Apparently the role of agriculture in the GNP expresses in quantitative terms the importance of that sector's shortcomings. As conventional wisdom had guessed for a very long time, these shortcomings were apparently serious enough to bring the silver boom to a sudden stop.

Rather than in the basic mechanisms of rural change, Brading was interested in the complex repercussions that change exerted on a more differentiated rural society than was previously allowed. The Bajío, an area that in the eighteenth century moved from the periphery of New Spain's economy to become its most dynamic center, offered an admirable vantage point to study these repercussions because in this region the impact of change had probably been more conspicuous than anywhere else. But for the same reason, it was not reasonable to expect the same developments in all of rural Mexico. What the Bajío revealed was, however, convincing enough completely to erode the authority of a book that had pioneered the field of rural history of colonial Mexico, François Chevalier's *La formation des grands domaines au Mexique*.[66] Brading fittingly opens his own work with a short and masterly historiographical essay that convincingly explains the reasons for Chevalier's long success and proves that these had little to do with the historical validity of his hypotheses.

Before Brading, William Taylor had already challenged Chevalier's views by offering an alternative "view from the South."[67] His dissidence was, however, less threatening to the then dominant interpretation. It essentially stressed that in Mexico the South is different, which is true enough. So different, indeed, was the Mexican southern region that Taylor's stress on control of land was here at least partially misleading. It would be difficult to guess from his admirably painstaking study of land tenure in Oaxaca[68] that the Indian communities that had kept control of their land much more successfully than in central Mexico were subject to alternative mechanisms of surplus extraction that brought them closer to the Mayan and Andean areas than to the Mexican core.

For that core, we have not only a more detailed general outline of rural socioeconomic change in the last colonial century than for any other Spanish American area but also a detailed sketch, which is being progressively fleshed out by regional studies (such as those of Eric Van Young and Claude Morin) and by specific consideration of social sectors and groups (as in John Tutino's very important unpublished dissertation on the landed elite in the silver age). The elaboration of a general view of the

Mexican colonial economy is much less advanced. For the merchant group, the thorough but relentlessly descriptive study by John Kicza does not add much to the brilliant—but admittedly sketchy and necessarily controversial—rehabilitation of Alamán's views offered by Brading in the midsection of his *Miners and Merchants*. An implicit global view of the Mexican colonial economy is, of course, hidden in the still sketchy quantitative reconstructions currently being attempted. In a much-attended book on Mexico's road from backwardness to underdevelopment, John Coatsworth promises to discuss it more directly than in his tantalizing quantitative explorations. Of course, attention to the Mexican economy as a whole is a necessary aspect of any economic, and not just social, study of colonial Mexico; and important insights can also be expected from Richard Salvucci's forthcoming study on the *obrajes*.

Even for Mexico, an area that more than any other attracted the attention of the historians of colonial Spanish America, a general view of the features and direction of socioeconomic change is just starting to emerge. For the rest of the Spanish empire, what we have is much more spotty. While some works deserve our attention for their methodological interest (such as Marcello Carmagnani's on the economic structure of colonial Chile or John Lombardi's on colonial Venezuela) and others for their wealth of suggestive, but not quite developed, insights (among them the brilliant essays of the late Mario Góngora),[69] these efforts are not really supported by the basic implicit agreements on priorities in the definition of issues to be explored and avenues to be taken, which would allow them to add up as effectively as for Mexico (and to a more limited degree for the Andean area).

Post-Independence Spanish America

The fragmentary character of our knowledge of post-independence Spanish America is even more marked. Here, it will only be possible to mark some trails and to indicate globally the vast territory they are haphazardly opening to further exploration, trying to impose on this barren and blurred landscape some semblance of regularity by looking at it first from a chronological perspective and then from a thematic one.

History 49

The independence period is only slowly emerging from a long historiographic slumber, which is the consequence of its having become the reserved domain of patriotic historiography. With many worthy alternatives available, few historians of sound sense felt the urge to challenge such bellicose institutions as the Instituto Sanmartiniano of Argentina or its counterparts in other Latin American countries. Since even Salvador de Madariaga, protected though he was by an international reputation and a British passport, found himself once unceremoniously expelled from Venezuela for his uncomplimentary opinions on Bolívar, such caution was very understandable; and its wisdom was again to be confirmed by the wave of organized patriotic indignation that followed the publication of a collection of essays on the independence of Peru edited by Heraclio Bonilla (tame enough except for the blunt introductory chapter authored by Karen Spalding and the editor). But the situation is perhaps changing more quickly than these episodes suggest. While managing to keep out of harm's way, Germán Carrera Damas has found it possible in Venezuela to challenge and tease in the most explicitly provocative ways the patriotic cult of Bolívar (by tactlessly stressing, for instance, that he was not a true democrat, a very distressing thought to right-thinking Venezuelans, and, even more cruelly, by devoting a brilliantly perceptive study to the historical roots of the cult itself).

This unexpectedly nonconflictive coexistence is made possible in part by the fact that the new interest in the independence period concentrates mostly on issues so far apart from those preferred by patriotic historiography that very few areas of contact (and potential collision) between the two have developed. These new interests focus on what the crisis of independence meant for Spanish American societies. The new shape the subject may take under this new inspiration is partially anticipated in John Lynch's general survey of the period,[70] which elegantly weaves together the new themes with those developed by liberal-nationalist historiography. The social impact of independence demands even more strongly than other subjects in Spanish American history a regional, and even subregional, approach. What has been done remains still uneven and for most areas pretty tentative. For Mexico, many years after Luis Villoro's pioneering study[71] on the reaction of different social groups to the final crisis of the colonial order, full of extremely perceptive insights but disconcertingly shifting constantly between "classes in themselves" and "classes for themselves," the preferred perspectives have become less panoramic. Thus, John Tutino has approached the Hidalgo rebellion in the context of the Bajío facing a critical moment in its economic course; and Hugh Hamill shed powerful, albeit indirect, light on the social impact of the rebellion by careful analysis of the revolutionary and counterrevolutionary propaganda. At the same time, Eric Van Young is starting a social study of the Hidalgo followers that, one hopes, will bring us far from the primeval horde suggested by Alamán (and, even if less shrilly, by other contemporaries of less firmly conservative convictions).

For Peru, both the important article added by Bonilla to the second edition of *La independencia del Perú*[72] and the studies of Christine Hünefeldt suggest that the independence struggle offered an opportunity for provincial elites in the Sierra to come into their own by proving themselves useful to both the local populations (by sparing them some of the ills of war) and the contending factions (by organizing on their behalf the mobilization of local resources). This insight is again confirmed by what Florencia Mallon found in the central Andes. But it is difficult to generalize from there, even for Peru. In Jequetepeque, his native corner of the northern coast, Manuel Burga has found instead that the new power, to the disadvantage of both communities and local elites, transferred the control of land to its mostly urban creditors (merchants but also public servants and army officers who had not been paid their salaries).[73] The same tantalizingly contradictory glimpses can be gathered from other studies that do not explicitly focus on the impact of independence; and it seems certain that in Mexico it brought about a temporary setback of the *hacienda*.

Concerning other areas, what we have is mostly indirect and spotty. For Venezuela, Germán Carrera Damas, in what started as a discussion of historiography, brilliantly showed why the movement led by Boves was not, and indeed could not be, a chapter in the rural masses' struggle for land.[74] In Uruguay, a dedicated team tried to prove an opposite conclusion—namely, that Artigas had led an agrarian revolution. While they did not convince too many of their readers (except for those already convinced), they were much more successful in reconstructing the inchoate social structure of Uruguay in its pioneering stage, by conducting a painstaking and thorough collection and an intelligent analysis of *all* documents available on land, trade, and credit. This is indeed a massive achievement, which has not been rivaled for any other area or period.[75]

Advances in the study of the independence era are also being made on a different front. Partly as an extension of what is being currently done on Spanish colonial administration, a new curiosity has developed (mostly among non-Spanish American scholars) about the astonishingly effective Royalist resistance. The study of the counterrevolutionary side of the struggle has progressed very considerably, especially in the mastery of detail. However, it cannot be said that recent contributions, even the excellent ones from Timothy Anna,[76] impose any drastic revision on our view of the process, and this is even less the case with Jorge Domínguez's *Rebellion and Loyalty,* which tries to integrate revolution and counterrevolution as alternatives available to colonial elites but, from an historian's viewpoint, manages to be at the same time obvious and farfetched. Even so, these studies open new access and offer the basic bearings for a new territory whose full exploration will necessarily introduce significant changes in our views of the revolutionary process.

The post-revolutionary order has the opening of trade as one of its foundations. No systematic exploration of the impact of this event exists beyond the argumentative and, on the whole, unconvincing general discussion by Christopher Platt.[77] This is indeed too bad because, even without the benefit of it, assumptions are being made about this impact that are being incorporated not only into the views that Latin Americans develop of their own past but also into the received wisdom of the historians' guild, not without danger for what is being built on these frail foundations. Our specific knowledge of the matter is still sketchy enough to allow for views that posit the unleashing of new, hurricane-strength trade winds at the moment of independence to coexist with those of Sergio Villalobos, for whom nothing of substance happened after 1810 because it had already happened before (a view that, while not widely shared, is, strictly speaking, still tenable).[78]

The political history of the independence struggle, both in its institutional and its ideological dimension, has been less affected by any recent historiographical renewal. In the first respect, David Bushnell's thorough exploration of the issues linked with the creation of a new political order under the circumstances of war in Bolívar's (and Santander's) Greater Colombia[79] has found few imitators (although William Lofstrom tackled similar problems for early independent Bolivia[80]). If one considers the staggering amount of disparate materials that Bushnell had to integrate into his study, this is not surprising. The ideological dimension of independence, until yesterday, attracted attention in Spanish America for basically extrinsic reasons. The search for *precursores* distinguished by an irreproachably orthodox Catholicism and firmly nonrevolutionary ideologies, while enthusiastically supported by the cultural organs of Franco Spain, was mostly inspired by the need to gain historical legitimacy for the growing conservatism of the Spanish American establishment. This need is now more frequently fulfilled in other ways, so much so that for a time Adam Smith appeared close to replacing Suárez in the devotion of these groups (even more easily because the devout but fickle followers that these considerable thinkers had found among the Latin American conservative classes very seldom had bothered to read either of them). After the ideological right decided to leave these issues very much alone, the ideological left is trying its luck at them and is now proposing a new understanding of Bolívar as the *precursor* of Che Guevara. But the narrower influence of the left in the scholarly establishment—and the usually marginal interest of the best scholars of this persuasion in political history—limit the possible impact of this even more open attempt at political manipulation of respected national symbols on the future course of Spanish American historiography. If this is reassuring, it precludes the probability that a new stimulus for explorations on the subject will soon be provided by the political and ideological travail of today's Spanish America; and the current comparative neglect is not likely to end soon. Nor does it appear likely that this neglect will be compensated for by the efforts of non–Spanish American scholars (the latest significant contribution to the study of the ideologies of the independence era coming from these quarters is probably Simon Collier's *Ideas and Politics of Chilean Independence*[81]).

For the times that follow, one finds only a few serious attempts at a global consideration of the national political process. Most of these rely on the division of the task among practically independent authors, which, at best, ensures complete coverage and reasonably reliable information at the expense of a really unified historical interpretation. More ambitious attempts at joining both are usually less successful. From this viewpoint, the political volumes of the *Historia moderna de México*,[82] which best reflect the historical views of its editor, Daniel Cosío Villegas, are quite exceptional for their ability to integrate a wealth of significant detail into a well-defined view of the Mexican past. (This is the view that, while identifying with what Mexicans like to call their liberal tradition, is painfully aware of the chasm that separates the political practices developed under its influence from all that is elsewhere understood as Liberalism.) Thanks to this unifying perspective, the work of Cosío Villegas successfully joins historical awareness and contemporary political relevance, an achievement reached with apparent ease by the founders of liberal-nationalist nineteenth-century historiography—the secret of which was lost to later Spanish American historians. This loss is so much in evidence that only Jorge Basadre's history of independent Peru[83] (in this reader's opinion, not as appreciated as it deserves to be by Peruvian historians of later generations) can in this respect be mentioned in the same breath with Cosío Villegas's impressive achievement.

The situation looks more promising when one looks, rather than at the global course of national political histories, at some specific issues or conflicts. It is here that outside contributions have been particularly significant. From Miron Burgin's *Economic Aspects of Argentine Federalism*[84] to Charles Bergquist's *Coffee and Conflict in Colombia*,[85] U.S. scholars have tried to shed new light on political conflict by calling attention to its socioeconomic background. Another area in which foreign contributions have also been important is political biography, a genre very marginal to Hispanic historiography and still at the core of it in the Anglo-Saxon world. Many are useful; few are more than that. Among them, John Lynch's recent *Argentine Dictator*[86] is exceptional for its vast historical ambitions. An attempt at least partially inspired by the recent barbarities, this treatment strives for a reciprocal illumination of Rosas and his national background that suggests the existence of deeper affinities between both than the most optimistic among Rosas's enemies had hoped to be the case. For all this we should be thankful; but it is much less than is needed to achieve a reasonably reliable sketch of the political course of nineteenth-century Spanish America. Paradoxically, the twentieth century, during which both the left and the right—from Lenin to Maurras—rediscovered the specificity and significance of the political moment, is also the century in which for the first time the legitimacy of political history has not been considered a matter of course. This is due in no small part to the fact that for most of the core countries its tasks have been already done, and perhaps overdone. The trouble is that this is not at all the case for Spanish America; and it is to be hoped that Spanish American historians will soon feel ready to have a try at political history (which, to be of any use, should be very different from the combination of mindless celebration and equally mindless fact-collection that we now so frequently get under that rubric).

If one leaves aside these exercises in academic history, the contributions of Spanish American authors to the political history of the nineteenth century are up to now mostly interpretative reconstructions that, at best, offer an irritating combination of shrewd insights and self-serving manipulation of the past. Indalecio Liévano Aguirre's overview of the history of Colombia, portraying this history as a series of conflicts between the oligarchy and popular leaders who periodically emerge to challenge oligarchic dominance and are subsequently destroyed and posthumously defamed as enemies of free government,[87] offers an extreme example that exacerbates the contradiction between the virtues and shortcomings of the genre. The basically arbitrary character of this historiographic exercise, even in its best practitioner, was revealed when Liévano Aguirre, grateful to President Lleras Restrepo for having included him in his cabinet, proceeded to cast this pampered son of the oligarchy as the new avenger of the downtrodden masses.

With the political history of the twentieth century, we are imperceptibly crossing the threshold from history to political science. Our historical view of the political changes that followed the irruption of the masses into politics owes as much, for example, to François Bourricaud's *Pouvoir et société dans le Pérou*.[88]

as to David Rock's *Politics in Argentina*.[89] More to the point, however, is that what our historical understanding owes to both is not that different in nature, although Bourricaud's book is as clearly a work of political science as Rock's is of history. We now also have interesting attempts at integrating both methodological perspectives, usually with a quantitative slant. Peter Smith applied it first to Argentine political history (with brilliant results in *Politics and Beef in Argentina*,[90] less convincingly in *Argentina and the Failure of Democracy*[91]) and then to revolutionary Mexico. He found in the study of political elites an admirable instrument for the historical exploration of this paradoxical mass revolution and used it with brilliant results in *Labyrinths of Power*.[92]

Other aspects of political-administrative history lend themselves to such quantitative approaches. James Wilkie used them to discover the actual policy priorities of the successive postrevolutionary administrations in Mexico.[93] On a very different issue, Herbert Klein (whose early *Parties and Political Change in Bolivia, 1880–1952*[94] is one of the few national political histories to achieve real historiographical distinction) recently co-authored *Revolution and the Rebirth of Inequality*,[95] which again uses quantitative methods to achieve new insights on the era of erratic political change opened for Bolivia by the 1952 revolution.

Post-independence political history offers, then, little more than a sampler of historiographical possibilities still to be fully developed. This is even more the case with other historiographic branches that are usually less set in their ways. For these also, the influence is even stronger of two opposite impulses—already present in the most interesting recent works in political history. While striving to achieve a stricter and more precise methodological approach to historical work, these impulses grow impatient with the limitations that the existing boundaries among different subdisciplines would impose, if taken too seriously, to the exploration of the past. The result is an intriguingly fragmentary historiographic landscape, only some of whose most prominent features can be examined here.

Economic history offers, of course, a comparatively well-defined field with an even better defined methodology; but straight economic history is only gradually emerging as a separate area of scholarly endeavor. Exceptional in his ability to build upon the contradictory foundations of the New Economic History and the ferment of his sociopolitical convictions, John Coatsworth provides a rich and insightful presentation of the changes brought to Porfirian Mexico by the introduction of the railways,[96] which effortlessly integrates historical and economic perspectives. Most of the recent works in the field place themselves instead at some point in the continuum between two disciplines whose approaches they do not integrate completely. Thus, the late Carlos Díaz-Alejandro, even if he included the word *history* in his title,[97] is very clearly an economist looking for examples in the Argentine past. Roberto Cortés Conde brings to his study of Argentina the historian's preferred interest in concrete processes of change.[98] For their part, Thorp and Bertram, in their insightful research on Peru,[99] constantly oscillate around the balance point (but mostly on the historical side).

Between the territories of economic, social, and political history, the retrospective dimension of the recently rediscovered interest in political economy is carving an historiographical space still sparingly colonized by scholars in what, until recently, was the undisputed domain of Spanish American essayists, who brought to it the same strengths and weaknesses we discovered in their explorations of straight political history. Only exceptionally did their essentially polemical and argumentative thrust inspire a sustained historiographical effort. Thus, Luis Ospina Vázquez's *Industria y protección en Colombia*,[100] an undoubtedly biased but admirably researched and cogently argued plea against protectionism, is less typical of Spanish American productions than Nieto Arteta's elegant *Economía y cultura en la historia de Colombia*,[101] a very attractive collection of educated guesses on the economic dimension of past Colombian sociopolitical conflicts.

The direction that the transition from essay to historical study is currently taking is well reflected, also for Colombia, in Marco Palacios's study of the social groups and policies developing around Colombian coffee agriculture,[102] an intricate rendering of a bafflingly intricate set of interweaving historical processes. Only for Uruguay do we have more than a sketchy general outline for a new view of the past. The massive work of José Pedro Barrán and Benjamín Nahum on a decisive turn in that nation's history, the failure of the Batllista faction of the Colorado majority party to impose upon the party and the nation an uncompromisingly and radically reformist course, provides an anticipation of what this new view of the past can potentially offer. Five volumes of the seven the authors have planned on the subject have already been published. The results are admirable in that they organize an overwhelming abundance of historical facts around a vigorous interpretation of the course of Uruguayan history that is as original as it is convincing.[103]

The Spanish American pioneers of this new historiographic territory, who usually share at least some of the ideological assumptions in the essayistic literature that they try to replace with sounder historical work, have learned from repeated experience that those essays are perhaps a useful source of imaginative insights but should never be accepted on trust. Their North American counterparts, however, are not always as wary as they should be of this seductive and dangerous essayistic legacy. Such misplaced trust partially limits the usefulness of otherwise admirable studies, such as James Scobie's *Revolution in the Pampas*,[104] and completely destroys others, of which E. Bradford Burns's *Poverty of Progress*[105] offers the most recent example.

In the field of social history, that of labor is only starting to emerge from the dominance of strictly partisan perspectives; and the study of urban history has been cultivated even more spottily than other subfields. (Richard Morse's *From Community to Metropolis: A Biography of São Paulo*,[106] was only to be followed at a distance by James Scobie's *Buenos Aires: Plaza to Suburb*,[107] but most of the growth is due here to studies that eschew the monographic consideration of a city to focus on specific issues of urban history as reflected in more than one urban center.) The historical study of the mostly (but not exclusively) urban sociopolitical tensions of our century is even less developed. We learn of this phenomenon mostly from the writings of sociologists and political scientists, who have also authored a rich literature on some related issues, such as the significance of urban squatters and shantytowns in twentieth-century Spanish American cities.

The most cursory look at some important recent works in the field or rural social history would reveal the diversity of themes, issues, and approaches that one finds in it. Arnold Bauer's

Chilean Rural Society from the Spanish Conquest to 1930[108] hides under its misleading title a brilliant reconstruction of the process of change that covers the eight final decades of that long timespan. This work focuses upon the impact of the changing market and transportation conditions on an agricultural sector that, after a short boom period, found its way to survival in a systematic avoidance of technological innovation; and it also examines the landowning elite consolidated under these unpromising auspices. *Historia rural del Uruguay moderno*,[109] the first important historiographic contribution of the Barrán and Nahum team, follows the modernization of the Uruguayan countryside under the social leadership of the landowning class and the intellectual and ideological guidance of the organizers of its corporate institutions, a process powerfully illuminated by the authors' twin interests in socioeconomic history and the history of ideas and ideologies. Ezequiel Gallo's recent *La pampa gringa*,[110] a social history that examines the first ventures in agricultural colonization by immigrant farmers in central Santa Fe, Argentina, during the 1870's and 1880's, is sustained by a delicate nostalgia that adds sensitivity and perceptiveness to its shrewd socioeconomic analyses.

The works of Bauer, Barrán and Nahum, and Gallo represent three vastly different historiographic enterprises. It is enough to put them together with Florencia Mallon's impressive book on the central Andes[111] to become aware that, for all their differences, all three works deal with a rural order defined in a wholly modernized context (even the Chilean and Uruguayan technological backwardness owes more to sound economic calculation than to any blind loyalty to tradition and routine). What lends additional depth and complexity to Mallon's study is its link with a different but equally Spanish American world where peasants who are still also Indians are entering a new transition that should make them either proletarians or farmers. (It is the world portrayed from the different viewpoint afforded by circulation and exchange of goods in Rodrigo Montoya's fascinating *Capitalismo y no-capitalismo en el Perú*,[112] where one can still discover the boundary that does not isolate, but rather integrates, a market economy and one still partially regulated by reciprocal ritual exchange.) This complex transition, in which the community has to struggle for survival against not only the vanguard of an invasive capitalism pressing from the outside but also the one emerging from inside the community itself, lends to Mallon's study its richness and suggestive power; yet it also contributes to some of the conceptual hesitancies (already reflected in its double title) that make the lesson of this admirable historical work less relevant to the search for general models applicable to the study of peasant societies in transition than is immediately apparent.

The abundance of precise and intelligent reconstructions of actual processes of change and (for all of Mallon's keen and sophisticated interest in "theoretical frameworks") the presence of unresolved uncertainties when trying to place them in a larger historical or conceptual horizon are features frequently found in the best works in the Latin American field. We shall find these uncertainties again in the studies on the history of ideas. In Spanish America, as in Brazil, the subject is in the process of dissolving into a myriad of potential research enterprises that follow specific directions defined not only by the context against which the study of such ideas is to be approached but also by an at least partial shift in the historian's emphasis. It is less and less clear whether the study of that background is deemed necessary for a better understanding of the ideas in question or is the main objective of the research, with the ideas playing an ancillary role as providers of new insights for a better understanding of the context. The last attempt to practice and justify a history of ideas for its own sake can be identified with the figure of Leopoldo Zea, and it owed much to the implicit assumptions that had guided the collective effort directed by his mentors from the Spanish diaspora, especially José Gaos. Admittedly, Zea was to advance from this starting point and to stress more and more, as his basic interpretive key, the specific position of an Hispanic world that at the same time belongs and does not belong in the West. He was to continue further on this line of historical speculation, bringing it close to the traditional domain of a philosophy of history. But this inclination, which reflects a less intransigently "pure" approach to the history of ideas than first seemed to be the case, leads Zea in a very different direction from more recent attempts to expand and enrich the empirical historical background against which the deployment of ideas and ideologies in time is to be projected. The examination of the historical context of ideas is, however, almost the only common feature that can be found among these more recent efforts, starting with Charles Hale's *Mexican Liberalism in the Age of Mora*,[113] in which the transition from the traditional to a more empirical approach to the history of ideas is already clearly (but barely) announced. Here, the shifts in liberal thought are linked with the political experiences of early independent Mexico with a precision and an attention to detail that contrast with Zea's readiness to hypothesize his social landscape from the landscape of ideas, egregiously reflected in his discovery of a rising bourgeoisie behind every advance of Positivism in Spanish America. Hale's work was just the beginning: we shall discover one of the possible outcomes of this transition by looking at Frank Safford's *The Ideal of the Practical*,[114] which joins an erudite study of the attempts made by some enlightened Colombian conservatives of the mid-nineteenth century to ensure a technical education for their children with a fascinating exploration of the meandering transition between the enlightened ideals of the Bourbon era and this strictly depoliticized cult of the practical. Safford provides a shrewd assessment of the influence that the new wariness of the old elite toward the social upstarts whom the schools of law were projecting into public life had in this surprisingly modern reformulation of its cultural ideal and, by doing all this, offers us both more and less than a traditional history of ideas.

With Enrique Krauze's *Caudillos culturales en la Revolución Mexicana*,[115] the ideas sustained by a generational group of intellectuals are used by the historian as part of his raw materials to make sense of these intellectuals' own sense of the course of their careers as they were pushed or derailed by the revolution. Hugo Vezzetti's *La locura en la Argentina*[116] again provides us with something altogether different: an impeccably Foucaultian development of an exquisitely Foucaultian theme, in which, of course, the ideas on madness current in Argentina at the turn of the twentieth century are expected to offer decisive clues for a general view of society that was intended to be also a theoretical and practical instrument for the more thorough domination of that society.

Here again, then, the search for new, precisely defined ways of exploring the past multiplies the perspectives and makes the achievement of a synthetic general view of that past an ever more elusive goal. But this shortcoming cannot be considered just the consequence of a restless exploration for new historical perspectives, which also affects other historiographic fields in which it does not achieve the same effect. The reason for this divergence is clear. Whatever heterogeneity in individual approaches one may posit, a common ground is usually provided for the core countries by the availability of a dense network of well-established historical facts that have become common patrimony for all historians. Very little of this exists as yet for Latin American history. The difference that this comparatively low density of historical research can make may be guessed by looking at a subject that, disadvantaged in comparison with most in core historiographies, is, however, exceptionally well covered by Latin American standards. I refer here to Mexico and its revolution.

For no other recent historical development do we have such books as Friedrich Katz's *The Secret War in Mexico*,[117] which adds to a detailed and exhaustive study of the revolution in a world context a first systematic exploration of the regional dimension in the revolutionary turmoil unleashed by the breakdown of the Porfiriato, *and* Héctor Aguilar Camín's *La frontera nómada: Sonora y la Revolución Mexicana*, a long book without a flaw, which triumphantly proves that narrative history, when properly done, can also be the best kind of analytical, problem-centered history.[118] There is also so much in addition to these two powerful works, from political biographies of almost all the main figures of the movement, starting with John Womack's deservedly successful work on Zapata (except, of course, for Villa, for whom Katz's sympathetic insights do not as yet add up to it), to analyses of regional movements and attempts at making sense of some typical secondary figures. All of this work, it would be pointless to deny, is not equally good; and much in its inspiration and criteria is as heterogeneous as for any other field. But the comparative abundance allows the reader to find out where these views dovetail or contradict each other and even formulate an opinion not only by choosing among the alternative interpretations available but by assessing them against his own interpretation, which will, be at least partially based on a common patrimony of facts that, for the Mexican Revolution, is getting close to the critical mass that makes at least plausible his attempt to build on its foundations a reasonably independent view of the process.

I would like to end on this mildly encouraging note; one that calls for a reassuringly conventional and uncontroversial conclusion. Whatever other points might be proposed at the end of this exercise, we have discovered one that is inescapable: there is still much to be done.

TWO

Political Science and the Study of Latin America

ARTURO VALENZUELA

There is no doubt that the field of Latin American politics has undergone significant changes in the last quarter-century; and twenty-five years is an appropriate span for appraising the progress we have made in understanding political change and political processes in that region of the world. In 1960, the field was in its infancy. Only a handful of universities offered a specialization in Latin American politics, and, with three or four exceptions, the leading departments of political science offered no courses in the area. A diligent graduate student could easily survey the literature on Latin American politics in a very short period of time.

Today, most of the universities granting Ph.D.'s in political science have a Latin American specialist, including the top-ranked departments in the field. During the last twenty-five years, we have witnessed the emergence of a new subfield in the discipline, comparative politics, which aims to explain the universe of political phenomena through new theoretical and conceptual frameworks. This effort was coincident with the expansion of area studies programs in the United States, including Latin American studies, whose growth was aided in no small measure by the Cuban Revolution and its implications for U.S. foreign policy. Hundreds of monographs have been published on a wide range of topics falling under the rubric of Latin American politics.

And yet, I wonder how much real progress we have made. I have the sense that the actual events in Latin America, the reality of Latin American politics, have often left us behind. If there have been changes within our field over the last quarter-century, they pale in comparison with the massive transformations that have taken place in Latin American social, economic, and political life. In the early 1960's, political scientists, following the cues of Fitzgibbon's periodic assessments of the progress of democracy in the region, were confident that there was an inexorable tide leading toward democratic institutions. And yet (if we exclude the Caribbean from our analysis), only Costa Rica, Venezuela, and Colombia remained democratic throughout the period, with Uruguay and Chile, the most democratic nations according to Fitzgibbon's rankings, succumbing to harsh dictatorships. In country after country, parties became irrelevant where they had once played important roles in the political process. Institutions such as the Catholic Church, which had become increasingly marginal to national political life, moved once again to center stage as guarantors of a measure of freedom and respect for human rights. Professional military establishments, which had been held out as the hope for less interventionist armed forces, proved to be more interventionist—claiming the right to intervene not only as a moderating force between struggling civilian groups but as rulers in their own right, seeking to reshape the fundamental basis of politics.

But it was not only democracy that failed; revolutionary experiments, with the dramatic exception of Cuba, also did not prosper. The death of Che Guevara in Bolivia and the defeat of countless insurrectionary movements underscored the fact that it was illusory to think that many Vietnams would appear on the continent. The overthrow of Allende in Chile and the reversal of state-sponsored revolutionary experiments in Peru, along with the rise of neoclassical doctrines of economic orthodoxy, seemed to put to rest the likelihood of socialist visions of the future. That appeared true at least until the overthrow of Somoza in Nicaragua and the rise of insurrectionary movements in Central America—events that were not fully anticipated and whose broader political meaning it is probably too early to judge.

In this paper, I will not attempt to present a detailed catalogue of the work in Latin American politics, evaluating its relative strengths and weaknesses. Rather, I see my task as giving a broader overall assessment of the direction of the field. My characterization is, I admit, closely related to my own concerns and research agenda. I have found that often our general theories or perspectives are dictated by the country or countries we know best. It is almost a rule of thumb: discover the country in which an author has spent the most time—or the country on which the author wrote his or her dissertation—and you will have a good sense of the scholar's vision of Latin American reality. We try to generalize or even elaborate a theoretical perspective based on our experience with Argentina, Brazil, Chile, or the Dominican Republic. In particular, there is a rather large gap in the vision of Latin American politics between those of us who see the continent from the experience of Central America or the Caribbean and those who see it from the vantage point of the Southern Cone—with specialists on Colombia or Venezuela providing something of a third view. Until the recent attention paid to Central America, much of the intellectual agenda has been set by scholars working on the Southern Cone. The great diversity of the region, which, as Abraham Lowenthal has noted, has increased further in the last twenty-five years, should continuously remind us of the pitfalls and difficulties of global generalizations.[1]

In reviewing the literature on Latin American politics, drawing in part on several assessments of the field by other scholars writing at different moments, we can divide the intellectual effort of the last twenty-five years into four phases: the public law phase, the modernization phase, the dependency phase, and the new phase of intellectual eclecticism.

The public law phase requires only a brief word. It consisted of the pre-1960's work of a handful of pioneering scholars in the United States, several of whom were professional historians.[2] In general, they sought to chronicle contemporary history, evaluate the prospects for democracy in the region, and describe constitutions, institutions, and formal processes in Latin America based on fieldwork as well as the writings of historians and legal scholars from Latin America. They wrote some comprehensive textbooks, some good monographic studies on individual countries, and classic studies on such topics as church-state relations and inter-American affairs.

However, this work came under heavy criticism by scholars in the mid-1960's because it was viewed as too formal, configurative, and descriptive. Merle Kling's 1963 assessment of the field is perhaps the most comprehensive statement of this criticism and reflects the beginning of the second phase, or modernization phase, of the study of Latin American politics.[3] Kling in no uncertain terms condemned the scholarship on Latin America for not adopting some of the insights derived from the revolution taking place in political science and embodied in the rise of the subfield of comparative politics. The broad objective of this revolution was to create a new science of politics—to explain and predict political phenomena in universal terms. This was to be accomplished by focusing on political behavior, as opposed to formal-legal processes, and drawing on conceptual schemes derived from structural-functional, psychological, and systemic frameworks.

Kling noted that there was an uneasy relationship between Latin American specialists and political scientists concerned with more general and theoretical issues. As he put it:

Political research on Latin America, rather than flowing into the somewhat turbulent mainstream of modern political science, often appears to drift in isolated channels of its own, with its sponsors perched along the banks of the more swiftly moving waters of the discipline. Authors of textbooks and treatises in the field of comparative politics therefore ignore Latin American data without evident pangs of remorse or expectations of censure for failure to recognize conspicuously pertinent research.[4]

Kling disparaged traditional political science's concern with "formal procedures, written prescriptions, interesting anecdotes, governmental structure, recommendations for public policy and normative judgments." In particular, he took scholars from Latin America to task for their disdain of empirical research. "Their academic culture and tradition," he wrote, "apparently has provided a congenial environment for speculative and philosophical excursions into nonlegalistic subject matter."[5] A similar view was expressed in crasser terms by Gomez, who argued in 1967: "It is difficult to find any considerable assistance [in the study of Latin America] in the works of Latin American scholars. In political science, there are very few studies that would be significant by North American standards." Many pieces, he said, were either legalistic interpretations or "European-style texts" relying largely on quotations or "highly partisan accounts . . . by bitter politicians whose detachment from an emotional motivation is quite in doubt."[6]

It was widely felt in the mid-1960's that the deficiencies of the scholarship dealing with Latin American politics could only be overcome by bringing Latin America into the mainstream of comparative politics. Kling, for one, called for the use of the "concepts of political development and modernization for ordering Latin American data." The research agenda should include "interests, parties, groups, elections, processes of decision making, operational rules of the game, conceptual self-consciousness, analytical devices, methodological rigor, and the potentialities of quantification."[7] He praised Fitzgibbon's attempts to measure the degree of democracy on the continent through panel surveys of experts, and he commended Robert Scott and George Blanksten for their attempts to bring Latin America within the framework developed by Gabriel Almond for the Princeton series on political development.[8]

The underlying preoccupation in this political development literature, so keenly illustrated in Scott's essay, was the relative degree of traditional versus modern orientations of these actors, and by implication their potential for political development. The basic assumption was that economic progress would lead to modern values, and modern values in turn would encourage modern groups and institutions—a necessary prelude to the establishment of stable democracies.

In the conference that served as the basis for the Kling paper, Samuel Huntington explicitly articulated this view, noting that each country in Latin America should be studied in "terms of its development progress in each of four separate dimensions: mass mobilization, interest articulation, elite broadening, and institutional development." Huntington also made very clear the policy implications of this work for U.S. foreign policy by adding that "where gross imbalances are discovered, American efforts should be devoted to pushing development in the channels where it has lagged the most."[9] Indeed, the assumptions of the modernization literature were variously reflected in U.S. aid programs, including the Alliance for Progress and Title IX of the Foreign Assistance Act, beginning in 1967.[10]

But what were the concrete results for Latin American studies of this modernization phase? I think that it is fair to say that we gained a substantial number of very valuable monographic studies in several areas. As Ranis noted in a 1968 survey of the field, the largest number of studies concentrated on parties and interest groups.[11] We learned a great deal about key institutions such as the military and the Church, and about the political role of urban dwellers, peasants, and students, all of which were studied as interest groups—that is, as actors within a political process of competing groups at different levels of modernization.[12] Several very good country studies also appeared, with Cuba, Mexico, Chile, and Brazil benefiting from a sizable body of writings on different aspects of their national political life.[13]

It is also true, however, that no matter how outstanding, this work did not enter into the mainstream of theorizing in comparative politics, nor did Latin Americanists trained in the United States provide new theoretical innovations for the field. The work on political parties, for example, was quite disappointing. A few solid and valuable monographs appeared for particular parties. Most stressed without adequate documentation the presumed hyperideological orientation of Latin American parties, the personalism of party followers, the lack of pragmatic orientations of elites, and their concern for such things as status as opposed to program orientations. It is notable that only one comparative volume on parties appeared during this period, and that generalizations about party structure and behavior were rarely subjected to careful conceptual and comparative analysis. Many important questions were never systematically considered. Why do most countries in Latin America have catchall parties, and what accounts for the development of mass-based parties in a few others? Why are parties and particular configurations of party systems so entrenched in countries as diverse as Chile and Colombia, and so ephemeral in other countries such as Brazil? Why do so many countries in Latin America have two-party systems, a phenomenon that is rare in other parts of the world? How important are party cleavages and party system variables in accounting for regime success and breakdown? What is the balance sheet of consociational efforts at party accommodation in countries like Venezuela and Colombia? What is the relative importance of cultural versus structural variables in accounting for party actions and behavior?[14]

The literature on the Latin American military generated in the 1960's and early 1970's, in contrast to the party literature, was one of the most impressive. First-rate monographs that caught the attention of specialists from other areas appeared for several countries. Abraham Lowenthal in his 1974 review essay of this literature highlighted some of the strengths of these works. And yet, Lowenthal also argued that we still did not know "how the political roles of armies evolved within different national contexts, why coups sometimes occur and sometimes not, why military regimes are sometimes brief and sometimes long, sometimes reformist and sometimes reactionary, how armies have been affected by macrosocial and institutional changes, and what effects various forms of military participation had on national politics and policy."[15] In a recent review of that same literature, I noted that Lowenthal's catalogue of unanswered questions is a more serious indictment of the literature than he himself was willing to admit.[16]

John Martz, in his 1971 review of the field, reflected some of the disillusionment with the failure of Latin Americanists to take up the challenge of bringing Latin America into the mainstream of comparative politics. According to Martz:

The record would seem to suggest that Latin American political studies have more often than not been unimaginative in concept and pedestrian in approach. A certainly healthy eclecticism has been diluted by a Pavlovian tendency to respond to passing fads within the discipline. Political scientists committed to Latin American studies have in recent years rushed to follow the comparativist pack. They have been distinctly trend-followers rather than trend-setters.[17]

But not everyone in the field was arguing in the early 1970's that political scientists dealing with Latin America should emulate and contribute to the political development literature. Kalman Silvert, one of the pioneers of the field and a scholar who sought in many of his earlier writings to apply modernization concepts to Latin America, articulated a sharp dissenting view in an essay published in 1975. He noted bluntly that "Latin American politics forces us to remember what we have been professionally taught to forget. To put it another way, the exercise of standard American professionalism is incompetence in explaining Latin American politics."[18] According to Silvert, "the factual material pressing in on us from Latin America, and indeed, from almost everywhere, demands theoretical, methodological, and technical change from us." U.S. social science was "designed to search out stability, conjunction, symmetry, intrasystemic extrapolations, manipulations of existing influence, the separation of ideas and actions, and the tameness of a citizenry led by an 'elite.'"[19] And yet, Silvert adds, even a cursory examination of Latin America suggests that concepts such as class, dictatorship, ideology, nationalism, torture, and power are commonplace. "To deal with Latin America, we must be able to explain instability, disjunction, asymmetry, intersystemic change, the creation and use of power, ideologies and behavior, violence, and so many other manifestations of a total situation in rapid and wrenching change."[20] The basic problem was not that scholars dealing with Latin America were ignoring the comparative literature. To their credit, they did not take it that seriously.

The difficulty with the literature on Latin America was not so much a Pavlovian reaction to modernization thinking as the lack of a series of conceptual tools capable of orienting the Latin American field toward dealing with the kinds of questions and issues that Silvert highlighted. New conceptual tools, however, did emerge, primarily from Latin America, not the United States. Martz makes no mention in his essay of the Latin American scholarship of the middle and late 1960's, a scholarship that would have a profound effect on the study of Latin America and Latin American politics. Indeed, it would inaugurate the third phase, or dependency phase, in our chronicle of the evolution of the field. This phase is not only characterized by a new paradigm that challenges the previous ones but also by the emergence and growth of social science research in Latin America. I will briefly review some of the assumptions of the dependency school and their particular reference to Latin American politics, then make a few comments about the production of social science research in Latin America during the last ten years or so.

The dependency perspective emerged as a critique of neoclassical assumptions in the literature on economic development as well as a critique of modernization and political development concepts in sociology and political science.[21] Both because of its intrinsic merits and the growing dissatisfaction with existing frameworks, the dependency literature and its offshoots, particularly the work on bureaucratic authoritarianism, catapulted Latin American studies into an entirely new position vis-à-vis other areas and fields. Rather than being the stepchild of area studies programs and a discipline incapable of generating more universal conceptual insights, Latin American studies would now have a distinct impact on the work in comparative politics and international relations dealing with the Third World. Whereas in the 1960's specialists on Asia and Africa were thought to be the real innovators, in the 1970's the work of Latin Americanists received considerable attention.[22]

Dependency writings called for a broad interdisciplinary perspective to explain the major themes of Latin American reality: economic underdevelopment, social inequality, political instability, and authoritarianism. They argued that change could best be understood as part and parcel of the global historical process of development. Change could not be understood by focusing on individual societies as the basic units of analysis. It was necessary to situate countries within a global context, stressing the fact that Latin America evolved on the periphery of the world system. External factors stemming from the international economic order affected in a complex and often dialectical fashion domestic factors, conditioning the prospects for self-sustained development.

It followed that the level of analysis should change from a preoccupation with culturally determined value patterns and motivations of individuals, whether members of the mass public or elites, to a preoccupation with the interrelationship between the economy, social classes, political alliances, and the state. The state, in turn, could no longer be understood as merely the end product of competing groups, or as an aggregate of bureaucratic agencies that claim a monopoly over legitimate force, but had to be recognized as an agent that directly and indirectly plays an important role in producing and reproducing the economic and social system, albeit with varying degrees of autonomy from social forces. Dependent, peripheral development historically produced an opportunity structure such that personal gain for dominant groups and entrepreneurial elements was detrimental to the collective gain of balanced development or the consolidation of representative institutions. There was room for variation, depending on the particular form of national insertion into the world system. There was also some room for choice, for individual human action, but this had to be understood to be severely limited by structural constraints.[23]

The dependency perspective implied not only important conceptual shifts but also shifts in the focus of research and the methodological tools employed. The study of individuals and groups, utilizing such techniques as survey research, gave way to broader, often more abstract and less empirical historical assessments of transformations over time. Most of the original work on dependency was preoccupied with attempting to explain why Latin America was historically underdeveloped in economic terms and how underdevelopment could be overcome. However, the dependency perspective also provided impetus for other research questions, most notably a preoccupation with the advent of new authoritarian forms of the state.[24]

The bureaucratic-authoritarian state, as Guillermo O'Donnell originally conceived of it, was the product of the political economy of a particular stage of dependent capitalist development. It resulted from the crisis of import substitution industrialization and the consequent failure of populist politics. The bureaucratic-authoritarian state was seen as a necessary political stage, dictated by an alliance of political forces intent on overcoming economic stagnation with a strategy of deepening industrialization in alliance with foreign capital.[25]

O'Donnell's work had a major impact on the field. It challenged in a frontal way the assumptions of some of the modernization literature, particularly those assumptions that held that economic growth inexorably leads to democracy by encouraging greater societal differentiation and communication, and greater professionalization and depoliticization of the military. Quite the contrary, economic growth, industrialization, and the rise of public and private bureaucracies and technocratic groups in mid-twentieth-century Latin America were associated with a particularly harsh form of popular deactivation and political authoritarianism. O'Donnell attempted in his writings to specify not only the origins of the bureaucratic-authoritarian state but also its overall characteristics and performance in different contexts, focusing on such features as the level of threat to the middle and upper groups, and the nature of pre-existing social and political arrangements.

Parallel to this theoretical innovation, reflected in writings on dependency and bureaucratic authoritarianism, was the burgeoning of social science research in Latin America.[26] In a real sense, the center of gravity of work on Latin American politics shifted from the United States to Latin America. In many countries—notably Mexico, Brazil, Argentina, Peru, and Chile—the research contributions of local scholars became so significant that by the early 1980's it became difficult to teach an undergraduate course and impossible to teach a graduate course dealing with any of those countries without a majority of the items on the syllabus being in Spanish.

The work by Latin American scholars was undertaken in a host of new research institutions, many of which were not university-based, providing them with the opportunity to structure broad interdisciplinary programs with collaborative research projects on particular questions. Few individual university or research programs in the United States could match by the late 1970's the research capabilities in Latin American social science of programs such as CIDE in Mexico, FLACSO in Santiago, IUPERJ in Rio, IEP in Lima, or CEDES in Buenos Aires, let alone the capability in those centers of research on the particular countries in which they are located.[27]

And while Latin Americans continued to pursue graduate work in Europe and the United States, regional programs such as the Facultad Latinoamericana de Ciencias Sociales, the Instituto Latinoamericano de Planificación Económica y Social, and the Social Science Program of Central American Universities, as well as research centers in Brazil and Mexico, became important training grounds for younger social scientists.

The most important research centers in Latin America, numbering over eighty, participate in CLACSO (Consejo Latinoamericano de Ciencias Sociales). CLACSO has held biannual assemblies since 1967 and provides a framework for coordinating research efforts of scholars from different countries through its interdisciplinary working groups and commissions. Among the most important CLACSO working groups of relevance to political scientists are the ones dealing with Population and

Development, Urban and Regional Development, Theories of Politics and the State, Bureaucracy and Public Policy, International Relations, and Transnational Studies. While fewer publications have resulted from the work of these groups than one would have hoped, they include notable efforts such as Norbert Lechner's edited volume *Estado y política en América Latina* and Cotler and Fagen's *Latin America and the United States*.[28]

I have dwelt on the importance of Latin American scholarship and its institutional manifestations to highlight the enormous differences between the state of affairs today and that described by Kling and Gomez twenty years ago. I do, however, want to stress one other dimension of the sociology of knowledge with respect to the study of Latin American politics that is of particular importance and that might be lost in my emphasis on the importance of research efforts in the region—namely, that some of the most outstanding efforts in the field have resulted from a close collaboration between Latin American and U.S. specialists. With the increasing cross-fertilization of ideas, the distinction between a Latin American and a U.S. approach to many questions receded. This was a major step forward and a difficult one, as it had to overcome not only the conceptual gaps that existed but real suspicions stemming from incidents such as Project Camelot and the close association of many U.S. scholars with the formulation of U.S. foreign policy in the early 1960's.

Genuine bonds of collaboration and friendship led to extraordinarily rich efforts in many areas: urban politics, international relations, U.S.-Mexican relations, and projects such as the work on the breakdown of democratic regimes, transitions to democracy, multinationals, political parties, and politics and labor.[29] These initiatives were aided by important institutional efforts, particularly the work of the Social Science Research Council—though other institutions played a role as well, including the Ford Foundation and the Inter-American Foundation. The Woodrow Wilson International Center for Scholars became, in the late 1970's and early 1980's a crucial forum for collaborative research and discussions.

But let me return to the substance of our research efforts. How much progress was made within the framework of the dependency perspective? Did the emergence of an alternative paradigm provide us with a new key to unlocking the basic questions of Latin American politics and development? The answers, of course, are mixed. While we have had many good studies and fruitful, even exciting, theoretical reflections, some of the fundamental questions about politics and political change in Latin America remain unanswered.

A few of the original formulations of the dependency thesis, which argued the impossibility of any kind of dynamic growth in peripheral capitalist societies, proved to be far off the mark.[30] And while the subtler dependency arguments such as those of Cardoso and Faletto spawned some very good work on the "new character of dependency" or "associated dependent development," their overall theoretical contributions did not improve much, either in terms of conceptual refinement or empirical substantiation.[31] Almost twenty years after it was written, Cardoso and Faletto's small volume has not really been superseded, and the leading theorists such as Cardoso and Sunkel have turned their attention to other pursuits. Indeed, the very notion of dependence has lost a good deal of its appeal, remaining more alive in some intellectual circles in the United States than in Latin America.[32]

There are some exceptions, such as the literature on multinationals already mentioned and some of the works of historians who have examined such questions as the relationship between export economies and labor movement formations. But the indepth historical, comparative, and interdisciplinary research efforts essential to fleshing out and confirming or disconfirming some of the generalizations of dependency writings—including many of the implicit assumptions about the relationship between dependent economic relations, class and political coalitions, and the state—have not been undertaken.[33]

Discussions surrounding the bureaucratic-authoritarian state have been more intellectually satisfying, but here again some of the concrete results have been disappointing. Many of the early assumptions about the direct tie-in between economic variables and authoritarianism have not stood the test of empirical reflection. Import substitution industrialization had different manifestations in different countries, and populist regimes were not as closely related to it as was once thought, though the strength of populism may be related to the intensity of repression in bureaucratic-authoritarian regimes. Some countries such as Colombia and Venezuela avoided bureaucratic-authoritarian regimes, and the critical variables that separated these countries from those that succumbed to military rule have not been fully clarified.[34] Nor have some of the global characteristics of bureaucratic-authoritarian regimes and their policy directions been consistent with some of the formulations in the model.[35]

My main problem, however, is not that some of the early generalizations have not stood the test of further reflection. My main concern is that, as with the general work on dependency, we have not developed enough good comparative and empirical research projects, not only to test propositions from the bureaucratic-authoritarian literature, but simply to understand more fully the characteristics and modes of operation of the Latin American military regimes of the 1970's and early 1980's. Such basic questions as the way in which the military governments in Uruguay, Argentina, and Chile organized themselves to enact laws, the degree to which they were willing to accede to societal pressures, and the concrete mechanisms for policy-making were never adequately fleshed out. What is the significance of the differences between the collegial style of policy-making exercised by the military in Uruguay and the far more centralized and personalized style of the Chilean military regime? While we often discussed the significance of the difference between a relatively autonomous civil society in Argentina and one that was more closely interpenetrated with parties and leadership networks in Chile, studies to investigate this critical element of the linkages between civil society and the state under authoritarianism were never fully developed. Our work remained suggestive, but too often general and abstract. There was a gap between this work and the multitude of more discrete studies on a multiplicity of questions that were carried primarily by Latin American scholars.[36]

Let me be rather bold by suggesting some of the reasons why it has been difficult for us to move to more concrete and empirical studies aimed at answering some of the large questions—why it is that what we promised at the theoretical level has produced fewer results than we might have expected. I believe there are two fundamental reasons for this—one having to do with broad epistemological issues, the other with the concrete reality of the research process, particularly in Latin America.

First, problems of epistemology. Robert Kaufman, in his excellent 1981 assessment of the field, put the matter this way:

> The positivistic sins of liberal social science may well have been the positing of oversimplified, linear relationships, specified in terms of arid abstract concepts, and tested with invalid quantitative data. But the new style of holistic and historical research contains epistemological sins of its own. One is the risk of lapsing into a theoretical or nondisprovable configurative analysis, in which the importance or weight of a given set of factors is simply assumed or presupposed. Another related problem is a tendency toward teleological reasoning which explains, *post-hoc*, any form of stasis or change in terms of the functional requirements or the dialectical contradictions of a given system.[37]

As originally formulated, the dependency argument was never advanced as a theory. It was, rather, a broad descriptive model of the evolution of societies from colonial times to the present. As an historical model, limited in time and space, it had no claim to universal applicability. Its historical and general formulation was such that it was true by definition—providing little room for a strategy of confirmation or disconfirmation of its major tenets. Its concern with broad characterizations of economic, social, and political phenomena tended to exaggerate the similarities of the Latin American experience while underplaying some of the important differences. This was particularly true from the point of view of political science, in which the framework tended to overstate the commonalities of Latin American politics without accounting for some important diversities.

The efforts to test dependency that were undertaken by U.S. scholars fell far short. They either completely missed the point about dependency writings—forgetting, for example, that these were intended to explain historical underdevelopment, not power relations among states in the contemporary world—or they extracted in an overly simplistic fashion a series of concepts, disembodied from the complex historical and dialectical nature of economic, social, and political relations.[38] But the inadequacy of these efforts does not mean that dependency analysis stood the test. We clearly need a maturing of the kind of systematic historical and comparative research that Cardoso and Faletto pioneered in order to do justice to their efforts.

To a much lesser degree as Karen Remmer and Gil Merkx have noted, the notion of the bureaucratic-authoritarian state also comes up short of being an explanatory theory. It is an ideal type, in which the relationship between empirical reality and the ideal type is problematic. As Remmer and Merkx note, "the latter is neither a hypothesis to be tested against the facts nor an empirical generalization based on them."[39]

But these epistemological problems could have been overcome. The absence of much empirical work on politics in the era of the bureaucratic-authoritarian state is closely related to more practical and immediate factors of greater significance—problems of the organization and execution of research.

First and foremost among these problems is the difficulty of conducting research under authoritarian situations. Political persecution in most countries led to the dismantling of much of the social science capability in universities. Promising research efforts and teams were broken up through the dismantling of programs and the exile of academics. And those research institutions that managed to survive did so with limited resources and with the constant threat of government intervention. That threat dampened the possibility of conducting many kinds of research; indeed, it encouraged more abstract and theoretical work of the kind that would be considered too esoteric for the authorities to be concerned about. In the same way that authoritarian regimes froze politics and political leadership, they froze much of the empirical research that could be carried out on political questions.[40]

Second, the political problems of everyday life in turn encouraged a preoccupation with the immediate, leading to a certain trendiness—a penchant for wanting to follow the events of the day. Our interest has moved in a rather dizzying pace from the breakdown of democratic regimes to the origins of authoritarianism, to the characteristics of authoritarianism, to the survival of civil society under authoritarianism, to transitions to democracy. Today, before we really have any kind of closure on these topics, we are moving to the study of the consolidation of democratic regimes. All of these efforts have barely kept up with the fast-moving events—and in turn they have produced somewhat general papers analyzing, often in very sophisticated fashion, some of the broader characteristics and implications of political regimes.

Third, this trendiness and absence of thorough empirical

work have been encouraged in Latin America by certain features of the organization and dissemination of knowledge—namely, the conference format and the reliance on soft money. As I noted earlier, conferences have contributed to some of the most innovative thinking in the field. However, the proliferation of high-level conferences has led, for the most part, to the production of general and theoretical essays rather than research papers or monographs. Because the number of full-time social scientists has been small and the top scholars have been in high demand, they often have not had the time or resources to undertake in-depth empirical research in preparing the next conference paper. This state of affairs has been encouraged by funding sources attracted to the conference format as a simple way of bringing together leading scholars of different nationalities to focus on common themes. It has also been encouraged by research centers in Latin America dependent on soft money from international foundations for basic survival. Honoraria for conference papers have been an important source of income for some of the leading researchers in Latin America committed to staying in their own countries despite the difficult conditions of survival under authoritarian rule.

These observations apply primarily to scholarship in Latin America. But we also need to consider various factors that are peculiar to the United States and help to account for a rather significant drop in scholarly research of an empirical variety in the United States.

The most important factor in this drop is the sharp decline of new cohort groups coming into the field. The diversion of the best students away from graduate training in social science, the reduced availability of funds for dissertation research (which seems to be getting progressively worse every day), and the growing attraction of other areas of study within comparative politics have meant that not as many graduate students are becoming Latin American specialists.

At the same time, the 1960's generation is finding it difficult to go back for renewed field research—there is the press of administrative duties, families, and research grants that are not comparable to salaries. There is a tendency for more established scholars to conduct less empirical work once the dissertation has been published.

In addition, among U.S. scholars there has been a clear distaste for authoritarian regimes, leading to a decline in field studies. Authoritarianism may have been considered too ad hoc a phenomenon, or too predictable, or too passing. Also, there may have been a perception that research would be difficult, when in fact foreign scholars could have undertaken countless research projects with much greater ease than local scholars. It is striking how little research U.S. scholars undertook on Chile, Argentina, or Uruguay in contrast with the research efforts of earlier periods. The work on Brazil, with some notable exceptions, has been carried out by Brazilian scholars. Growing attention paid by U.S. scholars to Central America has, by contrast, been a welcome trend—again, however, reflecting the importance of events in helping us to set our research agenda.[41]

Finally, the decline in research on Latin America has paralleled an increase in preoccupation with foreign policy questions and, in particular, U.S. policy toward authoritarian regimes and revolutionary transformations on the continent. Some prominent Latin Americanists have also turned their attention to other areas of study, such as European politics and policy-making.

Where is the study of Latin American politics going? We seem to be in a new and fourth phase, one in which there is some skepticism about global conceptualizations that aspire to characterize the whole of the region. As Robert Kaufman has noted, this is a phase of conceptual and methodological eclecticism, one in which we may want to pay more attention to middle-range questions and research objectives.[42]

We have been too willing in our theoretical frameworks to draw on broad cultural or economic determinants, to focus on abstract elements from "above" (the state) or "outside" (the international political economy) or on politics from "below" (the urban poor and peasants). We need to return to a concern for more discrete political elements: parties, elections, interest groups, bureaucracy, decision-making, and so forth.[43] In this vein, let me suggest four broad directions for future research, all of which focus in some way on the notion of state or regime.

First, we should consider the state and regime types. Indeed, there is a lack of a clear fit between underlying economic or cultural factors and regime types. This proposition is reenforced by the transition from authoritarianism to democracy in countries at substantially different levels of socioeconomic development, and by the fact that some countries have made the shift without a concomitant and fundamental reshaping of their own socioeconomic order. This suggests the importance of autonomizing political actors and the state itself. The political is much more secular than many of our formulations would have led us to believe. We need to revindicate the notion of regime as a focus for analysis—not just simply as an epiphenomenon.[44] The very economic determinants that may contribute to bringing a regime into being may contribute to undermining it, making more viable a democratic or authoritarian alternative. Clearly, however, as Cardoso and O'Donnell have reminded us, underlying structural features may contribute to a greater elective affinity to one type of regime or another.[45]

Among the basic questions we need answered is why Latin American countries with different economic or structural characteristics have sometimes experienced similar regimes, while other countries with similar economic or structural characteristics have sometimes experienced different regime types. Why, for example, were Chile, Uruguay, and Costa Rica able to establish democracies, while these proved so elusive in Argentina? And, more recently, why were Colombia, Venezuela, and Costa Rica able to maintain democratic institutions when all other regimes succumbed? Within the Central American context, what explains the difference between Costa Rica and other countries in the region in the development of democratic institutions? And what makes for the success of revolutionary transformations in one context and failure in others? Ad hoc explanations that draw on such answers as the existence of a larger middle class or of small independent farmers or a particular configuration of export economy are not fully satisfactory.

What is required is more systematic comparative efforts. The diversity of regime types in Latin America and the similarity of broad contextual variables make the continent an ideal place for comparisons with a small number of cases. These might focus on one case in comparison with a series of others, or they could be based on paired comparisons. Depending on the questions asked, comparisons with other non–Latin American cases might also be in order.

Second, we should look more closely at the state, society, and social subjects. During the heyday of authoritarian regimes in Latin America, scholars paid some attention to the survival strategies of political and social groups, be they unions, parties, or base communities. But with the partial exception of Brazil, not much research was carried out on this subject, and many of our observations may have come close to wishful thinking. We know little about parties, groups, and movements under authoritarianism or in a transitional phase toward democracy, or about their interrelations with other societal elements and with state structures. What are the mechanisms of co-optation and control, support and compliance, coercion and representation?

In other words, we need to return to a study of some of the political roles of societal groups, research that was rich in the 1960's but languished in the 1970's, with the partial exception of the very fine work on the urban poor. We need to study parties, interest groups, labor, business associations, students, and so forth.

But we should not undertake such an effort with the lenses of the modernization perspective. Our focus should not be on the degree of modernity of leaders or organizational structures. We should study them with the benefit of our journey from a microsociological bias to a concern for the contextual parameters under which groups operate and unfold, the broader relationships of representation and domination. In this effort we might profitably make use of insights from rational choice theories, taking care not to fall into a reductionist trap.

Let me stress that attention to these contextual variables is crucial. For example, if one were to study Chilean parties today with the perspectives of the 1960's, one would easily observe that they had ceased to be highly organized and disciplined parties with clear programmatic and ideological directions and impersonal leadership. In many ways the Chilean party system has become "Latin Americanized." Today, the parties are fragmented, hyperideological, and racked by personalistic conflicts. Old leaders still loom large, and new leaders have for the most part not appeared. Does this mean that Chileans have become more personalistic, less capable of programmatic orientations, more traditional in their political relationships? Or can we better understand the shift as a logical response to the impact that authoritarian rule has exerted on political organizations that for generations had been oriented to winning elections? The presence of the same old leaders, a perennial characteristic of Latin American politics, is not due to a sudden penchant for personalism in Chile, but to the freezing of mechanisms of leadership renewal through prohibitions of party meetings and the banning of elections.[46] And factionalism and hyperideological orientations are the clear result of the inability of individual leaders to demonstrate their authority through the winning of electoral contests and of the absence of an electoral calculus in defining party strategy. Party characteristics and behavior are to be understood as being related to the broader rules of the game. It is not modern parties that make for democracy, but democracy and democratic rules that make for modern parties. The calculus of leaders and followers is not determined by their individual proclivities per se, but by the broader context and the opportunity structures that help determine political action.

A similar argument can be made with respect to studies on the military. We simply cannot think of the military as a neutral actor, as one side of an equation in which it is counterposed to civilian institutions on the other side and intervenes as a response to the weakening of the latter. The military is an integral actor within the political system, not an institution outside of it. With its awesome power it helps to shape the very rules of the game, but it is also contaminated by its direct involvement in the political process. We need to rethink the role of the military in the light of its interrelations with other forces in society. It is not an autonomous agent.[47]

Again, the methodology should be more systematically comparative. We need to look at individual cases in the light of broad comparative questions. How do social cleavages translate into partisan attachments in different countries? Why do we have two-party systems in some countries and multiparty systems in others? Why is the incidence of polarized multiparty systems so rare?

And the fact that many countries have taken concrete steps back to democratic forms of government does not mean that we should not continue our attempt to study the role of political agents under authoritarianism. In many respects this is the time to undertake that kind of research. People are freer to talk, government officials and military officers have retired, and documentary sources such as lists of officials, minutes of meetings, and decrees and laws are more readily available for consultation.

Third, we should examine the state and political economy. It is very important that we continue the rich line of research dealing with political economy.[48] At a time when many scholars have been arguing that the dependency concept leaves much to be desired and the notion of interdependence seems more relevant, we find that Latin American countries have become extraordinarily constrained by international economic forces. Studies of international political economy are very valuable precisely because they are able to focus on the interactions of various levels: economics and politics on the one hand, and international, state, and class dimensions on the other. This work calls for a truly interdisciplinary effort. Indeed, as Kaufman so aptly remarked, the "growing interest in political economy . . . is at its best when it incorporates the proposition that the realms of the state and civil society *each* involve relationships of production and power which cut across the conventionally-defined realms of 'the polity' and 'the economy.' An understanding of these relationships will almost certainly require . . . a restructuring of the disciplines themselves."[49]

Beyond some very valuable studies on multilateral agencies and private corporations and the interplay between foreign and domestic capital and the state, we need more concrete and detailed studies of local institutions. In particular, we need good studies of finance ministries, state banks, state-industrial relations, natural resources, and public utility firms. We need studies of decision-making on key issues such as pricing, investment, trade, tariffs, and foreign exchange. How autonomous are these agencies? How do they relate to other agencies of the public sector? How do they relate to local and international capital? Are there substantial differences in policy-making under authoritarian and democratic contexts? What is the room for choice, for action that is responsive to democratic forces?[50]

Finally, we should focus on states and state structures. While I have already argued for greater attention to policy-making studies, I also want to stress the value of paying more attention to some of the formal aspects of government and politics in Latin America—a return to some of the themes of the public law literature of the late 1950's. With the behavioral revolution, and then with our preoccupation with broad and abstract categories such as the state, we lost sight of the formal, legal, and institutional aspects of Latin American politics. These aspects are not just figments of imagination; they are of central importance. We cannot lightly dismiss the significance of constitutions, rules, and procedures after observing the Brazilian military struggle for years to define rules of the game that would advance its interests, only to find itself trapped today by its own legality—a problem that the Chilean military shares to a more devastating degree.

We know very little about the similarities and differences between the governing structures of authoritarian and democratic regimes in Latin America. Yet, an important first approximation to these questions can be found in constitutions, decree laws, and rules. Excellent sources for these are law journals with commentaries on the generation of particular laws and their applications. As an example, I recently tried to figure out how the Chilean junta makes laws. The key starting point for this research was the legislative history of the formal rules defining junta powers and operations—a legislative history that is discussed in detail in several law review articles, complete with indications of relevant informal as well as formal pressures brought to bear at different points in the legislative process. Once the formal rules are clear, it then becomes possible through interviews with junta staffers, staffers in the office of the presidency, consultants to government commissions, relevant lobbyists of groups with access, and junta members themselves to understand how laws are made. A comparative study of the formal aspects of lawmaking in different countries under military rule would give us a good indication of the differences in governmental structure of no little consequence for broader questions such as policy-making and regime stability.

A preoccupation with laws and constitutions is clearly very relevant to our thinking during this period of attempted consolidation of democratic regimes. Constitutional frameworks, party laws, electoral laws, laws of succession, and rules and procedures governing military institutions and promotion systems do matter. They can either facilitate a process of democratic accommodation or hinder it.

Reflections along these lines should lead us to think such

heretical thoughts as whether or not parliamentary regimes would be better than presidential ones. After all, with the exception of the United States and the partial exception of France and Finland, Latin America is the continent of presidential governments. And this is despite the fact that its societal and political cleavages may be closer to those of Europe. Has the failure of democracy in Latin America been, at least in part, the failure of presidentialism? Is the success of parliamentary regimes in the Caribbean merely an accident of culture or history, or do parliamentary regimes afford sharply divided societies greater flexibility?[51]

In sum, this research agenda calls for an underlying concern for the following elements: (1) the degree of human choice within the parameters of various forms of structural constraints; (2) the broad historical-structural antecedents of current political issues and problems; (3) a preoccupation with formal, legal, and institutional dimensions as well as political behavior and political economy; and (4) a comparative methodology emphasizing the utility of small-n comparisons.

THREE

The State of Latin American Economics

ALBERT FISHLOW

It has now been more than thirty-five years since the Economic Commission for Latin America published its comprehensive analysis of economic development in the region. That occasion marked the formal debut of a structuralist economic approach, one that gained momentum and substance during the 1950's. By the end of the decade, the Commission's policy emphasis on domestic industrialization had found favor in most Latin American countries. An unusual consensus on both the method of analysis and the development strategy it implied pervaded the region. Orthodoxy maintained its hold on only a small, older generation of economists trained in the European tradition. Although international agencies defended the tenets of a universal economics during the 1950's, the heretical structuralists held sway and even gained adherents among sympathetic foreign academics.

Such a hold on thought and policy did not survive the crisis of the import-substitution model in the late 1950's and early 1960's. The economic reversal in the region was severe. As the Commission's report on the post-war period noted: "This downward trend became more general after 1955 and by the end of the fifties had led to stagnation in many Latin American countries and in some to a reduction of the absolute levels of real per capita income."[1] Attempts to adjust structuralist policies did not prove very successful. Even the mobilization of official external resources, first through the newly founded Inter-American Development Bank and then under the aegis of the Alliance for Progress, did not provide a solution. Nor was there a further round of intellectual innovations that tailored structuralist doctrine to the new realities.

Instead, structuralism increasingly came under attack for the inadequacy of its diagnosis. Reformism, because of its redistributive content, aroused an increasingly intense political reaction that was reinforced by deteriorating aggregate economic performance. A conservative opposition called for more orthodox economics and less state aggrandizement. In the name of private freedom and anti-communism, military governments replaced civilian leadership in Brazil and Argentina in the mid-1960's and promised an end to inflation and the beginning of sound economic growth.

At the same time, criticisms of structuralist doctrine mounted from the left. These reflected frustration at inadequate and incomplete implementation of far-reaching reforms as well as at the recalcitrant balance-of-payments problems that import substitution had not resolved. These criticisms became embodied in a dependency perspective that simultaneously rejected the new economic orthodoxy and the new political repression. Like structuralism, the dependency approach drew its inspiration from historical analysis and the regional experience. But it was also more comprehensive in its description of peripheral capitalist society and quite pessimistic about development prospects.

The next significant departure in economic analysis was largely a product of the changed circumstances of the 1970's. The 1973–74 oil shock quadrupled the price of petroleum and ushered in a period of larger capital inflows and more variable international economic conditions. While in some countries, principally Brazil, these developments led to a resurgence of import substitution, in others, like Chile and Argentina, international monetarism gained sway at the expense of traditional orthodoxy. Not only did money count, but domestic credit became the central determinant of the balance of payments.

This theoretical approach eventually fell victim to the Great

Latin American Depression of the early 1980's, even in Chile, where its adherents remain strongest. Yet, the same monetary approach is embodied in the stabilization programs of the International Monetary Fund (IMF), now found in virtually all the countries of the region. Such packages are necessarily more eclectic than theoretically pure, but they also make domestic credit management the central instrument for treating external imbalance.

While the IMF perspective now influences short-term stabilization policies in the region, a long-term analogue is almost as powerful. This outward-looking strategy preaches the advantage of an export and private-sector orientation. Getting prices right is argued to be a necessary and sufficient condition for international trade to become a reliable engine of growth and development. The strategy, adapted from its East Asian success, is a complete inversion of the structuralist, state-centered, import-substitution approach indigenous to Latin America.

Development thinking in the region has thus fragmented from the initial sway of structuralism three decades ago. Yet, under the impulse of the present crisis, despite the continuing and healthy economic policy debate in many countries, one also sees signs of a new convergence. To understand the antecedents of this emerging view, I begin with the characteristic features of the four economic models that have dominated Latin American economic thought for a generation: structuralism, dependency, international monetarism, and export-led growth.[2] I single out four issues to which Latin American economic thought speaks an increasingly convergent voice. By way of conclusion, I extend the discussion to the political economy of development strategy.

Structuralism

Structuralism[3] amended the orthodox full employment, capital accumulation driven, orthodox economic growth model in three important ways. One was the specification of macroeconomic equilibrium. The second was the characterization of underlying microeconomic relationships. The third was the definition of the role of the state.

The central macroeconomic novelty was attention to the foreign-exchange constraint. Access to foreign exchange, rather than domestic savings, was the critical determinant of economic growth in peripheral countries. For these economies, export earnings could be insufficient to buy the critical imports on which continuing growth depended. Reallocation of resources toward the export sector would not necessarily help because primary products confronted inelastic demand, with respect to both price and income. Reliance on trade in order to obtain industrial products via the intermediation of primary exports could therefore be less efficient than developing a domestic manufacturing sector. Static comparative advantage indicating primary specialization was a poor guide to dynamic efficiency.

In addition to the opportunity to utilize potential domestic savings, the industrialization strategy had a further appeal. Manufactures were regarded as the sector embodying advanced, and advancing, technology. The gains of increased productivity could be internalized and made independent of the adverse evolution of the terms of trade; for, contrary to classical theoretical expectations predicated on diminishing returns, historical experience was invoked to argue in support of deteriorating, rather than improving, terms of trade for primary producers. Later on, the virtues of indigenous technological capacity and labor force skill enhancement were added as sources of further external economies justifying priority for the industrial sector.

If this desired outcome were to be attained, however, barriers to competing imports were necessary. The function of commercial policy was not to temporarily equilibrate the balance of payments but to permanently restructure domestic relative prices in favor of the industrial sector. Internal terms of trade skewed against the export sector were the means of directing agricultural surplus to industrial investment. Where taxes could not be directly levied, market distortions were designed to serve instead. Such distortion extended to a differentiated tariff structure. While competitive products were to be excluded, complementary imported inputs were to be subsidized. As a result, the investment required to produce import substitutes domestically could be made more profitable.

At the microeconomic level, structuralism stressed discontinuities and imperfections. The agricultural sector was singled out as one important bottleneck. Relative prices were regarded as ineffective in reallocating resources, owing to concentrated landholdings and backward technology adopted in response to artificially cheap labor tied to the land. That system of land tenure inherited from the past was thus an obstacle to the provision of the larger food supplies required by a larger urban labor force; it was better suited to traditional, primary exports.

Other limitations of the market were also identified. The lack of coordination in early stages of industrialization meant that the investment opportunities in the industrial sector would not always be seized by investors keen on private profits. Since private producers were granted special privileges to induce investment, their protected position encouraged markup pricing rather than a competitive response. Apart from imperfections, there was the sheer sluggishness of private behavioral response. Private savers, for example, could not be relied upon to respond to interest rate incentives to expand the pool of funds available for capital accumulation.

These macro- and microeconomic conditions militated in favor of a strong state presence. The state was called upon to actively define and implement an economic strategy, rather than to accept the passive role Adam Smith advocated in *The Wealth of Nations*. That was a third decisive departure of structuralist economics. Development was a consequence of policy, not a natural evolution. The state's overall vision was called upon to substitute for the guidance of imperfect markets. Conscious and comprehensive planning was desirable. The state was to govern the accumulation of capital, both for infrastructure and for large industrial projects. The state was to operate public enterprises in activities that were beyond the capacity of private entrepreneurs. The state was to reform and regulate the private sector.

Structuralism was a Latin American theory of long-run development. Incidentally, structuralism was also a short-run macroeconomic theory that denied the effectiveness of orthodox monetary, fiscal, and exchange-rate policy in combating inflation. Reduction in nominal demands would induce reductions primarily in output, not in prices. Tighter credit and higher interest rates would only be passed along by firms to prices, even while shortage of working capital would cause them to restrict output. Reduced government expenditure would not "crowd in" private firms, but would lead to a contraction of complementary investment, and so, aggregate production. Devaluation would not correct a balance-of-payments disequilibrium by encouraging more exports and fewer imports, but merely succeed in fueling domestic inflation.

Structuralism was less explicit on what *could* be done in the short run to compensate for the inevitable shocks, international and domestic, to which developing economies were subject. Reform and structural change could be invoked for long-run development, but less persuasively in the short term. What emerged were two consistent reactions. The first was a greater official tolerance for inflation in Latin America than in other regions, a tolerance that had its basis not merely in the tenets of structuralism but also in long nineteenth-century experience with inconvertible exchange rates. The second was greater reliance on price controls and other practices to repress inflation when it threatened other objectives. That disguised the symptoms but not the reality of domestic disequilibrium.

Structuralism found favor in the vast majority of Latin American countries during the 1950's. It was a diagnosis that seemed to accord with the recent experience of the 1930's and 1940's. When countries applied trade controls and exchange restrictions in response to the crisis of the Great Depression, and expanded internal demand, the result was rapid recovery led by the industrial sector. Wartime shortages called new manufacturing capacity into being and continued protection of the old. In contrast, the foreign exchange reserves accumulated from export surpluses earned during the conflict rapidly evaporated with the end of hostilities and a return to freer international trade. There was soon a dollar shortage and reduced import capacity, and it became apparent that the United States intended to do nothing about it, at least for Latin America. The Marshall Plan for Europe amply demonstrated U.S. priorities and preoccupations. Latin America was forced to fend for itself and advised to rely on private capital inflow to help it do so.

While the economic analysis thus rang true, especially discounting the Korean War commodity price boom, its political implications also appealed to modernizing elites. Structuralism enhanced the power and prestige of the urban industrialists vis-à-vis the rural oligarchy. Not only were primary exports implicitly taxed by trade and exchange-rate policies, but the unequal pattern of land tenure was brought under direct attack as a barrier to continuing expansion of the industrial sector. While agricultural vested interests might prevail against agrarian reform, as they did in most countries, they fell easier prey to the relative favoritism displayed toward industry. The industrial bias also appealed to new political leaders desirous of enhancing their authority. On the one hand, a program of manufacturing expansion was easier to implement and produced a more evident public impact than a decentralized effort to increase agricultural productivity. On the other, the nationalist appeal of greater self-sufficiency strengthened the ability to deflect the wage pressures exerted by urban workers who wished to better their position.

The import-substitution strategy was therefore widely preferred to the alternative of turning the reins back to the international market and to the agricultural interests that benefited from it. It was not a model that would, or could, long endure. It deliberately provoked distortions in order to induce desired responses, but it did not adequately allow for the indirect and undesired consequences of the intervention. Three are especially important: the progressive imbalance in external accounts; the increasing sectoral disequilibrium; and the inflationary bias of more rapid growth.

The central paradox of import substitution—advocated to escape the foreign exchange constraint—is its tendency to cause even greater foreign-exchange vulnerability. In the first place, overvalued exchange rates adversely influenced the supply of future exports. At the start, it was possible to tax the agricultural sector because supply was inelastic in the short run, but thereafter producers adjusted away from export crops. They thereby evaded the tax and contributed to export stagnation. Indeed, import substitution was as successful as it was in Latin America only because it was initially implemented during a period of unusually favorable commodity prices induced by the Korean War; the result was windfall rents that could be taxed away without adverse balance-of-payments effects, thereby prolonging the viability of the strategy.

Secondly, import substitution produced an increased reliance on imports at the same time that exports were discouraged. As competitive imports were progressively produced domestically, the complementary imports that remained became ever more essential. Interruption in their supply would prejudice domestic production. Furthermore, once countries passed the easier phase of import substitution—and many had done so by the early 1950's because of their prior industrialization—complementary import requirements might very well begin to rise.

Resultant balance-of-payments problems in the 1950's were solved in part by direct foreign investment. Inflows on capital account helped to compensate for the stagnation of exports and resistance to import compression. There was a further advantage. Foreign investment in the industrial sector enabled it to use advanced technology to produce the modern goods that were most in demand in rising urban centers. The importance of foreign investment, and the ever more critical role it was forced to play, was an unanticipated and ironic consequence of a strategy advocated on the basis of domestic self-sufficiency.

Efforts to promote new exports might also have helped to close the payments gap, but few countries were prepared to undertake them. Some experimented with multiple exchange rates that favored nontraditional exports while taxing traditional commodities. On the whole, these initiatives fell short of success. They did so in part because domestic supply was unresponsive to modest incentives that were not a firm commitment to export promotion. Countries also encountered international obstacles. Although world trade resumed rapid growth in the 1950's, it was newly oriented to an exchange of manufactured products among the industrial countries rather than to the old patterns of North-South trade. Primary products declined in price from their Korean War peaks. While the exports of all oil-importing developing countries increased in volume by 5 percent a year between 1955 and 1963, their real purchasing power increased by only 2 percent a year. Latin American countries were not entirely idiosyncratic in their continuing belief in import substitution.

In addition to the balance-of-payments problem, import-substitution policies provoked serious sectoral imbalances. Industrial production was emphasized at the expense of agricultural output, with three consequences. First, food production did not keep pace with urban demand. Yet, a concern for inflation and rising urban wage costs prevented relative prices from reflecting, and possibly correcting, this inadequacy. Instead, urban incomes benefited relative to rural incomes, adversely affecting the equality of the income distribution. Second, capital-intensive industry absorbed smaller quantities of labor than rapid population growth and migration to the cities were making available. The other side of modernity and high labor productivity was a large number of poor, low-paying jobs. Third, physical targets dominated efficiency considerations. It was more important to construct and operate the steel plant than to calculate its comparative advantage. Opportunity cost considerations were played down, and sheer substitution of imports was played up, as if the premium on foreign exchange were infinite.

The third basic import-substitution disequilibrium was fiscal. As the initial real resources transferred from the agricultural sector began to give out, the state was increasingly called upon to subsidize the continuing investments in industry from its own revenues. Tax rebates and exemptions, as well as limited capacity to impose and collect new levies, constrained receipts. At the same time, expenditures were being rapidly expanded to satisfy the needs of the industrialization strategy. Government increased its participation in the economy, not only to provide complementary capital inputs but also to absorb potential urban unemployment. Government was the employer of last resort. The fiscal deficit reflected a growing disparity between commitments and the resources available for satisfying them.

Monetization of this deficit was the prelude to excess-demand inflation. Price increases generated an inflation tax that helped to finance the higher, and increasing, rates of investment. But accelerating inflation in turn aggravated the external problem by further overvaluing the exchange rate, while limiting the appetite of private-sector entrepreneurs for productive investment. Workers, too, soon recognized the reduced real wages that followed from the inability of nominal payments to keep pace with inflation. On the other hand, attempts to slow the inflationary process produced declines in output without parallel progress in stemming price rises. Inflation then became a cost-push phenomenon that was insensitive to the efforts to reduce demand.

In the last analysis, without a capacity to tax, and to restrain consumption, the state could play the role of capital accumulator only by stimulating inflation.

Alongside the gains in industrial production that at least the largest countries managed, an import-substitution crisis was thus created in the latter 1950's. It was especially severe for the smaller countries; for them, deviation from accommodation to the rules of the marketplace was more costly. But, for all, the favorable growth results were tainted by difficulties that had not been fully expected. Policymakers, wedded to a particular vision, failed to modify the strategy over time as implementation of its basic reforms became more problematic and its indirect economic consequences became more negative.

Eventually, structuralists recognized the need to amplify the policies pursued, if not the need to alter the underlying diagnosis. Three options presented themselves.

One was region-wide import substitution. Freer trade within Latin American countries could promote trade diversion for competitive imports and increase foreign exchange available for complementary imports from the industrial countries. So long as there was reciprocal trade growth, countries could all expand their regional imports and exports in a balanced way, easing the foreign-exchange constraint and benefiting from greater specialization. Theory did not work out in practice. While the large countries could sell manufactures to the smaller countries, the former had largely primary products to export, simply altering the source of their receipts rather than their amount. Large countries did not welcome competition from each other. Despite political endorsement at the presidential level and success in obtaining backing from the United States, the idea of a common market was never a relevant solution.

A second option was new inflows of official capital to supplement government revenues and alleviate the foreign-exchange shortage. That route led to establishment of the Inter-American Development Bank and later was a central part of the Alliance for Progress. But that policy also foundered. Early on, there were misunderstandings about the amount of public money available and its conditionality. Later on, changes in the goals of the Alliance made the structuralist objectives ineligible for financial support.

The third option was more radical. Those who advocated it ascribed the crisis of import substitution to the timidity of its implementation. Too much weight was being given to the private sector and not enough to the public. Too much attention was being paid to the balance-of-payments constraint and not enough to structural reform. Such a stance was a precursor to a dependency perspective. That transition quickly occurred once reformist governments passed to other hands, as many soon did.

For the option that prevailed was another. Brazil and Argentina returned to greater economic orthodoxy under the tutelage of military regimes in the mid-1960's. Yet, because industrialization had already left its mark, there was little question of returning to the status quo ante. Instead, the distinguishing characteristics of Latin American orthodoxy in the 1960's were short-term stabilization by means of monetary and fiscal instruments, and greater reliance on international market signals for the longer term. Growth took priority over distributional considerations. Reforms could wait, unless they were essential for efficiency and accumulation.

The bureaucratic-authoritarian model was more novel in its politics than in its economics. It was not export promotion, Asian style. It was not monetarism, either of the national or the later internationalist variety, although more attention was paid to monetary policy and interest rates than had been usual earlier, and much more attention was paid to financial markets. It was not a reorientation to agriculture and primary production, following natural-resource comparative advantage. Above all, it was not a return to private-sector preeminence and severely limited government participation in the economy. The economics of post–import-substitution populism, most prominent in Brazil but with vestiges elsewhere, was, in short, state capitalism that did not radically alter the import-substitution framework it inherited. Orthodoxy sought, instead, in a more favorable international context, to remedy some of the excesses of its predecessor.

Dependency Theory

Dependency theory[4] is much more a contribution to sociopolitical analysis than an economic model. Based on an historico-structural method, its originality derives from the use of position within the international system as a determinant of internal class behavior. It gained ground in the 1960's in response to the deficiencies of modernization theory as well as to the observed limitations of import-substitution industrialization. Dependency theory stood in stark opposition to the resurgence of orthodoxy and its external orientation.

Three economic propositions are integral to a dependency perspective. One is the principle of unequal exchange. The second is the adverse consequences of private foreign investment. The third is the disarticulation of the peripheral capitalist economy due to its skewed consumption pattern copied from that of the advanced industrial countries.

Unequal exchange directly follows, within a Marxist labor theory of value, from the large wage disparities between developed and developing economies. Low wages artificially reduce the prices of exports produced in the developing countries, benefiting the purchasers rather than the sellers. The basic idea is a familiar one. It can be rendered in neoclassical terms as an unfavorable division of the gains from trade, whether this be the result of excess supplies of labor or of high income elasticities of demand for imports. Trade can then impoverish rather than enrich. Staying in the international economy is a mistake under such conditions. Only elite groups stand to gain, which is how dependency analysis explains the long persistence of these disadvantageous trading relationships.

Open capital markets reinforce the costs of open goods markets. Direct investment provides an opportunity for multinational firms to pursue their global strategy at the expense of national concerns. There is a conflict rather than a coincidence of interest, and the greater power of the foreign enterprise, in conjunction with domestic class collaboration, is likely to prevail. Foreign capital, it was later argued, would typically associate with national capital or the state itself to pursue its aims. Dependency analysis saw the fatal flaw of the import-substitution policy, although cloaked in nationalist garb, as the concession of favorable treatment to foreign firms. More than static profits were involved: *dependentistas* further held that there can be no autonomous development so long as technology is externally supplied rather than indigenously created.

The third characteristic of dependent capitalist growth is its unequalizing quality. Industrial production may grow rather than stagnate, but only as a result of income concentration that supports demand for modern goods. But basic needs fail to be satisfied for large portions of the population who lack employment and effective demand. Aggregate growth may be sustained, but only at the expense of an unequal, and possibly increasingly unequal, distribution of income. External bottlenecks are primarily the consequence of the high import content of such a distorted consumption and production structure rather than of insufficient exports.

Dependency theory has been sharply criticized for the inadequacy of its interpretation of nineteenth-century Latin American economic development.[5] This debate will not be reprised here. What is more relevant for our purposes is the doubt cast by the contemporary East Asian export success upon the dependency perspective. Statements about inevitably adverse effects of international trade and capital flow in Latin America require qualification. The Latin American debt crisis stands in contrast to the continuing growth of many of the East Asian economies. Furthermore, Korea and Taiwan have seen an improvement in the income distributions. Economic models that seem to describe the region must also be confronted by comparative experience.

What I want to emphasize here, however, is the special place of the income distribution-consumption-production link within the dependency perspective. While that link is an implicit part of structuralist doctrine, a fuller elaboration was left to *dependentista* critics.

While theoretically sound, the relationship ultimately turns on the quantitative sensitivity of the consumption structure to income distribution, the consequent impact on foreign trade, and the productivity growth innate in the resulting production pattern. Relatively little evidence has been amassed in favor of very large beneficial effects.[6] Attempts to ascribe the large rise in Brazilian industrial production in the late 1960's and early 1970's to a deterioration in the income distribution have not proved persuasive. Neither in Allende Chile nor Sandinista Nicaragua, where the theory can, in some sense, be regarded as having been positively applied, do the experiences fully validate expectations. Shifts in income distribution and an orientation toward the satisfaction of basic needs did not alleviate the balance-of-payments problem; on the contrary, they were accompanied by a rise in the trade deficit. Continuing excess demands for many consumer goods could not be satisfied by a production structure that was prevented from responding to prices; and inflation, open and repressed, accelerated. While these experiments have been limited in duration and adversely influenced by external political pressures, and are therefore hardly decisive, the problems of economic management encountered do tell us something about the validity of the underlying theoretical positions.

Emphasis upon consumption patterns influenced by income distribution and by international demonstration effects contributes to inadequate attention to capital requirements and the determinants of technological change. It leads to false confidence in the capacity to escape from the balance-of-payments constraint without increase of exports. It makes the goal of improving the situation of the poor too easily compatible with continuing accumulation and growth. Just as modernization theory learned that not all good things come together, dependency analysts perhaps exaggerate the compatibility of the desired objectives of greater equality and sustained, autonomous growth through an inward-oriented style of development.

International Monetarism

International monetarism,[7] like many of modern economics' theoretical innovations, is a rediscovery of the classics—in this instance, David Hume's specie flow mechanism. Its underlying propositions emphasize the constraints imposed by integration into a world economy; in this sense, there is a shared acceptance with dependency theory of the key role of international interrelationships. In its simplest form, three propositions—two of them behavioral—suffice. The first is the law of one price: in all countries, the same goods cost the same (with allowance made for the small natural barrier of transportation costs and the potentially large unnatural barrier of trade restrictions). In a more aggregate incarnation, this is the assumption of purchasing power parity: the rate of domestic inflation is equal to world inflation plus exchange-rate depreciation. The second assumption is the existence of a stable relationship between the demand for money and income. This assures that changes in the money supply spill over to expenditure and income determination. The third equation required to solve the model is a monetary identity: the national money supply equals the sum of international reserves and domestic credit.

Then, in a world of flexible prices and wages and of fixed exchange rates—that is, in a world on the gold standard—the money supply is endogenous and self-correcting. Excess domestic credit creates internal demand, a smaller net export, and an eventual loss of reserves. This eventually contracts the money supply and thereby rights the initial rise in demand and prices and restores the trade equilibrium. Monetary arrangements are a superstructure; the real rate of growth is determined by underlying accumulation of capital. Demand is managed automatically through changes in the money supply and is sufficient to correct temporary problems in the balance of payments. If, for example, export prices fall and revenues decline, then reserves are lost, the money supply contracts, domestic prices and wages fall, and a new full-employment equilibrium compatible with external balance is achieved. Real income is lower as a result of the exogenous change in the terms of trade, but that cannot be avoided.

For the small economy, therefore, the role of policy is to enforce openness and price flexibility. Tariffs are to be substantially eliminated, and thus impediments to international price equalization removed, and a reallocation of resources compatible with comparative advantage encouraged. In addition, the public sector is to be limited in scope to assure the greatest latitude for private decisions, and its revenues and expenditures are to be kept in balance in order to avoid the prior claim of government deficits on domestic credit. Finally, foreign investment and loans are to be welcomed to compensate for the relative scarcity of national capital and to bring domestic interest rates into parity with international levels. Foreign debt, if contracted privately, should be no problem because it is determined by a profit calculus; and it is noninflationary because increased internal demand is accompanied by an increased supply of imports. If capital inflows were excessive, reserves would soon be lost, which would automatically reduce domestic demand and the current account deficit. The overall balance of payments is the ultimate test of the adequacy of domestic policy, and the evolution of reserves simultaneously signals and sets in motion needed adjustments.

Readers will recognize the theory not merely as a textbook ideal but as the inspiration for the Southern Cone stabilization and development strategy in the late 1970's. The initial application was a reduction of domestic inflation. The way to do this was by a pre-specified, decreasing adjustment of the exchange rate, using the law of one price. The way to keep inflation down, once it had fallen, was to adopt a fixed exchange rate. Free trade and capital movements would both facilitate stabilization and guarantee development.

International monetarism did not work as advertised. Its results in Argentina were a spectacular failure: a grossly overvalued peso that was sustained by a large increase in foreign debt and that contributed to rampant financial speculation and stagnation of the industrial sector. In Brazil, there was a brief and partial flirtation with the theory; the exchange rate was prefixed in early 1980 and was to be the key instrument for altering inflationary expectations. It did not. Instead, a large devaluation and an attendant rise in domestic inflation were later necessary to compensate for the intervening overvaluation. In Chile, the monetary approach had its longest and most successful run. As late as 1980, its adherents were persuaded that the growth of the Chilean economy would persist and that adjustment to adverse international conditions would be swift and without undue costs. In the end, Chilean per capita income declined by more than 11 percent between 1981 and 1984, and the country had the highest debt-income ratio of the hemisphere's debtors.

These results reflect three important limitations of the international monetarist analysis: an application to the short term of what are, at best, long-run equilibrium conditions; inadequate attention to the components of the balance of payments and concern only for a bottom-line total; and a focus on macroeconomic equilibrium rather than on economic development. These issues will be discussed briefly in turn.

Purchasing-power parity and the proportionality between the supply of money and nominal income are relationships that hold approximately only in the long term. A fixed exchange rate does require countries over time to keep their price levels in line, just as large increases in the money supply are associated with higher rates of inflation and nonconvertible currencies. It is another matter, especially in a developing country setting, to count on these relationships, along with instantaneous response and perfect price and wage flexibility, to automatically adjust the balance of payments in the short term. The right real exchange rate did not materialize, either during the boom or during the decline, as countries learned to their grief.

One important reason that exchange rates became overvalued, and were ignored, is the international monetarists' sole concern with an ultimate reserve position and their reliance on the wisdom of the market to make the right allocation between current account deficits and capital account surpluses. The symmetry is misplaced. Large entries of capital in response to interest-rate differentials may sustain exchange rates that prejudice the development of sustainable export capacity, and hence the ability to eventually repay debt. Because capital flows set up future streams of payments, they are inherently fraught with potential difficulty; the more so when loans are short-term, interest rates are readjustable every six months, and continuing supply of capital is uncertain. What appears to be a strong balance-of-payments position, measured by reserves, may quickly deteriorate because inadequate attention has been paid to the components of the balance of payments.

Not only does global monetarism approach pride itself in its holistic approach to the balance of payments, but it also ignores the sectoral composition of the economy. It can afford to do so because the exchange rate guarantees perpetual equilibrium. Unfortunately, what is right from the narrow perspective of the balance-of-payments position in the short term is not necessarily what is right for the longer term. Yet, policy intervention is ruled out to protect domestic activity, despite the possibility of irreversible changes in the production structure. In practice, the monetary approach in its Southern Cone application was equivalent to favoring services at the expense of tradable goods, particularly manufactured products. Industry was exposed to new competition from abroad and was unable to compete. Services were the answer. The trouble is that services are not an independent source of economic development. They respond passively to higher incomes emanating from other sources; they do not propel economies forward or provide the basis for continuing increases of productivity; nor do they guarantee a continuing stream of exports required in the future to service debt and pay for complementary imports.

These are the grounds for skepticism about the appropriateness of the international monetarist emphasis. They also apply in part to the IMF stabilization programs that incorporate some of the same analytic framework.

The IMF, however, modifies international monetarism in two important ways. First, it accepts the possibility of real devaluation as a source of expenditure switching as well as expenditure reduction via lower real incomes. Orthodox global monetarism would insist upon the futility of devaluation and call for internal restraint exclusively. Recognizing a place for devaluation corresponds to a greater concern with the specific state of the current account. Indeed, IMF programs explicitly limit public access to external capital markets, deliberately forcing the adjustment back on the current account. Second, the IMF recognizes that there is a time lag in adjustment and that internal markets are not perfect. The programs make explicit allowance, albeit perhaps not enough, for the role of international finance as a necessary adjunct to domestic austerity.

Despite these amendments, the IMF stabilization design suffers from its continuing insistence on an excess demand diagnosis in all countries at all times. What is appropriate to Mexico as an oil exporter in balance-of-payments and debt trouble in 1982 is not equally applicable to oil importers in the region or perhaps even to Mexico itself in 1985. Supply conditions are also a central part of the story, especially in Latin America. They operate in three important ways. First, there are significant lags between expenditure reduction in one sector and output increases in another. Second, demand management via high real interest rates and realigned exchange rates also affects firms' price and production targets. As shortages of working capital and imported inputs make themselves felt, output is diminished and prices rise to compensate for higher costs. Moreover, since financial costs are a large and increasing share of fiscal deficits, the government accounts may also deteriorate. Third, cutbacks in the public sector fall disproportionately on capital formation. Complementary private investment is also reduced and, with it, future supply. Disinflation, in other words, is more complicated than a simple reduction of demand and is not as central to the improvement of the balance of payments as the IMF analytic model insists. Indeed, they may even be incompatible: the changes in relative prices required to stimulate a trade surplus are likely to exert inflationary pressures. In practice, therefore, the Fund's programs are unrealistic in their targets, apparently deliberately so. In the words of one of the staff: "In general, corrective policy programs should aim at reductions in the rate of inflation that are perceived as significant—even if they do not appear particularly realistic—in order to influence expectations in the right direction."[8] But no one is fooled. All that happens is an inadequate combination of continuing price increases and excess capacity, and expectations that stabilization cannot be continued.

Export-Led Growth

Stabilization under the guidance of the IMF is policy for the short term. Export-led growth is development strategy for the long term, which advocates full integration into the international economy.[9] International demand is highly elastic and affords a reliable source of sustained growth. It remains only for developing countries to follow the signals of comparative advantage to exploit their cheaper costs in order to penetrate world markets. Such a strategy requires limitations on the intervention of the public sector and a correct alignment of prices. Exchange rates must not be overvalued, as they inevitably are a result of import protection. Interest rates must be positive in real terms, rather than negative, and must not subsidize capital-intensive, import-substituting industrialization. Real wages must be determined by international competitiveness rather than by fiat: balance-of-payments problems frequently stem from undisciplined excess factor demands.

The theory is not novel. It comes close to nineteenth-century laissez-faire. What has given the approach special weight in recent years has been the success of the East Asian countries. Exports have been an important ingredient in their rapid income growth. Despite the troubled state of the world economy since the first oil shock, these countries have managed to sustain their expansion. Economies committed to such an outward strategy have avoided a debt crisis like that limiting Latin American growth. It is an idea that apparently works.

As one of the advocates of export promotion summarizes: "Three main points have emerged from the experience of the countries that opted for export-led growth. First, their remarkable rates of growth were associated with the rapid growth of exports; second, for all countries where it was possible to contrast performance before and after the policy changes, the growth rate clearly jumped sharply after the adoption of the export-oriented strategies; and third, the sustained high growth rates indicated that outward-oriented policies created dynamic effects on the economies."[10]

Two sets of observations are in order. The first relates to the generalizability of the strategy; the second, to the means of implementing it.

Export-led growth is not a universal route to success. For one, there is a fallacy of composition. If all developing countries tried to pursue the strategy at the same time, the ensuing competition would push down the gain for all. Latecomers are likely to obtain less gain in pursuing the policy than those that preceded them. (This is even truer if early success provokes protectionist responses in importing countries.) What counts is not spectacularly high growth rates of exports, per se, but the differential advantage compared with an alternative allocation of resources. If exports must be sold at less profitable prices in order to compete, the foreign market is a less attractive source of dynamism.

Nor are the gains from trade linear. As economies become progressively more open, the marginal benefits diminish. The difference in domestic efficiency between exporting and importing the last trade unit is smaller than between exporting and importing the first. When exports come to represent high proportions of national income, the marginal benefits depend exclusively on the dynamics of productivity change in the export sectors, not on the static gains from trade. For large countries, diminishing returns set in much sooner. It is well to recall that

Japan only exports 15 percent of its gross product. Most is not necessarily best.

Much also depends upon the composition of trade. There is a difference between the resource-rich countries of Latin America and the low-wage, resource-poor countries of East Asia. Exports of labor-intensive manufactures from the latter are consistent with increased employment and greater income equality. Indiscriminate promotion of exports from the former can increase rents at the expense of wage share and actually prejudice the emergence of nontraditional exports.

Moreover, a high degree of openness is not an unmixed blessing. It makes the economy more susceptible to external shocks. An effective domestic response requires a high degree of internal price flexibility and resource mobility. If they are lacking, an apparently first-best strategy of international integration will prove inferior. The Latin American debt crisis stems in part from the *asymmetric* international integration of the region. It was easier to open capital markets than to establish the basis for continuing export growth; the one was a substitute for the other.

Empirical analysis, appropriately interpreted, bears out a more cautious view of what export-led growth can be expected to achieve for a broad cross-section of developing countries. Balassa correctly writes: "The increase in Korea's GNP would have been 37 percent smaller if its export growth rate equaled the average for the countries concerned. The corresponding proportion is 25 percent for Taiwan. At the other extreme, in Chile, India, and Mexico, respectively, the increase in GNP would have been 14, 12 and 8 percent greater if those countries had average export growth rates."[11] Yet, selection of such extreme cases exaggerates the true impact of more rapid export growth. That effect is typically between 0.1 and 0.2 percentage points of aggregate growth per percentage point of export growth, with a smaller elasticity as other causal variables are added. Thus, in a recent study, when export volume growth is introduced alone, its elasticity is 0.2; when the rate of investment growth is added, it has four times the influence of export growth—now reduced to 0.07—and the degree of total explanation increases markedly.[12] And when the independent influence of agricultural growth is also considered, its effect is almost six times as great as export growth, and more statistically significant.[13] Export growth is not a unique determinant.

Such statistical exercises do not really test the hypothesis of *export-led* growth, however. To do so requires calculation of the relationship between aggregate performance and the extent to which the rate of growth of exports *exceeds* overall growth. With such a specification, there is no statistically significant relationship. That is, the Korean and Taiwanese success stories of more rapid export expansion than output for the internal market are *sui generis*, and are not replicated in a larger sample of developing countries.[14]

Moreover, the observed simple relationship between product growth and export growth partially incorporates the structuralist argument of the importance of imports: exports are also an intermediating variable reflecting increased foreign-exchange availability for purchase of needed imports. For the same World Bank set of thirty-one developing countries for the decade 1970–80, substituting import volume for export volume as the causal variable increases the extent of statistical explanation markedly; $\bar{R}^2$ goes up from 0.29 to 0.48; its coefficient indicates that a point of additional import growth is worth 0.33 points of product growth, compared with the export contribution of 0.21 points. Neither, taken separately, constitutes an adequate explanation. When both export volume and import volume are introduced into the same equation, they are each statistically significant and positive; but import volume is much more statistically significant *and* has a coefficient of 0.27, compared with one of 0.10 for export volume.[15]

The point of these statistical calculations is to establish that export orientation is no more a panacea than import substitution proved. It is not to deny that an outward-oriented strategy may sometimes be indicated. But it does not rule out *efficient* import substitution as a sometimes preferable option for accelerating growth. There is no substitute for case-by-case analysis of appropriate development policies.

A second major objection to the insistence on export-led growth is its excessive bias against state intervention. By emphasizing the adverse effects of price distortion on growth, this theoretical perspective is clearly intended to discredit the "structuralist" view: "Their approach," writes Agarwala, "emphasized the role of the government rather than of the markets. . . . It was further assumed that government . . . can implement the necessary program of resource mobilization and resource allocation through administrative fiats."[16] The conclusion that distortions matter, and are primarily the product of state intervention, validates the neoclassical emphasis on getting prices right.

A key and increasingly recurrent claim is that these distortions add up to a statistically significant, and negative, influence on the growth rate. This finding was given prominence in the 1983 *World Development Report*: "The average growth rate of those developing countries with low distortions in the 1970's was about 7 percent a year—2 percentage points higher than the overall average. Countries with high distortions averaged growth of about 3 percent a year, 2 percentage points lower than the overall average."[17]

Such a conclusion, however, does not hold up very well under even casual scrutiny. The most influential component of the overall distortion index is the distortion of the exchange rate. Whether taken by itself or in conjunction with other components, incorrectly valued exchange rates explain the highest proportion of the variance in the aggregate growth rate. Its effect is central. Clearly, if exchange-rate distortion is an important source of poor performance, it should make its impact felt through lagging export volume. Yet, there is a statistically insignificant relationship between the growth of export volume and the exchange-rate distortion index! Indeed, the calculated $\bar{R}^2$ is −.01 and not remotely close to an acceptable level of explanation. In whatever way the calculated exchange-rate distortion index influences growth, it is apparently not via exports.[18] Another sectoral distortion index that can be readily tested is that devised for agriculture. Agricultural growth is also not associated with the measured distortion of agricultural prices.[19]

One cannot easily rationalize away these sectoral findings. It is difficult to argue that one is measuring one's distortions right if they fail to exert an influence where they are most relevant. My conclusion is that the statistical analysis is *not* "a powerful argument . . . in favor of avoiding high distortions in prices in trade, in factor markets, as well as in non-traded products."[20]

Rather, the widely publicized World Bank results are inadequately founded on a distortion index that has limited analytic content. These results obviously do not justify a policy of arbitrarily getting prices wrong. But neither do I want to confine myself to the bland conclusion that selective intervention may help to produce correct prices where the market does not; on that there is substantial conceptual, if not operational, agreement. The more fundamental proposition, rather, is that the correctness of the prices must be decided by reference to a comprehensive development strategy, and not independently of it. Overvaluation of the exchange rate during the early phase of the import-substitution period in the early 1950's played a positive role in many Latin American countries. It taxed excess profits on agricultural exports that were benefiting from the Korean War commodity price boom and transferred them to the industrial sector. In contrast, overvaluation of the exchange rate inherent in the Southern Cone strategy of reducing inflation at the end of the 1970's was a disaster. It is the appropriateness of the strategies that is at issue.

Getting policies right is more than a matter of getting prices right. To realign production correctly may require incentives that exaggerate market signals. Efficiency is frequently the eventual consequence of successful distortions: that is the typical latecomer story of successful economic development. Negative real rates of interest on credit in Korea in the 1970's did not hinder industrialization or exports; high positive real rates in Chile in the latter 1970's were no help in averting diversion of resources into speculative, nonproductive applications. There is substantial evidence establishing that the export-led success of Taiwan and Korea did not emanate from neutral state involvement but from coherent interventionist strategies.

Four Principal Issues

Contending economic ideologies have thus been a central part of the modern Latin American development experience. That debate currently continues under the impulse of the most severe downturn in economic activity since the Great Depression. Per capita income in the region has declined by some 10 percent in the early 1980's. For some countries, levels of industrial production are where they were a decade or more ago. A further novel, but welcome, ingredient in the present situation is a return to civilian governance and a process of redemocratization in many countries. Finally, because of the ubiquity of stabilization programs, the views of the International Monetary Fund have a large and captive audience throughout the region.

In the face of these influences, a pragmatic neostructuralism appears to be gaining influence throughout the region. Its features can be illustrated by reference to four principal questions that policymakers currently confront: the external debt, inflation, income distribution, and the role of the state.[21]

Latin American debt, as is well known, is disproportionately high relative to the exposure of other developing areas. As a consequence, countries of the region have been forced to make unprecedented adjustments to compensate for the adverse effects of high international interest rates, industrial-country recession, and limited capital supply from the early 1980's on. An external transfer of 5 to 7 percent of gross national product to meet interest obligations has required an equivalent internal transfer of real resources to the public sector, for most countries the principal debtor.

Thus far, with only a few exceptions, the payments have been made, despite a burden that is more than double the level of post–World War I reparations that Germany found intolerable. There has been little support for unilateral moratoria or rejection of continuing international economic relationships. Despite the long tradition of inward-looking development strategy in the region, there has been acceptance of the need for larger exports, as well as reduced imports. Trade surpluses in Mexico and Brazil have reached record levels.

But such accomplishments, on an emergency basis, do not mean that the present trade results can be extrapolated mechanically. There is little enthusiasm for an indefinite continuation of the present resource transfers from the region, even under conditions of world trade growth that might make the export surpluses feasible. There are valid reasons to resist. One is that the policies required to effect the transfers contradict the goal of stabilizing inflationary pressures. Devaluation, required to sustain the competitiveness of exports, adds to costs and hence feeds back upon inflation. Additionally, the needed large siphoning of resources by the public sector adds to inflation because of efforts by members of the private sector to defend their incomes. Cutting back on domestic governmental outlays is not an attractive solution because it carries the risk of overshooting and provoking a decline in output rather than prices. Financing deficits by debt rather than by printing money is roughly equivalent to printing even more money, because of the explosive interest payments that must subsequently be made. These are new structural components of the inflationary process.

Furthermore, the resources that have been transferred have primarily come at the expense of investment. Trying to compress consumption alone has not proved possible. There is resistance to further declines in living standards. But then the attempt to fully service large debts in the present prejudices the continuing ability to pay in the future. Exports to be made tomorrow require capacity increases today. But countries that are being forced to prematurely transfer such large proportions of their savings cannot afford to do so.

Neither short-term stabilization nor longer-term outward-oriented development strategy adequately respond to the problem. If one pursues immediate balance-of-payments objectives with high priority, inflation and low levels of domestic investment are likely to be the result. Relying on high rates of export growth to evoke new capital flows, and thus to reduce the size of present resource transfers, ignores the chilling effects of internal disequilibrium on potential lenders. The majority Latin American position supports continuing agreement with the IMF and negotiations with the banks, but also insists upon the importance of external debt relief as a necessary condition for sustained economic recovery.

The inflation problem, in this emergent neostructural view, is thus now related in many countries to management of the external debt, and more generally to shocks emanating from the international economy. There is continuity with structuralist doctrine denying the effectiveness of orthodox monetary and fiscal policies. But there is also a change. Inflation rates of more than three digits in Argentina and Bolivia, and running at about 200 percent in Brazil and Peru, no longer are tolerable. They provoke instability and uncertainty of real incomes, and threaten those segments of the population powerless to defend themselves. They distort economic incentives and detract from productive activity.

Nor have the experiments with IMF stabilization programs reinforced the penchant of even domestic conservative constituencies for greater austerity. Whatever the success in strengthening the balance of payments, it has not been replicated in the fight against inflation. Even in well-behaved debtors like Mexico and Brazil, progress has been limited. While it can be argued that conventional policies have been inadequately stringent in practice, there is more sympathy in the region than in international financial centers for why they never seem to be.

There is a growing appreciation that the high-inflation, indexed (formally and informally) Latin American economies require more than monetarist reaction or structuralist complaisance. An example of some of the new thinking on the subject is set out in a recent volume.[22] Even more impressive is the effort to apply some of the principles to the fight against accelerating Argentine inflation, in the context of an IMF agreement. These approaches, while they feature monetary reform and control as a centerpiece and call for fiscal control, also recognize that inflation is symptomatic of incompatible factor demands. An incomes policy, whether in the guise of price and wage controls, currency conversion schemes, or an explicitly negotiated pact, is therefore a critical component of an effective anti-inflationary package. While the priority attached to inflation continues to be an ideological litmus test, just as it was in controversies of the 1950's, there is greater consensus than there once was on this focal question.

The same is true with income distribution. Although short-term adjustment has monopolized attention, and concern with equality has apparently receded, the issue inevitably remains important in Latin America, owing to widespread poverty and dramatic inequality. Indeed, the stagnation and decline of recent years have quite possibly aggravated income differences. Real wage declines have been large in many countries even while returns to private asset holders, a select group, have increased. Yet, despite the probable magnitude of these distributional shifts, still not yet studied and documented, simplistic populist policies of large compensating nominal wage increases have not gained endorsement. Sacrifices have been made and continue to be acceptable, provided there is a reasonable expectation that they will amount to more than the enrichment of others.

There are limits. Real wages cannot always be the residual. Governments have recognized this reality and have not pushed unremittingly on the wage front or to remove price subsidies even when counseled to do so. There is wisdom in this softening of austerity. It will do little good to succeed, apparently, in stabilization at the expense of incompatible income shares that will later create new inflationary pressures. Nor can one design a development strategy any longer in which growth takes absolute precedence, with distribution to follow later. These are some of the lessons that the astute have learned and that the new politics in the region enforce.

The test to come is the capacity to allocate the benefits of renewed growth in a way that respects distributional concerns without succumbing to them. In this emerging middle ground, there is scope for public policy to influence production profiles in the name of employment objectives as well as to treat the excesses of poverty and unemployment.

This brings us to a final strategic issue that to some degree subsumes the others, the role of the state. The credibility of laissez-faire, perhaps because of the Southern Cone experience, is less than it once was in the region, or as it still seems to be among some economists in international agencies. But there is also less faith in *dirigisme* and the power of government to always intervene successfully. Proponents of exclusively market-oriented development strategies are not the only ones to criticize the performance of the public sector in recent years. Few would defend the proliferation of subsidies, tax exemptions, arbitrary regulations, proliferation of state enterprises, and increased expenditure of central governments during the heyday of capital inflows in the 1970's. Nor, for some time, has there been broad belief in Latin America that comprehensive planning should supplant market decisions.

The mood in the region is not in favor of development strategies that preclude a state role, but rather leans toward reconstruction of an effective developmental state. It is not an easy task to reconcile the diverse objectives and claims that a newly enfranchised civil society is vocalizing in many parts of the region. The days of the former alliance among foreign capital, domestic capital, and state technocracy are finished. New mechanisms of cooperation between the state and productive sectors, capital as well as labor, have to be forged. New bounds for state presence have to be defined, even as a restored ability to generate a public surplus must be found.

Difficult though it may be, there is a broad commitment in Latin America to harness and use government intervention more productively. That translates into (1) greater selectivity and decentralization of authority; (2) reliable access to real resources, rather than second-best measures that provoke other disequilibria; (3) attention to macroeconomic policy as well as to cost pressures that reproduce high rates of inflation; (4) adequate growth of exports to reduce the constraint to growth emanating from the balance of payments: exports are a means, not an end, important for their regular supply of foreign exchange rather than industrial dynamism; and (5) acceptance of integration into international financial markets, so long as they compensate for, rather than induce, vulnerability to external and internal shocks.

These are some of the central elements of the new economic thinking in the region. This emergent neostructuralism recombines rather than reinvents new theoretical perspectives. It has learned from the succession of models and development strategies that promised success. And perhaps above all, it reflects political reality: the new civilian governments, and the old, find this pragmatism and flexibility attractive. Development strategy encompasses more than technical models.

Political Economy

Despite signs of convergence in theoretical approaches to the principal economic problems of the regimes, obvious differences persist. They are likely to continue, despite further research and the accumulation of empirical evidence. No single and objective description of underlying economic relationships will be agreed upon by all. Diverse and contradictory views will continue to be espoused. Ultimately, the strategy chosen for policy implementation will depend upon political considerations rather than economic consistency. Those policies, in turn, affect not only outcomes but the underlying relationships themselves. That is what makes applied economics a handmaiden of politics rather than a pure science.

This characterization contradicts the still popular theory of economic policy pioneered by Jan Tinbergen. In that formulation, economic theory and econometrics yield a single underlying model specifying the interaction of economic variables, including their response to policy instruments. The task of politics is to choose a preferred solution among feasible outcomes by weighting goals like growth, price stability, income distribution, and so on. Values enter explicitly only in the choice of weights in the objective function.

Reality is not so neat. Underlying economic behavioral relationships are not known with certainty. Contradictory hypotheses enjoy a long life, rarely fully reconciled by historical evidence. Further information modifies the presentation of strongly maintained positions, but rarely leads to their abandonment: the twisting and turning of the monetarist-Keynesian controversy in the last fifty years is a striking example. There is good reason for skepticism in the absence of pure experiments. Evidence is not decisive when all other factors are not held constant. Ideology— a prior belief system—serves to identify the structure implicit in the mass of historical data generated under a variety of conditions. It is not readily abandoned. That is why some Chileans concede that Allende's policies may have failed but only owing to malevolence; and why others assert confidently that global monetarism remains valid, unfortunately cut short by the 1981 devaluation.

Underidentification is endemic not merely because of the complexity of economic systems but also because policies themselves influence behavioral responses. This is one of the valuable insights of the new rational expectations school of economics. It argues for the inability to predict from past evidence as one moves from one policy regime to another, since the observed responses of economic agents are adaptations to the expectations of the effect of policy interventions. The analysis is especially applicable to a Latin American setting subject to frequent, and sometimes dramatic, changes in development strategy.

Some of these advocates go further, insisting that the private sector anticipates perfectly, and thereby offsets the efficacy of, governmental intervention. Thus, rapid growth of the money supply, because it contributes to inflationary expectations, yields high, rather than low, interest rates. An important role for expectations does not imply their rationality, however. The public is not always right or omniscient. Effective policymakers also play upon and shape expectations, rather than being constrained by them. Expectations provide an additional and welcome degree of freedom, permitting policies that evade undesired trade-offs, even when conventional economic principles suggest they cannot work. Perón and others before him understood the irrelevance of past evidence well before academic economists discovered the precept. It continues to be invoked. That is what Reagan supply-side arithmetic and Sandinista socialism share in common.

In a world further complicated by imperfect knowledge of exogenous variables like international interest rates, world demand, terms of trade, internal supply disruptions, and so on, the Tinbergen policy process is inverted. Political leaders choose a specific model, and the economic advisers that believe in it, partially to rationalize the application of preferred instruments. Values emerge in the choice not only of ends but also of means. Reagan needed a theory to justify a tax cut and lesser government participation; the Sandinistas needed one to justify a transfer of income and increased public-sector planning. What differentiates ideologies is not so much goals—all agree upon the desirability of sustained and equitable growth—or even their weights. Policy instruments are what the debate is about. They embody the ideologies and are the symbols to which constituencies react.

Not all policies work, however skillful the job of selling them. Inflation does not decline, despite austerity; domestic output of wage goods does not increase markedly, despite increases in the wage share; import requirements do not diminish, despite investment in domestic industry; exports do not boom, despite real devaluation. Economic principles trip up policymakers not because they are always binding but because they are only sometimes binding. If one evades them long enough, moreover, success can be self-fulfilling. That is the promise held out by models of all stripes—populist or global monetarist.

The luxury of experimentation is not unlimited. The more

open the economy is, the more immediate and more restrictive any internal disequilibrium becomes, spilling over quickly to the balance of payments. Heterodoxy is correspondingly riskier and rarer in small open economies. It is not surprising, accordingly, that populists stress an internal rather than an international orientation. Insulation enhances the capacity to raise nominal wages and enlarge public expenditure. Conversely, conservative positions usually start from the priority of international market signals for the internal discipline they impose.

These considerations also illuminate why military regimes seem to find rigorous stabilization packages congenial. The preference does not stem from a firm belief in automatic market adjustment. Military instincts are interventionist. But military leaders can conveniently rationalize political repression in the name of needed price and wage flexibility. The objective is not adaptation to a given economic structure but radical reconstruction of civil society. Falling real income then becomes a symbol of policy success because it shows the determination to stay the course until the underlying economic model is applicable.

In a freer environment, however, stabilization is almost always subject to intense debate. That especially tries the patience of international technicians persuaded that *their* approach is the only right one. Politics can be tolerated only to explain the required policies but not to modify them. Lack of success in reducing inflation and restoring growth is blamed on inadequate implementation rather than inappropriate diagnosis. And success on certain indicators like the balance of payments, easiest to obtain because it is frequently at the expense of other objectives, is invoked to vindicate the policies.

But dogged persistence is not an invariable virtue, whether the model is heterodox *or* orthodox. Signals are not always meant to be discarded. They not only speak to the technical correctness of the theory but also have political consequences. Stabilization is a politico-economic project that is more likely to succeed through adaptive response than ideological rigidity. One of the lessons of this review of the state of Latin American economics is that technical economic models, even when very much in fashion, are not infallible. Another is that the choice and implementation of any model inevitably have a strong political component that is best recognized explicitly. A third is that the impact of economic policies is more predictable in a stable political context: what should be rigid is not the policies but the underlying policy environment.

These observations permit conclusion on a note of cautious optimism. Latin American redemocratization, although it inspires rising and inconsistent demands, can contribute to sound and consensual economic policies by institutionalizing legitimacy and promoting pragmatic flexibility. Strong representative governments can avoid the temptations of quick fixes, while not ignoring information on the adequacy of policies that have been tried. The state of Latin American economic thought is adequate to the task; one hopes that domestic political capabilities and the international climate prove equally conducive.

FOUR

Latin American Sociology in the Mid-1980's: Learning from Hard Experience

ALEJANDRO PORTES

The task of reviewing the state of Latin American sociology involves, at a minimum, two related but distinct concerns: (1) the situation and activities of Latin American sociologists themselves; and (2) those of foreign sociologists concerned with the region. A moment's reflection on these topics will persuade anyone of the magnitude of the task. The sociological enterprise is not homogeneous throughout the twenty republics and even less so if we include the non-Latin Caribbean. The disparities are even more marked among researchers from outside the region. In this case, differences in substantive topics and research traditions are compounded by a lack of consensus on the definition of the discipline itself and on what its goals and methods are. French sociologists working in Latin America come from a very different intellectual tradition than their British counterparts, and both are quite distinct from their North American colleagues.

Thus, if we are to tackle this topic with some hope of success, several limitations must be set at the start. The basis for exclusion of topics reflects more the context provided by a meeting of the Latin American Studies Association, in which the original version of this essay was presented, than any substantive evaluation of their importance. I will limit myself here to the Latin American republics, excluding the non-Latin Caribbean, and to the state of Latin American studies in U.S. sociology, excluding other foreign research groups in the region. Moreover, I will not delve in any great detail into the specific differences and characteristics of sociological research in each Latin American country. The limitations of space require that the picture be painted in fairly broad strokes, omitting many important particulars. The focus will thus be on major trends during the last two decades, and my main point of comparison will be the character of sociological research on the region as practiced in the United States and in Latin America itself.

Finally, I will not attempt any new definition of what sociology is, nor will I use this occasion to prescribe what it should be. Experience has taught me that definitions come and go and that prescriptions are politely listened to and then almost universally ignored. Instead, my approach will be strictly nominalist: sociology is what sociologists do, and the state of the discipline in any particular country or region is equivalent to the collective state of its practitioners. Thus, my primary concern here will be the *institution* called sociology and its evolution over time. In part, the reason for this preference is the context of the original meeting from which this book grew and, in part, the fact that reviews of the substantive sociological literature on the region are available elsewhere.[1] Nevertheless, the last sections will be dedicated to summarizing several of these thematic concerns.

Convergencies

Having delimited the task, we can first consider major trends during the recent past and the extent to which they have moved Latin American sociology as practiced in Latin America and in the United States closer or farther apart. The start of the 1970's offers a suitable point of departure, since this date approximately demarcates major social and political changes that had decisive consequences for the discipline in both parts of the hemisphere.

In Latin America, the beginning of the seventies brought an

end to the wave of revolutionary insurrections in the wake of the Cuban Revolution and the gradual fading of the populist and anti-imperialist project with which many sociologists and often sociology itself had become identified. Efforts to incorporate the masses into modern society and to liberate nations from external dependency gave way in many countries to a struggle for sheer survival as a new tide of repressive regimes gained dominance.[2]

In the United States, the rediscovery of Latin America in the aftermath of the Cuban Revolution also faded in the course of the sixties, along with the hopes generated by the Alliance for Progress. By the early seventies, the region had been firmly relegated to a secondary place in the North American public mind. Paralleling this shift, government and private support for research in these countries declined rapidly and, with it, the Latin-Americanist vocation of many U.S. social scientists.[3]

The last decade-and-a-half has been a period of rather humbling experiences for Latin American social science and, in particular, sociology. From grand visions of guiding or at least aiding major processes of societal change, sociologists in Latin America have been compelled to aim at increasingly more modest goals, including personal and institutional survival. Military regimes, in particular those of the Southern Cone countries, took aim at the discipline as one of their major intellectual adversaries. The career of sociology was abolished in several universities and relegated in others to an impoverished, quasi-professional status on a par, say, with nursing or elementary-school teaching. Many of the best thinkers and researchers were expelled from the official university system and compelled to seek refuge either abroad or in private centers supported by foreign foundations.

These precarious research centers came to represent in many countries the last flicker of independent scholarly inquiry. The restricted political space in which they existed and the constant threat of repression compelled their members to abandon broad ideological and philosophical debates to focus on more concrete and practical problems. Some examples of the topics of research that became popular during this period include family structure and dynamics, household strategies for economic survival among low-income groups, the emergence and dynamics of grass-roots organizations in poor urban settlements, rural colonization schemes and their impact, and the position of women in the family and society.[4]

Although much less severe than in Latin America, the history of Latin American sociology in the United States since the early seventies has also been fraught with difficulties. Unlike history, anthropology, and, to a lesser extent, political science, North American sociology has never developed a strong subspecialty on Latin America. At the start of the seventies, the field consisted in the United States of two frequently warring groups: first, mainstream scholars who viewed the region primarily as a laboratory to test extant theories of industrial development, political movements, modernization, and the like; second, radical sociologists who identified with the revolutionary project of the Latin American left and attempted to promote it through their personal and scholarly activities.

Subsequent events proved unkind to both groups. Large surveys and complex designs, which were the trademark of mainstream sociologists, fell prey to declining sources of support and to the negative reception accorded to many such projects in Latin America, especially after the Camelot experience in Chile.[5] Radical scholars, on the other hand, found the populist-nationalist project defeated in country after country. Just as the militant left was being repressed and weakened throughout the region, this group found itself on the defensive at home as well, because of the rapid turn of American sociology away from the civil rights activism of the sixties.

The harsh experiences during the last fifteen years have had a sobering effect on both Latin and North American sociologists. An unexpected outcome of these events, however, has been a progressive convergence of intellectual outlook and research activities on both sides of the hemisphere. In Latin America, earlier distrust of U.S. social science and frequent accusations of CIA links have all but disappeared. In part, this was due to the end of the massive research projects with transplanted methodology characteristic of the fifties and sixties. More important, however, may have been the solid support offered by the North American scholarly community to their Latin colleagues during times of political persecution. As the immediate adversary ceased to be foreign imperialism to become the newly installed domestic military regime, many Latin American sociologists came to find reliable and important allies in U.S. academic centers and foundations as well as among their North American counterparts.

The shifting character of sociological research also led to an increasing appreciation of the empirical side of the discipline in Latin America. A narrowing political space and the need to keep fledgling research centers alive dictated a move toward more modest and applied topics. Such work has generated, with time, an impressive research literature. Although Latin American sociology has never become as quantitatively oriented as the U.S. version, it has developed an increasing body of evidence and has come to rely progressively on fact over theoretical insight. As a prominent Argentine sociologist told me recently: "In meetings of CLACSO [the Latin-American Social Science Council] working groups, nobody 'drops' ideological lines any longer. We are all far more concerned with what is actually taking place."

Examples of this new genre of focused field research are the studies by Jelin, Feijoo, and their associates on social movement formation among women and among the impoverished population of the *villas* of Buenos Aires; those of Dagmar Raczinsky on survival strategies among *poblador* families in Santiago; a study of Bolivian labor migrants by a joint team of CERES (Centro de Estudios de la Realidad Económica y Social, the Center for the Study of Economic and Social Reality) in La Paz and CEDES (Centro de Estudios de Estado y Sociedad, the Center for the Study of State and Society) in Buenos Aires; studies of grassroots communities by Ruth Cardoso and other Brazilian sociologists; and studies of education, social stratification, and social mobility by Filgueira in Uruguay, and Pastore, Aguiar, and Magno de Carvalho in Brazil.[6] This type of research comes close to the everyday practice of the profession in the United States. Progressive affinity in specific research areas has led to an increasing number of reviews of the recent North American literature in such fields as the sociology of education, stratification and mobility, and the family by Latin American specialists and to the more frequent publication and citing of Latin American scholars in the United States.[7]

The trend toward convergence on the North American side is related, ironically, to the thinning ranks of sociologists working in the region. The "bad times" of the seventies discouraged many and led others to seek greener pastures elsewhere. As a collective enterprise, sociology in the United States has never regarded Third World studies as a priority area or particularly encouraged its practitioners. As an example, presidents of the American Sociological Association during the last twenty years do not include a single specialist in Latin America or, for that matter, the Third World or comparative development.

What is left, in the absence of significant economic or professional rewards, is a core group of highly committed scholars. Unlike many of their predecessors during the fifties and sixties, they went to Latin America neither to test pre-existing theories nor to aid or participate in revolutionary movements. Many lived in the region for extensive periods either before or during their first research efforts. As a result, their subsequent work tended to reflect more closely the realities of the Latin American societies that they studied. Contrary to earlier experiences, their topics of investigation frequently derived from theories and concepts born in the region rather than brought in from abroad.

Although dependency theory was known in the United States prior to this new generation of scholars, they were largely responsible for gaining it respectability by showing how it could generate hypotheses and guide serious research. Indeed, some of the best examples of the historical-structural method, long advocated by Latin American sociologists, have been produced in recent years by their North American counterparts. Representative studies of this "generation of the seventies" include Susan Eckstein's research on urban poverty and politics in Mexico City, Peter Evans' study of the "triple alliance" sustaining dependent development in Brazil, Gary Gereffi's analysis of denationalization of the pharmaceutical industry in Mexico, Karen Remmer and Gilbert Merkx's critique of the concept of the bureaucratic-authoritarian state, Stephen Bunker's study of colonization and underdevelopment in the Amazon, and Sherri Grasmuck's survey of Dominican immigrants in places of origin in the Dominican Republic and in New York City.[8]

It is my impression that these North American works are better known and have been better received in Latin America, at least in the countries where they were done, than the earlier products of multinational surveys or the lingering theoretical speculations on the "true" nature of dependency, imperialism, and the like. To summarize: in my view, the trend toward convergence started at a time when sociology in the United States and Latin America was a rather self-assured and sometimes arrogant enterprise. North American *hubris* was manifested in a view of Latin America as a laboratory either for testing functionalist theories of modernization or for implementing radical ones of revolution. On the other side, Latin American high hopes for egalitarian and anti-imperialist processes of change became embodied in a sociology defined as one of the intellectual guides and pillars of these processes.

The sobering experiences of the seventies took away some of the aura of excitement and self-importance of the earlier period and along with it, perhaps, the enthusiasm of many. Latin American sociology of the mid-eighties is a much more modest but also more mature enterprise. The increasing shift toward empirical investigation of specific social issues in Latin America coincided with the emergence of a novel style of research in the United States more steeped in Latin American realities and also more responsive to the emerging theoretical perspectives from the region. These trends, along with personal contact among a relatively small number of scholars over many years, have made communication easier and have facilitated collaboration between North and Latin American sociologists in ways that could not have been implemented in the past.

Divergencies

These developments are not the whole story, however. Although Latin American sociology in the region and its counterpart in the United States have points in common, they still remain very different enterprises. It is not that they lie at opposite extremes of any particular dimension, but rather that they possess distinct thematic priorities, interests, and goals. It is important to outline what some of these are as a counterpoint to the trend toward convergence.

As mentioned before, Latin American specialists represent a numerically insignificant proportion of U.S. sociologists, especially if attention is restricted to those involved actively in research. The costs of travel, the perceptible decrease in the number and sources of research support, and the secondary place accorded to Third World studies have all militated against the numerical expansion of this field. The core of U.S. Latin-Americanist sociologists also possesses several characteristics in common that set them apart from the sociological mainstream in the United States, as well as from regional specialists in other disciplines.

First, the typical research topics of North American sociologists working on Latin America tend to be far broader than those that are normative in the United States. Products of the "generation of the seventies" described previously actually fall in-between the scope of Latin American sociological writings, especially those of an earlier era, and the highly specialized ones commonly found in U.S. journals. Thus, for example, studies of urban poverty, peasant mobilizations, and the automobile or oil multinationals, although less broad than the history of Latin American dependency or the analysis of its state forms, are certainly far more encompassing than differences in aging by sex or determinants of mental disorders among urban minorities.

Second, although U.S. sociologists generally work in particular countries, the trend seems to be away from geographical specialization and toward increasing thematic issues, studied comparatively. Here, the main point of contrast is with Latin-Americanists in other disciplines. The latter tend to be more country-specific. It is more difficult to find full-time "Mexicanists" or "Brazilianists" among North American sociologists than among historians, anthropologists, or political scientists. Examples of the thematic comparative approach in sociology abound. They include Eckstein's analysis of the determinants of revolution in Cuba, Bolivia, and Mexico; Gereffi and Evans' comparison of patterns of dependency and development in "semi-peripheral" countries; Sassen-Koob's recent inquiry into the relationship between U.S. investments in export-manufacturing and out-migration from Mexico and the Caribbean countries; and William Canak's analysis of Latin American state-capitalist and bureaucratic-authoritarian regimes.[9]

Despite the shift into narrower research topics, dictated in part by political and economic considerations, Latin American sociology has been consistently characterized by its concern with "big" issues and by its overriding political orientation.

Research that focuses on the adjustment problems of various groups has occupied, until recently, a very subordinate position. Instead, attention has concentrated on the most general issues of social organization: class structures, state-formation processes, and the changing insertion of the region in the global economy. Reasons for this emphasis are not hard to find in a context in which the survival of various institutions, including sociology itself, has been frequently threatened by abrupt political and economic shifts. It has made little sense to study the adjustment of particular groups to a social order that is itself in a state of flux.

This macrostructural vocation of the discipline in Latin America did not disappear during the seventies but shifted direction somewhat. The new emphasis on the state by many sociologists signaled a move away from analysis of the external determinants of underdevelopment and toward the internal institutions that sustain it. This shift paralleled that occurring in many countries from earlier attention to foreign domination to a new overriding concern with state power run rampant on particular visions of the national future.

Latin American sociology has continued to follow very closely the drift of political events in the region. Just as the triumph of military reaction in many countries during the early seventies gave rise to writings on the character of the state and the concept of bureaucratic-authoritarianism, the recent demise of several of these regimes has produced the newest sociological themes. Among them are "redemocratization," broadly defined as the conditions necessary for establishing enduring democratic political institutions, and *concertación*, or the process by which different social classes and political forces can agree on rules of the democratic game.[10]

Two other distinct features of contemporary sociology in Latin America deserve mention. First, despite its move during the seventies toward applied and specific research topics and more field data collection, it continues to be a non-specialized discipline. A practicing sociologist in Latin America is, by and large, like a general physician; he or she investigates and writes on several topics that can change rapidly over time, depending on the political climate, sources of support, personal interest, and other factors. The medical analogy also fits the contrast with

U.S. sociology. In this case, practitioners, including Latin-Americanists, are, for the most part, specialists closely identified with a particular field of interest. Although, as noted before, U.S. sociologists in Latin America tend to cast their intellectual net wider than their home-based colleagues, the discipline still defines them as "specialists" in one area—namely, Third World societies or, more broadly, "development."

Like their U.S. counterparts, Latin American sociologists also continue to be excluded from major roles in social policy-making. In both contexts, sociologists as such are seldom called on to participate or advise in major policy decisions. This appears to be true even in those countries that have reestablished democracy after a long authoritarian period. The contrast with a related discipline, economics, could not be more dramatic. The reasons why economic policies are entrusted to economists whereas social policies are left in the hands of laymen are complex and would require a much longer paper to explore. The point to be stressed here, however, is a different one—namely, that some Latin American sociologists are moving into policy-making positions by directly entering the political process.

The numbers involved are small, but significant enough to merit attention. The transformation of one of Latin America's premier sociologists, Fernando Henrique Cardoso, into a major political figure in Brazil is perhaps the best example of this trend. The possibility of shifting in a relatively short period from academic research and teaching to political office is closely tied to the character of the discipline in the region, as described previously. Since many sociologists specialize in monitoring state actions and analyzing the ongoing political process, the gap that separates them from actual participation is, under some circumstances, fairly narrow. At present, it is not clear whether this apparent trend will continue or what effects it could have on the discipline as a whole.

A Changing Field: The Sociology of Development in the 1980's

As mentioned previously, Latin-America-oriented research in U.S. sociology is classified by the rest of the discipline within the field of development. Having examined the institutional evolution of the area during the last decades, I would like to briefly discuss substantive changes in research and theory that have taken place during the same period. Few specialties in sociology have experienced more drastic changes during the last decade than that of development/modernization. Before then, the main focus of interest in this area were those forces that produced sustained economic growth and improvements in mass standards of living or, on the contrary, maintained stagnation and backwardness in the less industrialized countries. A prominent American sociologist defined development in the sixties as a process that "proceeds as a contrapuntal interplay between differentiation (which is divisive of established society) and integration (which unites differentiated structures on a new basis)."[11]

Two assumptions were common to studies on the topic thus defined: first, that individual societies were the appropriate units of analysis, since it was within them that quantifiable economic growth and improvements in the quality of life, or the lack of each, occurred; second, that economic and social processes in the already industrialized world were qualitatively distinct from those in the less developed countries. Depending on the theoretical perspective adopted, "development" was therefore a matter of bringing these countries up to the level of the industrial world or of promoting a new "international economic order" in which both groups of nations—advanced and backward—would converge into a more egalitarian division of rewards.

Within this general framework, theorists of opposite persuasions debated whether it was the wrong kind of values and the persistence of tradition that generated underdevelopment or whether the latter was due to the continuous hegemony and exactions of the developed countries. Modernization and dependency became the accepted labels for this theoretical polarity.

Research in these traditions continues in sociology, although the limitation of resources prevents scholars from conducting extensive fieldwork, and thus published studies are increasingly based on the analysis of aggregate statistics or on reflections of general trends. One line of inquiry that continues the tradition of early modernization studies is the renewed interest in determinants of political democracy. Interestingly, the theme reemerged almost simultaneously in the U.S. and Latin America, although with very different methodological orientations.

In the United States, democracy is the subject of quantitative cross-national analyses aimed at discovering what combination of variables best "explains" the emergence and durability of democratic institutions around the globe. The recent work of Kenneth Bollen and Robert Jackman, among others, is illustrative of this approach.[12] In Latin America, the problem of institutionalizing democracy has a far more urgent character, and thus scholars can ill afford the time-consuming statistical analyses of their northern peers. Instead, studies of redemocratization are based on intense reflection on the authoritarian past of particular countries and comparisons between different national experiences.

In his *Autoritarismo y democracia*, Marcelo Cavarozzi analyzes, for example, prospects for building Argentine democracy.[13] His conclusions are not too optimistic: attempts at a comprehensive reordering of Argentine society in the past have led not only to compounded failures but to the abandonment of every rule of political coexistence. Although the country has demonstrated time and again its capacity to resist the authoritarian project, an entire generation grew up without even minimal exposure to democratic practice. Published at the start of the Alfonsin period in 1983, the book serves as a compendium of all the pitfalls confronting Argentine redemocratization.

An altogether different tack is taken by Fernando Henrique Cardoso, who analyzes the problem of democracy by focusing on its class underpinnings and by comparing the Latin American experience with that of the developed Western countries.[14] Unlike the classic European bourgeoisie, Latin American entrepreneurs have never shown a vocation for democracy, preferring instead to pursue a private dialogue with "their" interlocutors in control of the state bureaucracy. This entrepreneurial inclination explains, in part, why this class has seen no contradiction in supporting highly repressive regimes in the name of the free market and individual freedom.

In the absence of a democratic bourgeoisie, the primary structural support for democracy comes from an alliance of the working classes with salaried middle groups. This emerging alliance manifests itself through novel political channels—among them, church-sponsored organizations, trade unions, neighborhood committees, and women's associations. This alliance seeks to transcend the goals of traditional formal democracy by promoting its active participation in decisions that affect the material well-being of its members. For Cardoso, the challenge is how to expand the scope of state action while simultaneously giving a greater voice to these popular groups. How? By putting more issues to a vote, by decentralizing state agencies, and by de-mythologizing state officialdom through direct scrutiny by their constituents.

These U.S.–Latin American differences in the study of policy democracy—a theme that continues a central concern of the earlier modernization literature—find a counterpart in the respective approaches to the question of dependency. As a general paradigm, dependency has not been rejected but rather institutionalized in Latin American sociology. It is at present, however, less a substantive concern than a backdrop against which domestic issues are analyzed. As an example, the Cardoso analysis of redemocratization begins by reminding us that Latin America's condition of dependency means that many aspects of its political future have been fixed beforehand, but then quickly shifts to those still within the purview of domestic actors.[15]

Ironically, this turn away from external determinants of underdevelopment in Latin America coincided with a vigorous interest in "testing dependency" in North American sociology. This literature consists of various efforts to operationalize levels of dependency and examine their effects on such variables as economic growth and income inequality. Examples include the recent book by Volker Bornschier and Christopher Chase-Dunn, *Transnational Corporations and Underdevelopment*, as well as a number of articles in major journals by the same authors with Richard Rubinson.[16]

Despite greater empirical rigor, this North American dependency literature has had less impact on the general field of development than the original Latin American formulations of the theory during the sixties. It has been the target of several cogent critiques from authors of both hemispheres who have called attention to the futility of transforming a general perspective—dependency—into a set of statistical variables. Along similar lines, others have accused these studies of "consuming" the heuristic value of the concept without adding much to knowledge of the relevant processes.[17]

Despite these adverse comments, empirical research on dependency has made several valuable contributions, such as (1) refining the meaning of the concept by distinguishing between trade and investment dependence and, within the latter, between stocks and flows of investment; (2) establishing short- and medium-term effects of these different forms; and (3) tackling the thorny issue of countries that, although "dependent" by any definition, are still quite wealthy. A recent article on Canadian development patterns published in the *American Sociological Review* provides a good example of this line of work.[18]

Aside from these and other substantive topics that provide continuity with earlier modernization and dependency themes, the field as a whole has shifted in response to recent theoretical innovations backed by considerable research support. In the United States, in particular, the advent of the world-system perspective has come close to an intellectual revolution, raising serious questions as to whether the concept of "development" is still appropriate. Although the ideas at the core of the world-system approach date back to turn-of-the-century theories of imperialism, and although these ideas were extensively developed later on by Marxist economists such as Rosa Luxemburg and, more recently, Ernest Mandel, the approach is identified in U.S. sociology with the writings of Immanuel Wallerstein and his followers.[19]

World-system theory conveys with full force the idea that the global politico-economic system—and, in particular, the capitalist international economy—represents a valid unit of analysis and, moreover, that research at this level takes precedence over research on national and regional processes. For the sociology of development, this amounts to a complete reversal of method. In the past, the usual procedure was to first focus on a country or group of countries and then ask what factors—including external ones—accounted for their present condition or future prospects. Both modernization and dependency writings gave due credit to external forces as instruments either of cultural diffusion or of imperialist exploitation, but even the latter approach took as its point of departure the nation-state. On the contrary, the world-system approach proposes to chart global processes first and only then to examine how individual societies or other less inclusive actors adapt to them.

Although this point was first illustrated with historical material on the origins of capitalism in the sixteenth century, the facts that gained it greater credibility came from the contemporary world. Evidence of the interpenetration of national economies, the existence of social processes that transcend national borders, and the creation of a global culture is readily available anywhere. Research that backed this position has been frequently conducted by sociologists who started with one or another of the classic "development" paradigms and were then gradually compelled by their own data to abandon an exclusively domestic perspective and adopt a more global one.

Although dependency and subsequent world-system views are frequently identified as one, there are significant differences between them. Analysts of dependency tend to focus on the effects of foreign hegemony on subordinate nations rather than on the long-term dynamics of the system as a whole. The major goal of dependency writings has been to understand the origins of this condition, as it affects individual nations and regions, and explore possible ways out of it. The principal goal of world-system writings, on the other hand, has been to understand the evolution of the world economy as a unit over the last centuries, including processes by which previously "core" states became peripheral and vice versa.

The advent of the world-system approach weakened the previous assumption that nations represented the foremost unit of analysis and simultaneously rendered implausible the image of development derived from that assumption. Thus, the conflict between views of development as a process of imitating the industrialized countries or, alternatively, a process of gaining liberation from their hegemony has lost vigor as it became clear that most countries could do neither. Instead, the field shifted, particularly in the United States, toward a new interest in the forms of articulation of different actors—nation-states, cities, and social classes—in the global economy and the strategies and resources available to them. If "development" means anything in this new context, it is the alternative modes of adaptation by nations and other collective actors to broader structures that condition and constrain their options.[20]

This theoretical shift also undermined the second assumption of the earlier sociology of development—namely, the existence of a qualitative gap between societies and economies of the advanced and less developed worlds. It became increasingly clear instead that strategies of transnational corporations, processes of cultural diffusion, and global transfers of capital and technology tend to reproduce fairly similar structures in countries at different levels of industrialization. They also bind populations belonging to different national patches in ways that transcend those regulated and monitored by their respective states.

In general, the frontier of research in the field of development, particularly its U.S. variant, encompasses the study of four different flows across the center-periphery divide. These are flows of (1) capital, (2) technology, (3) cultural forms, and (4) people. Research on the first two has usually focused on the organization and strategies of transnationals such as automakers, pharmaceuticals, oil companies, and the like, and on locational decisions of entire industries such as garments, footwear, and electronics.

Examples include the previously cited research by Evans and Gereffi, as well as studies of locational patterns of high-tech industries such as biogenetics and electronics and the resettlement of labor-intensive industries in Latin America and elsewhere in the Third World.[21] A promising line of inquiry is the comparison of effects of foreign investment under different industrialization policies in Asian countries, such as South Korea and Taiwan, and in Latin America. This analysis also involves economists, but the distinct sociological focus is on those factors, including domestic class structures and the balance of political forces, that make possible the successful implementation of certain industrialization policies in some countries but not others.[22]

Studies of the reproduction of cultural forms on a global scale include at present two main currents: first, the research of John Mayer and his colleagues at Stanford on core-to-periphery cultural and institutional transfers; and second, studies of ideology, including social and economic doctrines, which provide explanations for inequality between countries or people and/or suggest solutions to them. Examples include studies of culture-of-poverty and marginality theories in Third World countries by Joseph Kahl, Janice Perlman, Susan Eckstein, and other North American scholars, and research on the impact of the neoliberal economic doctrines of Friedman and Von Hayek on development strategies by Latin American authors such as Guillermo O'Donnell, Norbert Lechner, Glaucio Soares, and Fernando Henrique Cardoso.[23]

The final thematic area is the uses and control of labor in different parts of the world economy. Included under this rubric are studies of international labor migrations—for example, from Mexico and the Caribbean to the United States. Also included are numerous studies of labor recruitment and labor practices related to the processes of industrial restructuring and plant relocation in such places as Haiti, the Dominican Republic, and the northern border of Mexico; and also Taiwan, Hong Kong, and other nations in Southeast Asia.[24]

The recent sociological interest in labor flows is grounded in what has been called, at the level of theory, the third "international division of labor." The first, or turn-of-the-century, division featured an industrial world producing and selling manufactures to the colonies and nonindustrialized countries, with the latter being assigned the role of raw material producers. The second, or post–World War II, division saw the more advanced peripheral countries become industrial producers of consumer goods for their own markets and net importers of heavy machinery and technology in the process labeled import-substitution industrialization. The third started around 1960 and spread across the globe in less than twenty years. John Walton describes it as follows:

> Capital and production are exported from the de-industrializing advanced countries for relocation in the hospitable confines of Third World assembly plants using low-wage labour and in "export platforms" from which goods are launched to yet other countries, or back to the home markets in the core. The Northeastern United States shoe and garment industries, for example, "migrate" to Mexico, Taiwan, or these days, Sri Lanka, but the products of cheap labour in those places resourcefully migrate back to Fifth Avenue and Mainstreet.[25]

It is likely that this process of mass transfer of labor-intensive industrial production has been exaggerated or has reached its limits. Electronics firms that were among the first to "run away" are now reported to have repatriated much of their operations. Far from disappearing, the U.S. garment industry continues to be one of the principal industrial employers, although it has been restructured to adapt to foreign competition. In another context, global "sourcing," as in the much-touted "world car," seems to have given way to attempts at plant reorganization in the United States.[26] Nevertheless, the situation is very fluid, and these comings-and-goings support Walton's basic conclusion that "footloose international capital and worldwide labour reserves, themselves capable of longer migrations, are now parts of a single system."[27]

Recent studies of what is variously called the "underground economy" or the "informal sector" in Latin American and U.S. cities offer also a valuable entry point for the comparative study of labor practices. Informality may be defined as the sum total of income-producing activities, excluding those that are contractual and state-regulated. As such, it covers a vast gamut of activities, from direct subsistence to petty artisan production and trade. Research on the informal sector is a promising line of inquiry because similar structural arrangements, involving the organization of production and commerce in microenterprises, persist and even seem to be expanding in countries that are at very different levels of industrialization—from the poorer Latin American countries to advanced ones and, in particular, the United States. In the latter case, urban informal activities appear to be growing on the basis of immigrant labor, mostly from Latin America and mostly undocumented.

There are differences, of course, because in Latin America activities outside the regulated economy have always been common or even normative, whereas in the United States the surge of sweatshops and homework appears to be a reenactment of practices that many believed dead and buried.[28] Still, the existence of this network of activities in countries at very different levels of industrialization offers another piece of evidence against the prior practice of limiting studies of development to the underdeveloped world. Also, by their very character, these activities offer a prime opportunity for sociologists to clarify how different sociopolitical contexts promote and constrain grassroots economic activities.

Conclusion

Looking ahead, most future developments are likely to represent continuities with those apparent today, at least in the short-to-medium run. Any attempt to outline future prospects of the discipline in either setting must take into account, however, two different questions: first, that of its internal structure; and second, that of its substantive content. Again for reasons of space, I will only deal briefly with each of them.

On the structural side, the first question is that of numbers. Latin American sociology is not likely to grow rapidly in either Latin America or the United States. This is so for two reasons. First, the enthusiastic promises made by or imputed to sociology in earlier periods dissipated long ago. The discipline is no longer seen as the key to discovering and perhaps exorcising the causes of underdevelopment, but simply as another limited intellectual pursuit. Second, the resources necessary to expand the scope of sociological research and significantly increase the number of its practitioners are no longer available.

In Latin America, these difficulties are compounded by the elimination or weakening of professional training programs. There is even concern in some countries that the discipline will disappear with its present members, since there are few institutional mechanisms to train a replacement generation. Although such fears are probably exaggerated, the present situation suggests that sociology as a profession is at least not likely to expand significantly in the short-to-medium run.

Another likely structural continuity is the setting in which most sociological research is done. In the United States, it will continue to be universities, especially those with well-established Latin American centers. In Latin America, the model of the private, independent research center is also likely to endure. Although created originally in countries like Brazil, Argentina, and Chile to meet emergency political situations, the independent centers have proven so productive and flexible that they will probably not be abandoned, even after their members have returned to regular university teaching. Indeed, the demise of these small but highly effective institutions would be a major loss not only for sociology but for all social sciences in the region.

Finally, the trend toward growing compenetration and collaborative activities between U.S. and Latin American sociologists is likely to continue. As noted previously, the numbers involved on both parts are relatively few, and exchange over a number of years seems to have facilitated mutual trust. An earlier and well-known example of such collaboration are the surveys of Balan, Browning, and Jelin in Monterrey, which remain to date one of the most significant contributions to the study of Latin American migration processes.[29]

Later examples that have yielded or promise to yield similar results include the work of the late A. Eugene Havens on Latin American rural structures in collaboration with Jorge Dandler in Bolivia, Bernardo Sorj in Brazil, and others; the program of analysis of Brazilian mobility and stratification on the basis of government surveys conducted jointly by José Pastore at the University of São Paulo and A. O. Haller at the University of Wisconsin; and the study of various aspects of the Brazilian development model by Glaucio Soares and Charles Wood at the University of Florida jointly with researchers in Belo Horizonte and in Rio de Janeiro.[30]

Despite these and other instances of collaboration, the substantive topics of interest to U.S. and Latin American researchers are moving in different directions, a trend that also represents continuity with the recent past. In the United States, research is likely to continue shifting away from individual country studies and toward substantive themes studied comparatively. Recent examples that reflect the growing influence of the world-system perspective have gone beyond comparisons within Latin America to include cases elsewhere in the Third World, primarily Asia.[31]

The severe economic crisis confronted by Latin America as a whole during the early eighties and the rapid political changes in many countries riveted attention on processes internal to the region. Knowledge of Latin America's dependent position and the vast significance of external forces and constraints on its development remains a constant backdrop of studies by Latin American sociologists. Yet, much contemporary research takes such factors as given, in order to explore those internal variables that can contribute, for example, to the emergence of broad-based class alliances, revolutionary movements, or a resilient democratic order.

Despite this topical divergence, studies of development in both regions, but particularly in the United States, appear affected by a certain loss of focus. The problem may be summarized by noting that many specialists on the question of development cannot tell at present what is distinctly "sociological" about their approach, as opposed, for example, to economic or political. This loss of bearing actually began with the demise of modernization theory. Despite its limitations, amply criticized in the development literature, modernization was a more sociological viewpoint than those that followed it, for it focused on the effects of institutionalized values on economic and political action. Dependency, on the other hand, has been a more economic-oriented approach, for it focuses on the mechanisms of surplus extraction via foreign investment and trade. Needless to say, this emphasis on global economic structures has been reinforced by the advent of world-system theory.

This is not the time to return to the notion that instilling the values of the Protestant Ethic will turn Haiti into Sweden, but it is time to take seriously the notion that economic action does not occur in a vacuum. To the extent that development is primarily an economic phenomenon (growth and distribution), it is the task of sociology to refine and correct the notion of the relevant actors (nations, local communities, and individuals) as unconstrained maximizers. As Mark Granovetter has reminded us, economic action is still social action, and, as such, it is embedded in a structure of preexisting social relationships that largely determine its course.[32]

Social embeddedness of economic action goes a long way toward explaining, for example, why multinational strategies that prove successful in one country fail in another and why development policies effective in Southeast Asia are mostly inapplicable in Latin America. It is also the key to understanding how "invented" informal employment in the margins of the modern economy not only provides a means for survival for the urban poor in Latin America but also supports, in manifold ways, the visibility and growth of the modern sector.

It is for this reason that research is so promising on multinationals as *social* organizations, on the dynamics of negotiation between transnationals and nation-states, on the global diffusion of cultural patterns and institutional forms, on the social processes underlying internal migrations, and on the modes of articulation between formal and informal sectors. Such research can restore direction to sociological studies of Latin American development by revindicating class structure, social networks, social norms, customs, and charisma as significant factors affecting the course of adaptation to the global system and the chances for economic growth of individual countries and the region as a whole.

FIVE

Anthropology in Latin America: Old Boundaries, New Contexts

LOURDES ARIZPE S.

In the last twenty years, anthropology in Latin America has renewed its theories and methods as never before. The burst of energy that allowed it to overflow its old thematic and disciplinary boundaries was generated by its openness to changing social and political contexts and by its close association with other Latin American social sciences during this period. New analytic tools as well as new research methods were tried out.

Now that the tide has subsided, valuable research and important intellectual imprints are left that must be evaluated. At this ebb tide, though, it is not quite clear whether the surge has marked a radical departure from previous anthropological work. Nevertheless, if it did not bring about a revolution in anthropological research, as many prophesied in the sixties, it did indeed stimulate evolution. Not an evolution based on the normal accumulation of data, but one splendidly brought about by a deep questioning of the role of anthropology, and of social science generally, in the social and political life of Latin American societies, and by an awakening to the fact that, if social science is to respond to relevant concerns, not only its theories but also its practice must change.

Though the questioning was radical, the solutions proposed—that is, the research projects that ensued—have not coalesced into a major theoretical or methodological breakthrough. At present, anthropology in Latin America is still seeking new solutions, and hence its research is interesting and relevant at this time, but the terms are modest.

Although anthropology in most of Latin America, as in the United States, retains its wide disciplinary character, in this essay I will only review research in social anthropology and ethnology. Other specializations such as archaeology, physical anthropology, ethnohistory, and linguistics, as well as emerging subdisciplines such as ecological or symbolic anthropology, would require a different approach and will not be dealt with here. Also, social anthropology and ethnology are the nearest to the other social sciences—economics, history, political science, and sociology—under review in this book and thus will be enriched by cross-references.

The Latin American Social Science Boom

Innovative thinking in the social sciences in the region, as Fishlow notes in his chapter, began with structuralist economic theory in the 1950's. However, problems faced by the import-substitution model at the end of that decade soon led to mounting criticism by orthodox economists and by left-wing researchers.

By that time, anthropologists had become increasingly dissatisfied with traditional ethnographic research. Anthropological studies in Latin America had been carried out by foreign researchers since the beginning of the century. They followed two main ethnological traditions: Boasian cultural relativism from the United States, and the Mauss school of ethnology from France.

By the fifties, three major trends were present in anthropology in Latin America. The more classical ethnological studies focused primarily on registering vanishing Indian cultures. Methodologically, they concentrated on standard ethnographic fieldwork with the aim of classifying and describing the cultural diversity of Indian groups. This research developed especially in countries such as Brazil for the study of Amazonian peoples.[1]

In countries such as Peru, Mexico, and Colombia, because most Indian groups are peasant societies with a richness of culture that spans several centuries, research developed around community studies, following the research methodology set by, among others, Robert Redfield, Manuel Gamio, George Foster, and Oscar Lewis in Mexico, Bernard Mishkin in Peru, and Sol Tax in Guatemala.[2] During the fifties, this methodological perspective also became important in applied anthropology. Rural development policies were applied through *"desarrollo de la comunidad"* ("community development") programs as the microcounterpart of ECLA (United Nations Economic Commission for Latin America) and Alliance for Progress policies.

A third important trend in Latin American anthropology at that time, which may be considered its most original contribution to world anthropology, was the theory and practice of *indigenismo*, Indianist state policy. Initially, this policy was based on the assumption that Indian cultures were a hindrance to modern progress, and therefore efforts should be directed toward integrating Indians into national society through acculturation.

By the beginning of the sixties, the dissatisfaction of the new generation of anthropologists with strictly ethnographic as well as community studies, and with the failures of Indianist policies, coincided with the critique of ECLA economics and the emergence of political and guerrilla movements in many Latin American countries.

Intellectually, the ground had already been sown for a deep questioning of the prevalent assumptions of cultural relativism and functionalism in anthropology. Following the lead given by Julian Steward and Julio de la Fuente a decade earlier, Gonzalo Aguirre Beltrán and Eric Wolf opened a new perspective by analyzing the relationship between Indian and non-Indian peoples as one of domination, within the context of center-periphery exchange.[3] Indians were no longer primarily seen as holders of "other" cultures, or as pure descendants of native populations, but as colonized peoples and exploited peasants.

This line of research in anthropology converged with developments in Latin American sociology and history in the mid-sixties through the work of Rodolfo Stavenhagen, José Matos Mar, and Orlando Fals Borda. Stavenhagen had initially trained as an anthropologist and later became a major exponent of Latin American sociology. One of his major contributions, the theory of internal colonialism, provided a microregional counterpart to dependency theory.[4]

José Matos Mar, Augusto Salazar Bondy, and Julio Cotler were responsible for opening up this new perspective in Peru in 1968, in their classic study *Perú problema*.[5] In this book, which led the way for most rural studies in the seventies, the main themes were unequal regional development, pluralism, and the culture and mechanisms of internal domination. All of them converged in a major framework, that of dependency, which was being developed by Latin American historians, economists, and sociologists.

In Colombia, Orlando Fals Borda and his group developed a major methodological tool that was to influence anthropology deeply.[6] The latter, all during the sixties, faced a relentless questioning of its aims and methods from a political and moral standpoint. Do outsiders have a right to intrude on native people's lives? Aren't standard ethnographies no more than cultural booty that end up exclusively enriching metropolitan countries or national elites? Are anthropologists no more than sophisticated spies?

One solution to these dilemmas was found in action-research, which converged with the *concientización* movement born of Paulo Freire's *Pedagogy of the Oppressed*.[7] Fals Borda became one of the main theoreticians and practitioners of this method. In different countries, among anthropologists, it ranged from denouncing conditions of repression and exploitation of Indian and peasant groups to actively engaging in land invasions, mobilizations, and community militancy.

It is clearly significant, at this point, that the disciplinary boundaries between anthropology and sociology, as well as economics and history, practically disappeared. Anthropology, though, had a special contribution to make. In the words of Cynthia Hewitt de Alcántara: "If it was Latin American sociology which most thoroughly explored the theoretical implications of superimposing geographical or sectorial forms of domination upon class relations, as the concepts of colonialism, neocolonialism and dependence implied, it was anthropology which provided the much needed perspective on the third dimension of the generically colonial situation: ethnic discrimination."[8] By studying discrimination against Indians, anthropologists were able to provide theoretical tools for the study of all forms of domination.

By the end of the sixties, guerrilla insurgency, peasant impoverishment, massive rural-urban migration, and patchy reforms to failing economic policies in most Latin American countries demanded new interpretations from social scientists. Very soon, though, as is mentioned in other chapters, political repression quickly ended challenging intellectual activity in Brazil, Chile, Argentina, and Uruguay.

It is interesting to note, however, that in such countries anthropological methods became useful to carry on with research. Large-scale surveys could no longer be carried out, and censuses were not published. Interviews and participant observation, though, were useful to continue unobtrusive research in low-income urban and rural households.

In the first half of the seventies, in those countries where it was still possible, social anthropologists were deeply involved not only in describing but in bringing about social change. Anthropology, as defined by Rodolfo Stavenhagen, echoing the intellectual climate of the time, had to be radical, committed, and active. *"Antropología comprometida"* became the rallying cry for the new thrust in anthropology.

Regional Boundaries and Intellectual Debate

Developments in anthropological research in the region have been described, up to this point, mainly in their relationship with internal factors—that is, the boom in Latin American social science and political and cultural movements. Yet, it is quite clear that intellectual currents and political events outside the region were also influential—among them, the civil rights and anti-Vietnam War movements in the U.S., and also the rise of Marxism, especially its application to anthropology by writers such as Maurice Godelier, Claude Peter Worseley, Claude Meillassoux, and Phillipe Rey. Equally important was the growth of a Third World perspective, through the work of anthropologists such as André Betéille, Talal Asad, and others.

Some of these anthropologists came to Latin America to do research or to teach. But relations with non–Latin American researchers were not easy at the time. As a result of rising political consciousness, distrust grew against outside researchers, especially when some anthropological projects, such as the famous Camelot project in Chile, were found to have hidden political agendas. The link of other institutions such as the Summer School of Linguistics to nonresearch activities helped to deepen distrust. In that situation, some foreign colleagues chose to work in greater contact with Latin American anthropologists, and very fruitful collaboration was achieved as a result. In other cases, however, foreign anthropologists retreated into more academic debates centered around their own universities back home.

It is important to say that non–Latin American anthropologists are caught in a double bind: if their research touches on sensitive economic or political issues of Latin American countries, they may be open to uneasy questioning from their local counterparts or from governments; and if they focus on more symbolic or strictly cultural or extremely specialized debate, it may be said that their research topics are irrelevant. There is no easy way out of this dilemma, and, unfortunately, hemispheric academic associations that could find ways of easing this situation do not exist, with the exception of the Latin American Studies Association.

However, it must be pointed out that national anthropologists are also, in a sense, caught in a similar double bind, which is analyzed below in the section on the "Insider Versus Outsider Debate."

For their part, many non–Latin American anthropologists, taken aback by the political militancy of most Latin American anthropologists during the seventies, took a dim view of research being produced in the region. This was especially the case with colleagues from countries with a strong empiricist tradition, such as the United States and England. It is true that many of the debates on social issues of the seventies in Latin America rose to meaningless heights of abstraction. This was especially so when modes of production were endlessly discussed with little empirical data to back up different positions. But it is also true that heaping empirical data upon empirical data with no theoretical direction was an equally meaningless exercise. It seems to me that the empiricist project in anthropology came to an end, in fact, when the painstaking, meticulous efforts of the Human Area Files failed to produce any major breakthrough in explaining human society on this planet. The need for new theories, then, is certainly there.

The deeper level of these intellectual differences, though, seems to me to stem from the attempt made by Latin American social scientists in the sixties and seventies to root the basic assumptions and issues of their research in national and regional concerns. It should by now be a well-established fact that European and U.S. social science is indeed rooted in deep philosophical concerns that grew out of the social scientists' historical experiences. Among such concerns are individual freedom versus social constraints, sentiment versus rationality, culture versus nature, and the search for "rational" man. Such questions do underlie Latin American culture, obviously, but our historical development, at this stage, gives priority to other concerns. Some of these are unity versus diversity, imitation versus isolation, authority versus corporatism, and the violence of Nature versus the violence of imposed civilization. These issues had begun to emerge by the mid-1970's. Unfortunately, many of them were straitjacketed in rigid theoretical terms, especially in neo-Marxism, and thus creativity was stifled.

But the original thinking, creative search, and self-awareness of anthropology in Latin America in the seventies show that this is the right road. Conditions have now reverted, and the vicious cycle of intellectual dependency may be setting in again. But Latin American anthropology, and social sciences generally, have shown that, given appropriate conditions, they can make an important contribution to world social science. Let us hope that economic and political constraints do not continue to stifle them.

Old Debate, New Terms: Ethnicity and Ethnicism

The shift in theory that defined Indians no longer as members of autarchic cultural entities but as subordinate communities within a large-scale structure of domination made the old classical debate on the nature of their relationship to the national society and the State go quite a few steps further.

Being Indian designated not only those who "felt" that they were Indians, following Alfonso Caso's famous definition a few decades earlier, but those who, according to Darcy Ribeiro, had gone through the passage from tribal Indian to generic Indian.[9]

Throughout the seventies, anthropological research in Latin America, as well as in other parts of the world, explored this view further. A study in Hueyapan, Mexico, showed that Indianness there constitutes a negative identity, independently of the content of the villagers' culture, since it is defined by the fact that they continue to lack what the elite continue to acquire.[10] Another study compared two neighboring peasant communities—one, Mazahua; the other, mestizo—that had been granted land during the Agrarian Reform.[11] Forty years later, the Mazahua community was poorer, a fact that could be traced to unequal access to land, to jobs in the growing capitalist sector and in the bureaucracy, and to political office.

Against both the previous view that considered Indian cultures as dying remnants about to fall off the modern world and integrationist policies that sought to acculturate Indians, the new trend argued that development could in fact be achieved while maintaining divergent cultural traditions. As a matter of fact, it was stated that development could not come about otherwise, since the discrimination against Indians did not, among other things, allow them to challenge the notably unequal distribution of income that had resulted from development policies.

This debate, held both in academic and official institutions, strongly influenced Indianist policies. In the seventies, the new term of *"indigenismo participativo"* was coined.[12] One of its major proposals is that Indian communities should have a greater say in decision-making and in applying programs and projects in their regions. As part of this discussion, bilingual and bicultural educational policies were widely discussed in many Latin American countries.[13]

As part of their theoretical proposals, exponents of this current also argued that, far from being handicaps that slow down national progress, native cultures are intrinsically valuable for their human and social creativity. Anthropologists the world over, of course, had been putting forth this idea for decades. Now it was expanded and related to democracy and the structure of the State. Indian cultures, it was stated, represent viable social and political entities. Thus, instead of the State denigrating or trying to eliminate their cultures, it should recognize that both their historical and their ongoing cultural creativity can actively contribute to building national culture and identity. Accordingly, the term "plural society" was resuscitated from early anthropological literature on the colonial situation and given new life through the concept of "cultural pluralism."[14]

Although this discussion is being held in most Latin American countries where Indian cultures have a strong cultural profile, up until now only Mexico, as recently as 1982, has made cultural pluralism its official policy toward Indian groups. However, a new, even more open policy is coming into the light and will probably become an important issue in Latin American anthropology in the years to come, as the Nicaraguan government goes ahead in granting autonomy to its coastal Pacific region, where the majority of Misquito, Rama, and Suma Indians live.[15]

The trend under review also stresses that not only Indian groups but also peasant and low-income urban groups can create highly original and vibrant symbols and performances, just as worthwhile as those of more academic or elite traditions. This proposition also mirrors an old debate, leading back to Herder and folk culture in Germany at the turn of the last century. Social conditions seem to have made it just as relevant for Latin America at the turn of this century. The new term that refers to this is "popular cultures."[16]

Why popular cultures and not folklore? A different set of assumptions is behind each term. Folklore collects finished products of open-ended social groups, with a view toward preserving and comparing such items. Popular cultures, on the other hand, record the cultural dynamics of the way of life of low-income groups in urbanized and semi-industrialized societies. The Gramscian influence is evident here. It came through the writings of Italian Marxists and anthropologists, especially those who looked at *clases subalternas* ("subordinate classes") within capitalist society.

This view blended with that of Latin American social anthropologists already mentioned, who were trying to place Indian groups within the context of underdeveloped capitalist countries. The new perspective of popular cultures breaks down the old boundary between Indian and non-Indian groups (peasants, migrants, and urban low-income groups), all of whom, in any case, share the same structural position in such countries.

Another difference from previous anthropological work is that the perspective of popular cultures is action-oriented. It tries not only to record and to preserve but also to stimulate the cultural creativity of such groups. In this respect, it also ties in with the heightened interest in action-research that, as mentioned, has been evident in the social sciences in the last fifteen years, especially in Latin America, but also in other regions.

However, the new trends mentioned above—that is, the reappraisal of Indian identity, the shift toward policies of cultural pluralism or regional autonomy, and the interest in popular cultures—may never have happened in anthropology if it had not been for a major social development in the seventies and eighties in Latin America: the rise of ethnic consciousness and militancy among Indians.

The Insider Versus Outsider Debate

Parallel to the developments mentioned above, and in close connection to them, the seventies witnessed an unprecedented historical event in Latin America: the rise of ethnic militancy among Indians. They reclaimed their right to speak for themselves and to preserve their cultural heritage.[17]

This is clearly not a unique Latin American phenomenon, but one shared, it seems, by almost all regions of the world, and is undoubtedly linked to the questioning, on a grand scale, of the economic, political, and cultural world order, based on nation-states and capitalism. In Latin America, the social and intellectual conditions that gave rise to this ethnic revival came hand in hand. One could ask: did the political struggles in Latin America in the sixties drive ethnic groups to greater militancy, thus putting anthropology, in turn, in the defendant's chair? Or were the self-doubting questions that anthropologists began to ask about their right to intrude in other peoples' lives and cultures the breath that brought forth flames from the smoking embers of

Indian consciousness? Obviously, there is no clear-cut answer, but, as Levi-Strauss would say, putting it in this way may be useful for thinking about it.

The salient feature in this development in Latin America is the uneasy ambiguity that now shades relationships between anthropologists and Indians. A large number of Latin American national anthropologists have supported the rise of Indian consciousness and organizations to a greater extent, perhaps, than anthropologists from the North. The reason is clear: while Western anthropologists usually study peoples in other countries, national anthropologists study their own co-citizens as alien peoples. The ensuing intellectual and moral discomfort often leads to social guilt, to retreat into glacial scientific "objectivity" or to committed social science.

Most often, Latin American anthropologists have taken a moral stance of defense of Indian peoples. Because native peoples in Latin America—as in most other regions of the world—usually occupy a subordinate and therefore muted political position, anthropologists, quite naturally, came to fill this political void and thus became spokespersons for native peoples. It is interesting to note that, in more backward situations, it is priests who have historically taken on this role, as tradition since Fray Bartolomé de las Casas shows. With development, it is anthropologists who step in, both as researchers and as administrators of Indianist institutions.

This helps to explain why anthropology in Latin America has developed more as advocacy for the Indians than as a scientific endeavor. Now that Indians in some countries are able to voice their own demands and to fill political positions, one may predict with some confidence that this will lead to important changes in anthropology.

A few anthropologists are feeling threatened. They feel that Indians may eventually take over not only all ethnological and anthropological fieldwork but also administrative positions within government institutions working in those areas. It must be remembered that governments are the main, and sometimes the only, employers of social anthropologists and ethnologists in most Latin American countries.

A more legitimate concern has led some left-wing anthropologists to oppose Indian movements on the grounds that they may ultimately lead to conservative positions on political matters and may be class-divisive. Other anthropologists, conscious of the need for national unity, are worried that ethnic militancy may become exacerbated and lead toward separatism, which can easily be manipulated by foreign powers.

In contrast, the fact that foreign anthropologists are not touched by such national concerns, although some are aware of them, has turned many of them into ardent supporters of Indian movements.

Indian anthropologists have traditionally been scarce in Latin American universities and museums, but they are growing in numbers with every generation.[18] In Mexico, several groups of "ethnolinguists," all native speakers of Indian languages, have been trained to do ethnographic and linguistic work among their own peoples. In the field of history, Indian historians have been especially successful in reinterpreting historical texts by reading documents in their native languages with their own worldview.[19] Documents describing newly formed Indian organizations, the emerging ethnic consciousness, movements, and strategies are circulating widely in Latin American countries. A major source of such documents is the journal *Civilización: configuraciones de la diversidad*. Other organizations outside the region, such as IWGIA (International Work Group for Indigenous Affairs, Copenhagen) and Survival International, help to document the situation of Indians.

That ethnic movements have deeply changed the traditional role of anthropologists and have questioned their role as researchers is evident in the fact that the relationship of anthropologists to their informants continues to be one of the major concerns in the mid-eighties. Clearly, these movements will help to mold social anthropology and ethnology into a different kind of endeavor, hopefully more relevant as well as more scientific.

New Debate on an Old World

The Old World that anthropologists embraced as their own in the New World was, of course, that of ancient Indian civilizations. Halperín gives an excellent review of historical studies in Latin America, so it is not necessary to go into them in this chapter. However, it is worth mentioning that, in the last twenty years, anthropologists have done distinguished work both in Mesoamerican and Andean social history.

In the first region, however, the research findings on pre-Hispanic Mexico, related to topics such as demographic patterns, the structure of the State, social organization, agriculture, and irrigation, have not had a direct bearing on present-day anthropological themes, most probably because the demographic, technological, and ecosystemic base of Mesoamerican societies was totally altered during colonial domination.

In contrast, such research in the Andean region has found a problem that is still relevant today, related to the ecological adaptation of agricultural producers to geophysical conditions. In this sense, the tools developed by anthropologists to study human adaptation and reciprocity were useful for historians in analyzing the problem.[20] And the anthropologists' historical work, as can be seen in Halperín's chapter, has added depth and insights to research done on present-day Andean peasant communities.

Historical research showed that the "vertical control of ecological levels" was one of the main principles of Andean social organization.[21] A complex system of exchange, both of basic foodstuffs and ritual goods, evolved during the Tiwantinsuyu (the period of expansion of the Inca Empire). This system gives a distinct pattern to the economic and social organization of communities today. One of the books that makes the link between the two epochs is Karen Spalding's aptly titled *From Indian to Peasant*,[22] which, to paraphrase Darcy Ribeiro, describes how the quichua speaker went from being a *generic Indian* to becoming a *generic peasant*.

Such research had its counterpart in early community studies, which later developed into regional studies. Of the latter, the best known are those by Allan Holmberg and Mario Vázquez in Callejón de Huaylas in Ancash, and the Peru-Cornell Vicos Project,[23] conceived by Mario Vázquez.

As current problems swept rural communities in the Andes, as mentioned earlier, anthropologists focused on cultural domination and on agrarian problems. José Matos Mar and researchers at the Instituto de Estudios Peruanos centered on agrarian reform;[24] and, among others, Rodrigo Montoya looked at peasant movements and the new agricultural associations created by the Velasco military government.[25] These topics were to be widely debated in Latin America.

As mentioned earlier, the other major contribution of anthropology in Latin America in the seventies was the debate on the peasantry. It was both interdisciplinary and international, with wide participation by non–Latin Americans.[26] It touched on a whole range of relevant topics: agrarian reform, the peasant economy, agrarian capitalism, rural-urban migration, and peasant movements. Thematic diversity was offset by theoretical convergence. One theoretical question gave an unprecedented consistency and continuity to this debate—namely, will peasant economies in Latin America survive the spread of agrarian capitalism?

Related questions set off in different directions. Are agrarian reform programs the solution to increased landlessness, impoverishment, and decline in agricultural production, or are they a mere reformist attempt to stem peasant revolutions? Do the social, cultural, and human advantages of small-scale peasant societies offset the gains in economic efficiency and productivity of high-technology agribusiness? Is the rural exodus a net loss for peasant communities or the only way to improve standards of living and avoid massive unemployment? And, a more general question, closely related to dependency theory: are peasant communities a handicap for national development because of their traditionalism, or are they artificially preserved in a nondeveloped state in order to be exploited by the capitalist sector as labor reserves or producers of cheap commodities? And, finally, are peasant movements retrograde political forces or progressive movements that could lead or be allied to major revolutions?

On the central questions of how Latin American peasants are resisting the increasing monetization of their economy and the relentless extraction of their resources by capital, studies clustered roughly around two positions. Historical structuralists and cultural ecologists focused on the dynamics of peasant production and culture, with Chayanov as one of their major theoretical sources,[27] and stressed that such communities would and should continue to exist. Thus, in this view, peasant institutions and movements should be supported and traditional technology and community organization preserved. Those holding this view were labeled "*campesinistas,*" a term derived from "*campesinos*" ("peasants"). The term in fact hid more diversity than unity in actual theoretical positions, but it was popularized by the late Ernest Feder, one of the most influential researchers in agricultural economics, in his famous article "Campesinistas y descampesinistas: Tres enfoques divergentes (y no incompatibles) sobre la destrucción del campesinado."[28]

On one side of the debate, the exploitation of agricultural producers was linked to the role of the State, to the political control of peasant organizations, and to the workings of the national and international markets. The exponents of this view emphasized that peasant culture plays an important part in allowing communities to resist the pressures of the market economy. By preserving traditional social and cultural priorities, peasant communities were able to escape the "maximizing mentality" that would fully integrate them into the capitalist system. Among anthropologists, this issue had, of course, links with the substantivist-formalist debate in economic anthropology. Thus, peasant communities were not to be seen simply as the historical residue of a previous mode of production but as viable societies that defend their right to exist as an alternative way of life.[29]

It followed, then, that wage labor and migrant labor constitute survival strategies that enabled low-income rural households to go on with their agricultural production. Peasant society adapts in this and many other ways to the predatory capitalist environment. In fact, the resilience of peasant societies is emphasized, pointing toward the possibility that they might even survive modern industrialism.

The opposing position in this debate took the more orthodox Marxist view that the historical progression of modes of production made the disappearance of noncapitalist modes—among them, those pertaining to peasant communities in Latin America—both inexorable and inevitable. Accordingly, those holding this view were labeled "*descampesinistas*" by Feder.

Those holding this view agree that proletarianization is the only fate open to the peasantry in the shorter or longer term, but disagreement flares as to the precise definition of the mode of production to which they belong. A wide-ranging debate evolved on whether it was a feudal or incipient capitalist mode of production. This discussion developed especially among historians. Among anthropologists, positions ranged from positing a "peasant mode of production" to envisioning several kinds of pre-capitalist modes, such as the simple mercantile economy.[30]

The important point, however, is to ascertain the kind of relationship that such pre-capitalist modes of production have with the capitalist sector, since this would clarify how resources are being extracted from peasant communities. For some, the peasant sector is an autonomous entity, exploited indirectly, mainly through extraction of surplus and labor; for others, it is totally embedded in the capitalist sector, so that capital directly exploits the labor of peasants.[31]

New Boundaries, New Debates

A distinct feature of Latin American anthropology in the seventies was the diversification of its themes. Research in urban anthropology began early in Peru, with studies on migrants' adaptations and voluntary associations. It developed further through research on the urban poor in several Latin American cities, which centered around the issue of whether these groups are "marginal" to the urban economic and social system. Their "survival strategies" have become a major theme of research.[32]

Another important research topic having a long-standing tradition in Latin America is medical anthropology, which had mostly dealt with traditional pharmacopoeia and therapeutic practices. Interesting debates have developed in this area in recent years. One of the subjects researched has been the role of protein in defining size, density, and settlement patterns in indigenous populations in the Amazon Basin.[33] Another is the effect of coca chewing on the physical condition of high-altitude populations in the Andes, a debate that is both relevant and timely in view of government actions and legislation related to coca in particular and drug use in general in Peru.[34]

During the seventies, another important theme, that of women, seen from an entirely new perspective, burst boldly on the horizon. Again, disciplinary boundaries have been superseded in this research area, although most anthropologists have focused mainly on rural women. Early ethnographic studies on women at the beginning of the seventies provided the basic data on women's lives in such communities. By the late seventies, a debate had evolved as to whether women in Indian and in traditional rural communities have a relatively higher status than women in capitalist societies, which would mean that the spread of capitalism is detrimental to women. Research found, however, that there was no single direction in such change, but rather that the interplay of women's roles in social reproduction and economic production has to be carefully analyzed before any conclusive judgment can be brought to bear.[35] Accordingly, significant work has been done in examining women's roles in migration, in poor households' survival strategies, in community organization, and in population processes.[36] In the eighties, attention shifted to women's land tenancy rights and their integration into agricultural and agribusiness wage labor, offshore assembly plants, and home-based work.[37] Important new insights have been gained about these central issues, which are only now being taken up in general discussions of development. In the Latin American social sciences, an attempt to deal with this new perspective is being made by trying to build an intermediate social parameter—either the family or the community or barrio—to bring together, once again, the micro- and the macroview of society.

Conclusions

Together with other Latin American social sciences, anthropology in Latin America had one of its most ebullient periods in the last twenty years. This surge grew out of the critique of anthropological theories and methods of the fifties and developed in the following decade in close association with social, political, and ethnic movements. Most importantly, anthropology expanded largely because other social sciences grew as well, overflowing old academic boundaries between them. From Latin American history and sociology, as Halperín and Portes describe them in this volume, anthropology took the "historical-structural" perspective. This provided the macrocontext in which to develop the views on center-periphery exchange and internal colonialism that were already being debated in anthropology. From heterodox economics and from political science, as explained by Fishlow and Valenzuela, anthropology took a diachronic view of development and an interest in political movements and the State. From Marxism, it took an interest in social and political movements and the long duration span that rendered ahistorical ethnographic studies obsolete.

What it gave back to other disciplines during this period came out of intensive field studies. These provided valuable microsocial data on many of the issues being explored by other social sciences. Anthropology showed that the weavings of the international market penetrate even to the most remote villages; that in spite of macrohistorical trends, peasants take up strategies that may still change the course of history; and that individuals are inextricably linked to families, identity groups, and communities, and this determines the pattern of social change.

Although, in comparison with sociology, economics, and political science, anthropological publications in Latin America are few and the field's topics and methods so diverse as to appear fragmented, the discipline has had a modest impact in social research in the region during this time. Through its in-depth qualitative studies, it helped to persuade sociologists and demographers to use the family, rather than the individual, as the basic unit of analysis in their surveys. Importantly, it showed that peasant communities subject to the pressures of the monetization of their economy resist such pressures in diverse ways, thus altering the effects of development policies proposed by economists. In studying the strategies for survival of rural households, anthropologists further extended this analysis, which now constitutes a tool for sociologists in understanding the myriad strategies of groups in the urban context.

As a discipline, Latin American anthropology also broke down its internal boundaries during this period. It no longer studies only Indians and peasants, but also workers, women, urban groups, and the researchers' own middle-class environment. In terms of topics, the new contexts, such as urban social movements, Indian ethnic militancy, or the permanent links of communities to international migration, are constantly opening new areas for research by anthropologists.

However, it is clear that, whatever its theoretical problems, historical structuralism did provide a necessary macrocontext for anthropologists' work. Now that it has been questioned, anthropologists once again face the problem of not having a macrosocial background in which to place their microanalyses. Most importantly, historical structuralism also provided a unified vision of social development that gave cogency to the diverse and partial approaches taken by the different social sciences. Without it, theoretical concerns and research topics seem to be drifting apart, both between and within Latin American social sciences. And this also has an effect on the field of Latin American studies in U.S. and European universities.

Finally, of course, the weakening of the institutional and financial support for the social sciences in general in Latin America is also slowing down progress in anthropology in particular. Fieldwork is costly and requires long periods of time, so that few institutions are able to finance it. Publishing is also becoming more difficult, and this makes it impossible to maintain an ongoing debate that will cohere the results of research and bring them forward.

But the last twenty years of questioning, exploring, and proposing in anthropology in Latin America, as haphazard and uneven as they may have seemed, were absolutely necessary. The grounds for greater precision and convergence have been set. If there is still time, and if financial woes do not engulf us, anthropology may yet overstep old boundaries into a new era.

SIX

Spanish-American Literary Criticism: The State Of The Art

SAÚL SOSNOWSKI

The limitations of this survey, which considers neither the vast body of work pertaining to Brazilian literature nor the production that refers to the literature of the non-Hispanic Caribbean, are evident from the title. This is, in part, a function of the conditions that govern any overview of this type, and reflects neither prejudice nor elements that are endemic to literary criticism. Literature departments in both the United States and Latin America, where most universities are still dominated by national(istic) concerns, are a study in fragmentation. The effect is to marginalize both Brazilian literature and the work of writers from the English and French Caribbean from the mainstream of Latin American production as a whole. Such academic fragmentation only reflects the overall cultural and political fragmentation that characterizes the continents.

This chapter, then, focuses on a specific context and on a praxis centered on "academic criticism"; it considers neither the substantial body of journalistic commentary at hand nor the occasional notes that appear in nonspecialized publications. It does include the images of Spanish-American literature that

---

This chapter is translated from the Spanish by Katherine Pettus and Helene Anderson.

emerge from journals of literary criticism, both those with an explicit ideological position and those that, while not appearing to do so, reveal their sympathy for a stand that transcends the generosity of true objectivity. Like any so-called absolute freedom, the freedom of these publications is also conditioned.

Recent years have seen the publication of an assortment of evaluations and surveys of the state of the art. The publication profiles themselves constitute an ongoing tally of certain tendencies.[1] Among these is the recent and growing polarization of ideological markings already evident in the new stage ushered in by the triumph of the Cuban Revolution and the international acclaim that greeted a select group of Latin American writers. The considerable volume of scholarship that has already been devoted to the impact of the Cuban Revolution on Latin American cultural relations—not to mention its more direct and less mediated impact on political relations—renders any reiteration of the different positions superfluous. There are at least two trends: one that insists on celebrating the word and indulging, with the skill of a professional makeup artist, in the creation of meticulously manicured critical glosses, and the other that encourages literary practice to incorporate the cultural into the social sphere. The former sees in the production of self-referential languages the opportunity to sustain paraphrases built on structures that should also be read and deconstructed, while the latter leads to a growing academic preoccupation with the relation between the intellectual and society and the role of literature in social processes.[2] These ongoing debates continue to be rooted in the agenda imposed by the reading public, by the writers themselves, and by their increasingly visible social function.

Focusing on narrative, when the Boom is employed as an organizational category for study sequences, "extraliterary" considerations begin to affect the evaluation of the texts. The fact that a new literary constellation was calling for formal literary discourse to both integrate and be integrated into speeches, declarations, and critical reflections, and for some authors to become their own critics and thus transform their work into a double frame of (self-) reference, also contributed to the creation of a conditioned circuit. All this, in turn, meant a transfer, a "shift" of emphasis, with all its attendant ideological baggage, from an inquiry into the factors that motivate or inspire the production of a literary work, to an analysis of the multiple interpretations that compete for the meanings of a text, to the role that the text plays (by itself or with its author) within the system as a whole. Clearly, these shifts are partial, and all the various approaches still populate the pages of literary criticism.

The opinions that authors such as Carlos Fuentes, Julio Cortázar, and Mario Vargas Llosa have voiced on literature and the public function of the writer have meant that the literary canon is no longer confined strictly to their novels and stories. The literary/publicity boom transformed the author into a "superstar," a transition that was marked by changes in the perception of the writer's responsibilities to the public.[3] It was a new social contract wherein the intimacy of reading was transplanted from the private sphere to the public, to the platforms and podiums of plaza and conference hall. Given the level of everyday violence characterizing the struggle taking place on Latin American soil, the debate on the role of the informed and responsible intellectual can only be viewed as an impatient and caustic reply to such post-structuralist concerns as the survival or demise of the category "author." Nonetheless, in the name of a critical approach strictly bound to the text, others tolerated the excision of extraneous elements so that minute attention to the word might circumscribe all critical practice. Although critics were allowed to "go out and play," the newly opened doors threatened to expose the extent to which academic pursuits were artificially isolated from the reality of the street, thereby challenging the comforts and privileges of the academic career.[4]

Inevitably, we must consider the resources at the disposal of the academic market, given the fact that, quantitatively, priority is still being given to the epigones and to prestigious literary figures. Bibliographies, for example, confirm the ongoing cult of Borges, whose name appears in a disproportionate number of trivial publications as well as in several meritorious studies.[5] Similar treatment is lavished on the works of those identified with the Boom as well as on those who have benefited from the by no means unjustified attention being paid to Latin America. Consequently, knowledge of some contemporary writers has improved, and precursors such as Felisberto Hernández, Macedonio Fernández, and Roberto Arlt have been reclaimed and incorporated into required reading lists. This process has not, however, resulted in the establishment of a literary tradition or an historical continuum.

Redoubled efforts to have the new "superstars" resurrect writers whose work had been left to gather dust or to be read by a select few (Cortázar on Felisberto and Lezama Lima, for instance) reveal how few critics are prepared to engage in in-depth analysis of new writers or to study the complex processes of cultural formation. Playing it safe, many stick with the authors whose complete works have been sealed by their death or by some other sort of prolonged silence. Critics seem to find reiteration a gainful source of employment, either lighting upon (yet another!) "new approach" that will end up in a future literary history as a scribble in the margin of a footnote, or arriving right on cue with their review of the hallowed one's latest publication, regardless of whether or not this merits the follower's rapt attention.[6] Instead of shifting the focus from the familiar and overcoming their enthusiasm for studying the various literary figures in isolation, they intensify their quest to the bitter end, until the fragment that will justify more freshly printed pages is actually unearthed. But such justification is addressed only to the institution that set the rules of the game and sponsors the plethora of reviews whose one reason for being is to act as a forum for this type of findings, as opposed to shedding such light as would stimulate new and more relevant studies.

The "publish or perish" policy, whose original purpose may have been to stimulate research and disseminate scholarship, more often than not serves as a sententious end to the silence that is printed and quantified in the annual reports. These reports could be more positive were they to pluralize their subject matter, give heterogeneity priority over reiteration, and, on other grounds, declare their independence from the academic caciquism whose intricately woven webs reap only a desultory harvest of provisional recognition within each respective clan. While respect, admiration, emulation, and identification with the masters may be salutary sentiments during the initial stages, when confined strictly to what has been bequeathed they do not lend themselves to new interpretations or to the generation of new knowledge. As long as the spotlight is held on the same texts, figures, tropes, and devices, the same material will be grist for the ever slower mills that eventually grind the interstices from every page ever written by every epigone, condemning literature (and its unfortunate professional reader) to a slow death from massive and concentrated doses of tedium. Still, as we shall see below, there is no need to resort to parricide, to the mortal blow that may inaugurate a new series of critical options.

Although this is by no means the only impression that remains with a reviewer of recent Spanish-American literary criticism, it is a dangerous and proven symptom of the waste that can befall practices not dedicated to the production of knowledge from perspectives that are nourished and regenerated by new theoretical frontiers or by readings that obviate the official stamp of approval issued by academia. Such readings would include the substantial and positive contributions of the 1960's and 1970's, such as those based on the works of Amado Alonso, that broke with traditional stylistic analyses. Although wary (and justifiably so) of sociologism, the critical production of a considerable sector has focused more on the texts and on partial or complete analyses of given works than on the mechanisms of literary production, whose relevance is a bone of contention within the formal framework of literary studies. The time has also come to evaluate the study of fantastic literature and the disproportionate emphasis on the variants of "magic realism" and "the marvelous real" as a generic category rather than a description of an essentially thematic phenomenon.[7]

Since the 1960's, as part of the international critical context, Latin American literary criticism has exhibited a healthy tendency to bring psychoanalysis, structuralism, semiotics, and deconstructionism and its projections to bear upon theoretical consideration of the texts. Some critics have incorporated these components into a Marxist perspective with an eye to generating a still broader cultural analysis of intellectual production. As ever, though, fashion has made its presence felt. Numerous published studies, whether in absolute and appropriate seriousness[8] or in a no less obvious bid to be playful or superficial, display reams of footnotes that, depending on the particular moment under consideration, refer to Barthes or Genette, Greimas or Kristeva, Todorov or Lacan, or, more recently, Bakhtin or Jameson, regardless of whether these references impact directly on textual analysis. While they do call attention to the critic's updated bibliographical currency, these pages are the least relevant, being overshadowed by critical readings that do use a theoretical approach in order to describe, dismantle, and finally reconstitute the texts that conform Spanish-American literature. One cannot help recognizing that these studies aspire to scientific validity and, having discarded the constraints of any Latin American specificity, to the award of a central and strategic place within the forefront of Literature with a capital L. They accomplish this by focusing almost exclusively on fiction—one legacy of the Boom, whose major works slipped quickly into the Western domain—rather than on poetry, whose avant-garde stage anticipated the experimental features that took hold in fiction decades later, and which established its residence in the Spanish language. Moreover, critical discourse was assimilating the observations of various authors on the renewal of forms in an ostensibly avant-garde gesture (which as an act of faith in its own progress distanced itself from the poetic avant-garde) that was an attempt to synchronize historical with literary progress. Once the dialogue of languages had been joined, the attempt was made to move gradually toward the universal codes wherein the literary is subjected to an inquiry into its origins prior to any territorial claims and definitions. Ahistoric discourse reveals the ideological options that inform both the criticism and teaching of literature; these are also clear in the other series of options that are informed by the social sciences and in the essays that, from heterogeneous and hybrid references, attempt to formulate readings that account for both the literary specificity and its particular focus. Ideally, this dialogue between literary approaches (text and context, theory and textual description) would embrace the possibility of a (re)integration into its home territory—in other words, consideration of what is specifically Latin American.

Periodicals devoted to Spanish-American literature run the gamut of theoretical and critical options and reflect, either tacitly or explicitly, their own ideological preferences and orientations. These are revealed as much by their declarations of principles as by their selection of material. The rough outline that follows should be seen neither as judgmental nor comprehensive in terms of the breadth of the concerns that pertain to each journal.

The spectrum ranges from *Dispositio* (Ann Arbor, Michigan)

Literary Criticism 169

and *Lexis* (Lima), which exhibit a clear preference for semiotic analysis and theoretical approaches, to *Ideologies and Literature*, whose title defines its agenda, to those journals that favor the study of the relations between literature and society, although not to the exclusion of other approaches. These include the *Revista de crítica literaria latinoamericana* (Lima), *Hispamérica* (Gaithersburg, Maryland), *Escritura* (Caracas), and *Texto crítico* (Xalapa, Veracruz), and publications such as *Punto de vista* (Buenos Aires), a journal devoted to cultural politics. Official journals such as *Casa de las Américas, Conjunto* or *Unión* (Havana), and *Nicarahuac* (Managua) clearly respond to the ideological lines informing their editorial policy. While many academic publications such as the *Revista Iberoamericana* (Pittsburgh, Pennsylvania) define themselves as open spaces, certain emphases define preferential positions. Wide cultural dissemination is served by journals such as *Cuadernos Hispanoamericanos* (Madrid). Of yet another register is *Review* (New York), which is dedicated to publication of English translations of works by Latin American authors. *Review*'s commitment is to internationalizing a particular area of literature that begins with the writers of the Boom and caters primarily to those of its heirs who might be of interest to the U.S. market. A similar tendency to prioritize recognized authors and textual issues is also evident in journals not exclusively devoted to Spanish-American literature, such as *Books Abroad—World Literature Today* (Norman, Oklahoma), *Modern Language Notes* (Baltimore), *Hispanic Review* (Philadelphia), or *PMLA* (New York), which occasionally feature Latin American writers. Insofar as special monographic issues are devoted to specific authors, the tendency is to select, among others, Borges, Cortázar, Fuentes, Rulfo, and Paz; in other words, those who guarantee the apparently insatiable attention of academia.[9] Fortunately, publications such as those of the Poitiers Seminars have broadened the spectrum by incorporating meticulous analyses of the works of Felisberto Hernández, Roberto Arlt, Carlos Droguett, and Augusto Roa Bastos. Be that as it may, this is only a foretaste of the work that still remains to be done before all that preceded these new trends can be reclaimed and assigned a place in the ongoing task of constructing a literary tradition.

Both those who base their argument for the contextualization of literature on the premise that it is an expression of a specific social state of affairs, and those who demand that everything extraneous to the first level of the text itself be excluded, have their own channels of communication (journals, primary and secondary spokespersons, conferences, and symposia). The respective groups use these in their quest to establish the properties of the meanings of literature and the role it does or does not play in the system. Interestingly enough, the participants will wrangle over interpretations of the stellar figures, in each case switching back and forth between the textual focus and its respective general framework. In the final analysis, the issues lead to the appropriation of the author, to what implications can be ascribed to the reading of given texts, and, in some quarters, to how those same readings contribute to a broader understanding of the world to which they refer. In other words, the theoretical and critical reflections presuppose a revision of the academic literary canon that ideologizes the map that is drawn out of Latin American cultural production as an activity taking place on this side of every work of literature. This is exactly the point at which critical practice departs (should depart?) from any vestige of casual "divertimento" in order to fit even the aesthetic encounter and the sense of playfulness into the space from which it originated. The main purpose is not to diminish or void the joy of reading but to determine, through professional critical activity, what is actually meant by the game, the laugh, or the caress that slips out of the pages.

Our task up to this point has been to highlight an activity that at one extreme trains its sights on the literary text as a mediator, filter, or transparency of the referential, and at the other discovers the entire meaning of literary production in the opacity of these same texts.[10] These may not even represent the actual poles, and a full spectrum of preferential readings lies between both extremes, some of which attempt to formulate heterogeneous systems capable of rendering the complexity of any given literary text. Advanced literary forms may be useful as a point of departure, not so much because the greater degree of theoretical modernization is especially suited to a reading of the ultramodern—a pose that proved irresistible to critics of the "cosmopolitan avant-garde"—but because they give us immediate access to the multiple meanings of those advanced forms and of their technification.[11] Once again, it is history that imposes its conditions.

The correlation between the recent rise of Latin American literature and its enthusiastic reception in Western intellectual circles has already been amply demonstrated. While I decline to go into further detail about what the Boom actually means and how it can be defined, suffice it to say that the vicissitudes of the debates about Cuba, from the springlike beginnings to the probing questions that accompanied the "Padilla Case" and the public disassociation from the Revolution of some eminent writers,[12] have left their mark on this process of literary notoriety.

Nor has the exile of a considerable number of middle-class Cubans, who have been assimilated into the U.S. academic world, been without repercussions, most obvious among which is the list of authors, particularly Cuban authors, that has been incorporated into the academic curriculum. The arrival of newly exiled writers has two particular effects on the field: it both enlarges the spectrum and shrinks our channels of available information on the island's cultural production. The disproportionate emphasis accorded a select group of exiles—notably Guillermo Cabrera Infante and Severo Sarduy—reflects, apart from their indisputable literary merits, a political option whose reverberations are felt in the analyses of Alejo Carpentier (or, with variations, in those of José Lezama Lima) and, of course, in the study of those who continue to participate in the revolutionary process.

The fact that the wave of fascism that swept over the Southern Cone generated new studies and debates on the subject of literature and exile legitimizes neither the facile and tendentious homogenizing of exiles nor the statements that exile has become a literary trope or a reflection on literature itself. If there is any recent phenomenon that lends itself directly to an analysis that is stamped indelibly by the historical process, it is the literature of exile. And in this case, particular attention must be paid to the individual signs of these exiles and to the specific circumstances that conditioned the production of every literary page. The fact that the subject of "exile" has been used to lend some publications a semblance of democratic openness does not automatically make it a literary category or a label that can be applied to define a particular body of work. Its place is in, and should be referred back to, the appropriate framework of the respective national literatures.

We have yet to examine the problem that arises from adhering to too strict a definition of the "national." Scrutiny of the relation between works produced abroad and those written within established frontiers only exacerbates this problem. Included in this category, albeit under very particular conditions, are Chicano works vis-à-vis Latin American literature[13] and the multilayered island/mainland Puerto Rican literature, clearly exemplified in essays on nationality and in solid anthologies of poetry and fiction. These literatures are all generated under the pressure of hegemonic forces bent on paring down and undermining cultural diversity. The intercontinental journeys that have become cosmopolitan hops for a growing number of writers, their resonance with worlds that have preserved pre-Hispanic elements, and their championship of the vanquished voices are not, however, mutually exclusive. Moreover, such multivalent heterogeneity serves as a challenge to the brand of criticism that takes refuge in a neutral instrument so as to approach all cultural manifestations with equal ease, disposing of the object's specificity and therefore obtaining predictably uniform results. This state of affairs underscores the need for theoretical propositions that are adapted to the specificity of the object under scrutiny, even at the risk of being forced to assimilate the proposals that are inherent to the text, and of succumbing to purely reiterative statements that echo the original texts with empathy.

Instead of which, what emerges from a panoramic overview of the authors and themes subjected to critical review (especially in the U.S., which because of its central position is less concerned with national particularities) is a tendency to concentrate on those authors who have contributed to the internationalization of Spanish-American literature. Although a certain amount of quantitative oscillation does take place, and a not inconsiderable bibliography has been compiled that includes writers such as Manuel Puig, José María Arguedas, and Severo Sarduy, who from different vantage points have also made key contributions to a universal literature that resists any attempt at homogeneous definition, the works of Borges, Cortázar, Onetti, Donoso,

Vargas Llosa, García Márquez, Rulfo, Fuentes, Paz, Carpentier, Cabrera Infante, and, more recently, Roa Bastos keep heading the list of the "contemporaries." The propensity for established "cult" figures and those who are inevitably and justifiably ranked in the literary canon—José Martí, Rubén Darío, César Vallejo, Vicente Huidobro, and Pablo Neruda, to name the undisputed authors of another literary series—remains a constant, although these authors are not universally regarded as founders of subsequent ongoing trends, despite important critical evaluations of Modernism. Their ongoing presence is largely a function of their widely acknowledged literary centrality and, in terms of the study of recent authors, of the above-mentioned aspects of academic organization and politicization that inform the selection of mandatory readings. Such selection often leads to the dissemination of decontextualized, often fragmentary or barely unified information. The continental map that would emerge from such studies, were they to be quantified, would be a distorted geography of the mountain ranges and rivers of Argentina, Chile, Mexico, and Cuba.

Several brief conclusions can be drawn from the foregoing considerations: critics persist in circulating a literature written by epigones; they propose thematic approaches that cut across specific differences, and chronicle literary periods on the arbitrary basis of set numbers of years or the author's chronological age. More particularly, they concentrate on partial versions of literary production, all of which tend to overlook a cardinal factor— namely, that the cultural clocks of the various Latin American regions are not synchronized. Not only do they measure time differently, but the literary production that pertains to the tempo of each corresponds to the level of development of the particular area under consideration. Thus, when literary experimentation is used as a criterion for selection, vast regions whose literary response is adequately served by modalities discarded by more cosmopolitan zones several decades earlier are denigrated for their "antiquity" or simply left out of the picture entirely. Likewise, a reading concentrating on urban production (certainly a valid literary segment) presupposes a series of questions about the meaning of that production from the standpoint of its uniqueness vis-à-vis the other texts that also constitute its local base. Insofar as any selection implies the ability of that text to represent a segment that in fact goes beyond its representational competence, to concentrate systematically on only some variants of Spanish-American literature—the experimental wave, for instance—distorts not only the literary text as a whole but also the world that has generated those pages.

In more general terms, an entirely opposite option organizes all literature under the rigorous but not totally inflexible principle of periodization. While this may contribute significantly to systematization, it runs the risk of being too sketchy once the points of identification, contact, and similarity of the layers common to any history have been staked out and the focus is trained on the heterogeneities defining a continent that is far from uniform. Certain questions may underscore the shortcomings of strict periodization. Can it, for example, access a comparison between the fiction and the poetry of the 1920's and 1930's, as well as an evaluation of how the relation has changed in recent decades? Such questions highlight the need to account for the asynchronicity of literary series and to incorporate a solid and organic literary history into the realm of criticism.

A desire to organize Latin American letters in a manner that would account for its multiple facets produced several generational studies. The laudable and valuable efforts of Pedro Henríquez Ureña were followed by the adjustments proposed by José Juan Arrom and Cedomil Goić, among others.[14] The need to incorporate the reading of literature into a critical analysis of the historical processes from which it emerged led Alejandro Losada to propose research strategies that would lead to a general periodicity model of literary processes in Latin America.[15] The creation of such a model demands an integral, interdisciplinary approach that is free from any hint of schematicism and that articulates, first on a general level and then in greater detail, how social systems correlate as conditioners of any and all literary expression. While this approach may account for the kind of literary response that accompanied the transition from colony to liberal republic, it would also have to consider the variations in the meaning and experience of modernity for the different regions and political processes of the continent.

The risk of generalization is inherent in every new approach, and a balance must be struck between universalization of the processes and the precise detailing of the works that tend to be

Literary Criticism 175

seen as epiphenomena within the more abbreviated national or regional pictures. One example would be to study the foundational nature of Modernism as an integral component of the literary sequence and tradition it inaugurated, rather than as an isolated fragment. Many of Angel Rama's proposals about the literary system and the exemplification of some concrete proposals, such as his analysis of the works of Martí and Darío in the context of the forces that gave Modernism its particular meaning, or his definition of the lines of the ongoing debate between internationalism and regionalism, were characterized by a balance between these different analytic possibilities. Although Rama was not unique in this endeavor, his work is significant in terms of what it reveals of the will to integrate advances in literary theory with profound reflection on the historicity of the literary phenomenon, and its tendency toward an inclusive perspective that is combined with detailed focus on the specific texts and the expression of judgments on their worth. Rama is also notable for his flexibility in the face of rigidly orthodox formulations[16] and for the generous criteria with which he (and others) formulated the Biblioteca Ayacucho project.

The detailing of numerous analyses, and fluctuating or dramatically transformed social and historical conditions, call for an approach that forces the study of literature to come to terms with the instruments of its analysis. I have already mentioned the use that a core of critics has made of the propositions advanced by several variants of structuralism and post-structuralism, especially through readings that dispense with any frame of reference beyond the language of the text. Their universality accounts for the discreet charm of some analytic approaches and also explains, for instance, the reasoning behind Fernández Retamar's argument for a distinctively Latin American literary criticism. Following a similar line, Françoise Pérus proposes a critical model, of demonstrative value, from a materialist perspective that systematizes its readings and, paradoxically, offers another model of abstraction, to which some of Hernán Vidal's propositions attempt to respond.[17]

Such distinctions as can be drawn between the critical enclaves or schools that favor greater theoretical emphasis and those whose predilection is historical remain provisional. As I proposed earlier, however, we can arrive at the different versions of the same literature that emerge from these discrepancies by underscoring the characteristics of each camp. The splinters can largely be attributed to the partialization of literary studies and the kind of overconcentration on authors or national literatures that make a vision of the whole difficult or impossible to come by. This is exacerbated when isolated and marginal themes are selected but not incorporated into the general analytic canon for an exhaustive examination of their true meaning from that all-inclusive perspective. Clearly, this category excludes the publications that still see literature as an expression of the artist's mood, and criticism as the representation of plot or the summary display of descriptive fragments. In the best of cases, readers will be able to combine those approaches into a more integral reading. As some critics have demonstrated, insofar as specific ideologies do not intercede in order to block access to the text, a first recourse to semiotic tools, for example, does not invalidate a second contextual and historicist stage, which in turn describes/explains how the mechanisms internal to any text actually function.[18] Although the orthodox practitioner may have difficulty accomplishing this, it is a feasible task for the heirs to heterodoxy.[19]

This combination is also found in thematic analyses, as demonstrated in the renewed attention commanded by the "dictator" as a result of the recent novels of García Márquez, Carpentier, and Roa Bastos, among others, which is also clearly associated with the recent proliferation of dictatorial regimes. It can also be identified in the reexamination of issues related to indigenism in the Andean zone[20] and bilingualism in the Quechua-speaking areas and in Paraguay. We come across this topic again in relation to the more recent problems of literary production within non-Spanish-speaking countries of exile, and even within Latin American countries whose Spanish resonates differently from that of the homeland. This perception of difference goes beyond the confrontation with language to anchor itself in multicultural manifestations foreign to the countries of origin. In so doing, it dictates reassessment of the nineteenth- and early twentieth-century migratory waves vis-à-vis those journeys undertaken by liberal "gentlemen" who sought inspiration and wisdom in European centers, as well as the flights of citizens rejected in more modern times as undesirables by their own governments. All of which, without resort to any sleight of hand whatsoever, reiterates the need for a multivalent approach that accounts for the complex processes that resist any one interpretation or any one channel of reception.

A related process is accompanying the growing and justified attention being paid to analyses of some Spanish-American women writers. A canon of feminist criticism has developed swiftly and effectively out of the initial stage of identification of women writers.[21] Social changes and the implementation of appropriate theories have begun to inform the specificity of the ongoing debate concerning "women's writing"; and the discussion, which is also framed within the study of national literatures, is now being transferred to the Latin American context as a whole via conferences and specialized journals. The emphasis is not merely conjunctural; it responds to changes in perception and to a heightened awareness of women's multiple social functions.

The growth of "testimonial literature" is indicative of yet another measure of literary transformation aimed at integrating a specific reading with the demands of the public and of history. Heretofore seen as part of a more political continuum, developed by such different writers as Rodolfo Walsh and Miguel Barnet, it is also the foundation, for example, of aspects of Elena Poniatowska's work. Criticism has only recently begun to interpret those processes of literary production that cut across formal categories, molding them to their own purposes and image, and to study the alternatives these texts offer to the official rubrics that sanction literary genres. Added to this is the possibility of linking the approach of these works with the transparent immediacy that characterizes the Colonial chronicles: ineluctable gambles, perhaps, on literary intervention as it attempts to organize worlds that exceed the limits of the word.

How social transformation has intervened in contemporary analysis is also found in the teaching of drama as text. It must be borne in mind that this is a relatively new area of criticism, and that this fact conditions certain appraisals.[22] While theater seems to be the field that has least absorbed the theoretical approaches that pepper the critical readings of fiction and poetry, the options that emerge from, for instance, a comparison of bourgeois and alternative collective theater reinforce arguments that advocate a more in-depth scrutiny of the critical tools employed to date. The ongoing alternation between performance and reading mandates a consideration of the interaction between the text and social conditions, especially in recent cases wherein censorship and repression become active participants in the drama of daily life. (Argentina's "teatro abierto" is, in this sense, an exceptional case.)

Simply naming the many themes and listing the authors considered in recent years would hardly amount to a complete picture of the state of the discipline, a task undertaken, moreover, by specialized publications. Although the mere quantity of pages written is no guarantee of any new corpus of literary knowledge, it is a sign of the growing professionalization of criticism. While some pages are obviously expendable, there is a very significant body of studies that cuts across all areas of literary history and that should be seen as required reference material. In spite of the reiteration and, as I have mentioned, the insistence on a relatively small number of writers, recent years have seen the publication of important studies on Colonial literature that range from the discovery and recording of neglected materials to exhaustive analyses of some chroniclers and a select group of distinguished Baroque figures.[23] It is still difficult to ascertain whether the renewed interest in the Colonial period can be attributed to its affinities with contemporary narrative modalities—or to the exhaustion faced by these modalities—or to a new awareness of the need to conduct a meticulous and scientific exploration of Latin America's origins. Clearly, related questions could be asked about the revival of the debates on national literatures, on mestizo culture, and on the ideology of those intellectuals who participated in the formation of the liberal republics and in subsequent nation-building projects. Such questions might illuminate the experiments of avant-garde poetry and its more recent echoes, the practice of poetry as a constant breaking with itself, and the dispersion of voices and texts as a direct result of violent dictatorial regimes as compared with other experiences of repression in black, mestizo, and Indian communities in other areas of the hemisphere. Also included in this category are the more recent debates about the identity of Hispanic communities in the United States, certain

Literary Criticism 179

dead-end literary experiments, and the asynchronicity of history and literature. The insistence on theoretical approaches and on a variety of critical paths also indicates that the critics have not left unexplored the contributions of linguistics, semiotics, deconstruction, or the theory of reception, for example. Equally pressing is the need to discard fashionable clichés that merely echo passing trends.

The fact that a significant group of critics argues for a broadened definition of literature, or at least what falls within the competence of the literary field, denotes the already existing schism between "higher" literary forms, acknowledged traditionally and aesthetically as such, and popular literature. Moreover, the schism derives from a conviction that "higher" and "popular" comprise areas of culture that encompass nonliterary forms and are accessible to those elements that confirm that no text is "an entity unto itself." The annual *Studies in Latin American Popular Culture* (Morris, Minnesota; Las Cruces, New Mexico) has started to gather empirical data and to sponsor the necessary theoretical considerations.[24] The incorporation of the literary into the space of everyday life may have resulted from an approach that, in the best of cases following Michel Foucault's teaching, opts for the study of intellectual history and changes in the forms of intellectual relations, rather than limiting itself to the specificity of the literary text. Such an option evidently carries an ideological mandate that is not averse to accepting the mutual interaction between the intellectual product and the social context, and their subsequent mutual transformation. This, in turn, implies the definitive and explicit incorporation of literary criticism into ideological fields of which it is already a part. Therefore, any expansion of the limited concept of "the literary" would have to constitute a strand of the debate on aesthetics. Moreover, in order to untangle the intricate weave of effects and causes that governs those broadly defined literary products, it would have to situate the debate alongside an analysis of the ideological relations between social classes.

Other horizons may open up when the boundaries of the traditional genres are thrown into crisis by the reduction (or expansion?) of the parameters of literary products to one vast text compiled by a tradition that defines the survival of the classical. Once the era of "God and Golem, Inc.," in the words of

Wiener, is inaugurated, and literary artifacts commune with other expressions of stellar cybernetics; when categorical divisions begin to mute their sharp edges and are subsumed under the rubric of "communication"; and when experiments on a page yearn to become other writings and readings that can dispense with print, critical discourse will inevitably expand, at least in order to keep itself up to date. When soap operas and comic strips and the heroes of other media invade the terrain of "literary formality," it will be up to the reader to plunge back into the original materials, and then to consider them not just as tributaries to "higher literature" but as texts written for the general Latin American public.

This critical expansion need neither stretch the prevailing literary canon to include all manifestations of popular literature and culture nor treat the canon as inflexible. However, some preliminary and heretofore neglected phases must be completed. Among these is the incorporation of little-known national literatures, particularly those of Central America, knowledge of which has been largely confined to the region. Although the works of Ernesto Cardenal, Pablo Antonio Cuadra, and Sergio Ramírez, to name three Nicaraguan writers, have been receiving more attention, the various features that comprise an ethnically and socially diverse literature still remain the patrimony of the few who have access to the handful of journals that publish this work.[25] Thus, for many, there is little incentive to seek explanations for the new proximity that characterizes the narrative and poetry of such countries in new stages of national development as Nicaragua and Cuba, as opposed to the processes that prevail among the countries still fixed upon the liberal projects of the nineteenth century. This is just one of the many topics that clearly calls for specialized scholarship but always squarely situated within the framework of global Latin American perspectives that should heed the ongoing dialogue with other cultures.

To sum up, although the mechanisms of marketing and distribution are partially responsible for the problem, it can also be largely attributed to the predilection of potential readers to itemize segments of "metropolitan literatures" within Latin America. While not disparaging the limitations and pressures intrinsic to the work of the academic enterprise, it is possible to anticipate a growing focus on younger authors—who should not have to die to win a permanent place in the academic world—and on those writers who, while not having ascended into the modern international constellations, still contribute to the significance and internal debates of their respective countries and cultural areas. Colonial letters are certain to receive increased attention, which should yield critical editions of extant manuscripts as well as rereadings of the better-known Colonial texts. Likewise, growing interest in periods of national formation will inform a broader understanding of foundational texts. I share Jean Franco's recognition that the emerging feminist criticism is based not only on the initial identification of women writers but also on an analysis of their work that is founded on sociocriticism, psychoanalysis, and the mechanisms that operate within the ideology of the texts, mechanisms that should certainly be analyzed in all writing. Moreover, it will clearly be necessary to fill in a gap that also yawns within these pages, and integrate the Spanish-American with the literatures of other parts of Latin America.

Undoubtedly, the divisions and dichotomies will persist, and some readings will still be denied; believers will cling to their faith and indulge in tautological discourse: the pretense that the image in the mirror actually belongs to someone else. There are difficulties, however, in settling down at the extreme poles of the debate. While not reducing literature to the function of a mere filter or transparency, we can see it as an artistic mediation that, above and beyond the proper functions of re-cognition and pleasure in the text, leads to a new look at what lies beyond and on the fringes of its literary presence. In this sense, the literary matter we scrutinize is a kaleidoscope that is constantly reorganizing its components as it redefines its parts, with chance *and* the reader's voice that sustains it participating in the marvel (or horror) of seeing it all from within and knowing that it can also be so. Moreover, the extremes can be feasible points of departure in the search for a balance between the actual analysis of the text and its referents; such a balance would avoid not only confusion between the various levels of meaning but selection of only one of them. For the one would result in impoverishment of the overall meaning, while the other would reduce critical reading to an exercise whose pleasure reverts to the same hand that fashions arabesques or simply points to the harmonious architecture of an empty palace.

It was the "sect of the monotones" that inspired incendiary polemics and justified an invisible duel wherein the contestants eventually recognized one another. Only when they were in Paradise and in the presence of the Divine were Juan de Panonia and Aureliano able to comprehend that "the orthodox and the heretic, the hater and the hated, the accuser and the victim . . . were one and the same." The reference to Borges's "The Theologians"[26] is not meant to be sanguine, especially in the light of episodes of denunciation and silence that have fueled other fires. It alludes, rather, to the fact that, wherever fanaticism and unfettered dogmatism are absent, dialogue and collaboration have a chance to prosper, and there is room for options whose diversity constitutes a point of departure. This leads eventually to interpretations that share a common purpose—namely, a more profound grasp of the complete meaning of the texts and heightened receptivity to the rules that govern literary systems. Knowledge and acceptance of these systems also invite, as every literary page does, a whole host of multiple and legitimate readings.

Notes

Notes

MITCHELL: Introduction

1. Charles Wagley, ed., *Social Science Research on Latin America* (New York, 1964); Manuel Diégues Júnior and Bryce Wood, eds., *Social Science in Latin America* (New York, 1967).
2. Howard F. Cline, ed., *Latin American History*, 2 vols. (Austin, Tex., 1967).
3. Roberto Esquenazi-Mayo and Michael C. Meyer, eds., *Latin American Scholarship since World War II* (Lincoln, Neb., 1971). Geography and studies of economic integration are also represented by one essay each in this collection.
4. Robert S. Byars and Joseph L. Love, eds., *Quantitative Social Science Research on Latin America* (Urbana, Ill., 1973). Byars and Love dealt with archaeology and social anthropology separately, and included (as did Wagley nine years earlier) a chapter on scholarly developments in the geography of Latin America. Economics was not covered, however, partly on the ground that quantification was already so common in that field.
5. For key works that develop or expound these approaches, see, on dependency: United Nations Economic Commission for Latin America, *The Economic Development of Latin America and Its Principal Problems* (New York, 1950); Fernando Henrique Cardoso and Enzo Faletto, *Dependencia y desarrollo en América Latina* (Buenos Aires and Mexico City, 1969). On clientelism: Julio Cotler, "The Mechanics of Internal Domination and Social Change in Peru," in Irving Louis Horowitz, ed., *Masses in Latin America* (New York, 1970); James M. Malloy, ed., *Authoritarianism and*

Corporatism in Latin America (Pittsburgh, 1977). On bureaucratic authoritarianism: Guillermo A. O'Donnell, *Modernization and Bureaucratic-Authoritarianism: Studies in South American Politics* (Berkeley, 1973). On internal colonialism: Rodolfo Stavenhagen, *Social Classes in Agrarian Societies* (New York, 1975).

6. A few of the most important contributions to the growth of Brazilian studies are Fernando Henrique Cardoso, *Empresário industrial e desenvolvimento econômico no Brasil* (São Paulo, 1964); Peter Evans, *Dependent Development: The Alliance of Multinational, State, and Local Capital in Brazil* (Princeton, 1979); Albert Fishlow, "Brazilian Size Distribution of Income," *American Economic Review*, 62 (May 1972): 391–402; Celso Furtado, *The Economic Growth of Brazil* (Berkeley, 1965); Alfred Stepan, *The Military in Politics: Changing Patterns in Brazil* (Princeton, 1971).

7. See, among many others, David Collier, *Squatters and Oligarchs* (Baltimore, 1976); Henry A. Dietz, *Poverty and Problem-Solving under Military Rule: The Urban Poor in Lima, Peru* (Austin, Tex., 1980); Abraham F. Lowenthal, ed., *The Peruvian Experiment: Continuity and Change under Military Rule* (Princeton, 1975); Cynthia McClintock and Abraham F. Lowenthal, eds., *The Peruvian Experiment Reconsidered* (Princeton, 1983); Richard C. Webb, *Government Policy and the Distribution of Income in Peru, 1963–1973* (Cambridge, Mass., 1977).

8. See Wayne A. Cornelius, *Politics and the Migrant Poor in Mexico City* (Stanford, Calif., 1975); Janice Perlman, *The Myth of Marginality: Urban Poverty and Politics in Rio de Janeiro* (Berkeley, 1975); John D. Powell, *Political Mobilization of the Venezuelan Peasant* (Cambridge, Mass., 1971).

9. Future "overview" panels—to be sponsored by the Latin American Studies Association—may well evaluate the progress of interdisciplinary research in the hemisphere.

10. Florestan Fernandes, "The Social Sciences in Latin America," in Diégues Júnior and Wood, eds., *Social Science in Latin America*, pp. 19–20. Fernandes singles out (p. 35) some of the writings of Kalman H. Silvert as exceptions to this generalization.

11. See Carmelo Mesa-Lago (with Sandra E. Miller, and Shirley A. Kregar), *Latin American Studies in Europe* (Pittsburgh, 1979); Carmelo Mesa-Lago with Shirley A. Kregar, *Latin American Studies in Asia* (Pittsburgh, 1983).

12. This progress may be traced to factors including the rapid recruitment of young scholars into hemispheric studies beginning in the mid-1960's, the frequency of their alienation from U.S. official policies at the same period, and the professionalism and leadership shown by scholars from both halves of the hemisphere.

13. This circumstance may result from the two fields' rootedness in shared national experiences and their relative distance from the scientific aspirations of the other disciplines examined.

14. Such links have included informal scholars' briefings for departing U.S. ambassadors who requested them, and the periodic Scholar-Diplomat Seminars conducted by the Department of State. Some academic specialists in Latin American affairs were also included in the initial meetings (under the Carter administration), which proved to be precursors for the (Reagan) Caribbean Basin Initiative.

15. Two exceptions to this generalization are provided by the reports of the Commission on United States–Latin American Relations, informally known as the Linowitz Commission: *The Americas in a Changing World* (New York, 1975); and *The United States and Latin America: Next Steps* (New York, 1976). An illustration of limited political impact may be found in the Latin American Studies Association's long series of resolutions critical of varied United States policies in Latin America.

16. Direct press coverage has been sought, for example, by the Latin American Studies Association's group of observers at the 1984 Nicaraguan election, by PACCA (Policy Alternatives for the Caribbean and Central America), and by the Inter-American Dialogue for its recommendations since 1983. The Dialogue has also recently launched a project to generate and place op-ed contributions by researchers on inter-American themes in U.S. newspapers.

17. On these subjects, see John Coatsworth, *Growth Against Development: The Economic Impact of Railroads in Porfirian Mexico* (De Kalb, Ill., 1981); Sherri Grasmuck, "Immigration, Ethnic Stratification, and Native Working-Class Discipline: Comparisons of Documented and Undocumented Dominicans," *International Migration Review*, 18 (1984): 692–713; Albert O. Hirschman, ed., *Latin American Issues: Essays and Comments* (New York, 1961); Richard M. Morse, "The Heritage of Latin America," in Louis Hartz, ed., *The Founding of New Societies* (New York, 1964).

HALPERÍN DONGHI: History

1. Franklin W. Knight, *The Caribbean: The Genesis of a Fragmented Nationalism* (New York, 1978).
2. Laird W. Bergaad, *Coffee and the Growth of Agrarian Capitalism in Nineteenth-Century Puerto Rico* (Princeton, 1983); Francisco A. Scarano, *Sugar and Slavery in Puerto Rico: The Plantation Economy of Ponce, 1800–1850* (Madison, Wisc., 1984).
3. Ramiro Guerra y Sánchez, *Azúcar y población en las Antillas*, 3d ed. (Havana, 1944).
4. Levi Marrero, *Cuba: Economía y sociedad*, vols. 1–8 (Río Piedras, 1972–80).
5. Ramiro Guerra y Sánchez, *Manual de historia de Cuba* (Havana, 1938).
6. Julio Le Riverend, *Historia económica de Cuba*, 4th ed. (Havana, 1974).

7. Manuel Moreno Fraginals, *El ingenio: El complejo económico-social cubano del azúcar*, 2d ed., 3 vols. (Havana, 1978).

8. Raúl Cepero Bonilla, *Azúcar y abolición: Apuntes para una historia crítica del abolicionismo* (Havana, 1947).

9. So much so that they are not even mentioned in Ramón de Armas's warm presentation of Pérez de la Riva ("Prólogo" to J. Pérez de la Riva, *El barracón y otros ensayos*; Havana, 1975), which is otherwise remarkably frank, to the point of acknowledging the overwhelming Jewish presence in the Cuban Communist Party of the twenties (for obvious reasons, not a popular subject in Cuba in the mid-seventies).

10. Franklin W. Knight, *Slave Society in Cuba During the Nineteenth Century* (Madison, Wisc., 1970).

11. Louis A. Pérez, *Intervention, Revolution and Politics in Cuba, 1913–21* (Pittsburgh, 1978); idem, *Cuba Between Empires, 1878–1902* (Pittsburgh, 1982).

12. Kenneth R. Maxwell, *Conflicts and Conspiracies: Brazil and Portugal, 1750–1808* (Cambridge, England, 1973).

13. Fernando Novais, *Portugal e Brasil na crise do antigo sistema colonial, 1777–1808* (São Paulo, 1979).

14. Dauril Alden, *Royal Government in Colonial Brazil, with Special Reference to the Administration of the Marquis de Lavradio, Viceroy, 1769–1779* (Berkeley, 1978).

15. Stuart B. Schwartz, *Sovereignty and Society in Colonial Brazil: The High Court of Bahia and Its Judges, 1609–1751* (Berkeley, 1973).

16. John Leddy Phelan, "Authority and Flexibility in the Spanish Imperial Bureaucracy," *Administrative Science Quarterly*, 5 (1960): 47–65.

17. Raimundo Faoro, *Os donos do poder: Formação do patronato político brasileiro*, 2d ed. (Porto Alegre, 1975).

18. Carlos Guilherme Mota, *Nordeste 1817: Estruturas e argumentos* (São Paulo, 1972).

19. Leslie Bethell, *The Abolition of the Brazilian Slave Trade: Britain, Brazil and the Slave Trade Question, 1807–1869* (Cambridge, England, 1970); Robert J. Conrad, *The Destruction of Brazilian Slavery, 1850–1888* (Berkeley, 1972).

20. Thomas J. Flory, *Judge and Jury in Imperial Brazil: Social Control and Political Stability in the New State* (Austin, Tex., 1981).

21. Fernando Uricochea, *The Patrimonial Foundations of the Brazilian Bureaucratic State* (Berkeley, 1980).

22. Joseph L. Love, *Rio Grande do Sul and Brazilian Regionalism, 1882–1930* (Stanford, Calif., 1971).

23. Eul Soo Pang, *Bahia in the First Brazilian Republic* (Gainesville, Fla., 1979).

24. Ralph Della Cava, *Miracle at Joaseiro* (New York, 1970).

25. Maria Isaura Pereira de Queiroz, *O messianismo no Brasil e no mundo* (São Paulo, 1965).
26. Thomas E. Skidmore, *Politics in Brazil, 1930–1964: An Experiment in Democracy* (New York, 1967).
27. Boris Fausto, *A Revolucão de 1930: Historiografia e história* (São Paulo, 1970).
28. Antônio Cândido, *Formação da literatura brasileira (momentos decisivos)*, 4th ed. (São Paulo, 1971).
29. Florestan Fernandes, *A integração do negro na sociedade de classes*, 3d ed. (São Paulo, 1978).
30. Emilia Viotti da Costa, *Da senzala à colônia* (São Paulo, 1966).
31. Carl Degler, *Neither Black nor White: Slavery and Race Relations in Brazil and the United States* (New York, 1971).
32. Maria Sylvia de Carvalho Franco, *Homens livres na ordem escravocrata* (São Paulo, 1969).
33. Stanley J. Stein, *Vassouras: A Brazilian Coffee County, 1850–1900* (Cambridge, Mass., 1957).
34. Warren Dean, *Rio Claro: A Brazilian Plantation System, 1820–1920* (Stanford, Calif., 1976).
35. Thomas H. Holloway, *Immigrants on the Land: Coffee and Society in São Paulo, 1886–1934* (Chapel Hill, N.C., 1980).
36. Caio Prado, Jr., *Formação do Brasil contemporâneo* (São Paulo, 1942); idem, *História econômica do Brasil* (São Paulo, 1945).
37. Roberto Simonsen, *História econômica do Brasil, 1500–1820* (São Paulo, 1937).
38. Celso Furtado, *Formação econômica do Brasil* (Rio de Janeiro, 1959).
39. Stanley J. Stein, *The Brazilian Cotton Manufacture: Textile Enterprise in an Underdeveloped Area, 1850–1950* (Cambridge, Mass., 1957).
40. Warren Dean, *The Industrialization of São Paulo, 1880–1945* (Austin, Tex., 1969).
41. Boris Fausto, *Crime e cotidiano: A criminalidade em São Paulo, 1880–1924* (São Paulo, 1984), with a clear shift in emphasis from his *Trabalho urbano e conflito social, 1880–1920* (São Paulo, 1977).
42. Sergio Miceli, *Intelectuais e classe dirigente no Brasil (1920–1945)* (São Paulo, 1979).
43. Antonio García Baquero-González, *Comercio colonial y guerras revolucionarias: La decadencia económica de Cádiz a raíz de la emancipación americana* (Seville, 1972); Baquero-González, *Cádiz y el Atlántico, 1717–1778: El comercio colonial español bajo el monopolio gaditano*, 2 vols. (Seville, 1976).
44. John H. Parry, *The Sale of Public Office in the Spanish Indies Under the Hapsburgs* (Berkeley, 1953).
45. Mark A. Burkholder and D. S. Chandler, *From Impotence to Au-*

thority: The Spanish Crown and the American Audiencias, 1687–1808 (Columbia, Miss., 1977).

46. Mark A. Burkholder, *Politics of a Colonial Career: José Baquíjano and the Audiencia of Lima* (Albuquerque, N.M., 1980).

47. See, among others, Allan J. Kuethe, *Military Reform and Society in New Granada, 1773–1808* (Gainesville, Fla., 1978); Christon I. Archer, *The Army in Bourbon Mexico, 1760–1810* (Albuquerque, N.M., 1977).

48. John Lynch, *Spanish Colonial Administration, 1782–1810: The Intendant System in the Viceroyalty of the Río de la Plata* (London, 1958); John Fisher, *Government and Society in Colonial Peru: The Intendant System, 1784–1814* (London, 1970).

49. John Leddy Phelan, *The Kingdom of Quito in the Seventeenth Century: Bureaucratic Politics in the Spanish Empire* (Madison, Wisc., 1967); idem, *The People and the King: The Comunero Revolution in Colombia, 1781* (Madison, Wisc., 1978).

50. Woodrow W. Borah, *Justice by Insurance: The General Indian Court of Colonial Mexico and the Legal Aides of the Half-Real* (Berkeley, 1983).

51. Robert Ricard, *La conquête spirituelle du Mexique* (Paris, 1933).

52. Nancy M. Farriss, *Maya Society Under Colonial Rule: The Collective Enterprise of Survival* (Princeton, 1984).

53. Charles Gibson, *The Aztecs Under Spanish Rule: A History of the Indians of the Valley of Mexico, 1519–1810* (Stanford, 1964).

54. Severo Martínez Peláez, *La patria del criollo: Ensayo de interpretación social de la realidad colonial guatemalteca* (Guatemala, 1970).

55. William B. Taylor, *Drinking, Homicide and Rebellion in Colonial Mexican Villages* (Stanford, Calif., 1979).

56. Nathan Wachtel, *La vision des vaincus: Les Indiens du Pérou devant la Conquête Espagnole, 1530–1570* (Paris, 1971).

57. Karen Spalding, *Huarochirí: An Andean Society Under Inca and Spanish Rule* (Stanford, Calif., 1984).

58. Steve J. Stern, *Peru's Indian Peoples and the Challenge of Spanish Conquest: Huamanga to 1640* (Madison, Wisc., 1982).

59. Brooke Larson, "Rural Rhythms of Class Conflict in Nineteenth-Century Cochabamba," *Hispanic American Historical Review*, 60 (Aug. 1980): 407–30.

60. Carlos Sempat Assadourian, *El sistema de la economía colonial: Mercado interno, regiones y espacio económico* (Lima, 1982).

61. James Lockhart, *Spanish Peru, 1532–1560: A Colonial Society* (Madison, Wisc., 1968).

62. David Brading, *Miners and Merchants in Bourbon Mexico, 1763–1810* (Cambridge, England, 1971).

63. Enrique Florescano, *Precios del maíz y crisis agrícolas en México, 1708–1810* (Mexico City, 1969).

64. Woodrow W. Borah, *New Spain's Century of Depression* (Berkeley, 1951).
65. David Brading, *Haciendas and Ranchos in the Mexican Bajío: León, 1700–1860* (Cambridge, England, 1978).
66. François Chevalier, *La formation des grands domaines au Mexique: Terre et société aux XVI–XVII siècles* (Paris, 1952).
67. William B. Taylor, "Landed Society in New Spain: A View from the South," *Hispanic American Historical Review*, 54 (1974): 387–413.
68. William B. Taylor, *Landlord and Peasant in Colonial Oaxaca* (Stanford, Calif., 1972).
69. A good selection that reflects Góngora's wide-ranging interests is offered in Mario Góngora, *Studies in the Colonial History of Spanish America* (Cambridge, England, 1975).
70. John Lynch, *The Spanish-American Revolutions, 1808–1826* (New York, 1973).
71. Luis Villoro, *El proceso ideológico de la revolución de independencia* (Mexico City, 1967).
72. Heraclio Bonilla, "Clases populares y estado en el contexto de la crisis colonial," in Bonilla et al., *La independencia del Perú*, 2d ed. (Lima, 1981).
73. Manuel Burga, *De la encomienda a la hacienda capitalista: El valle del Jequetepeque del siglo XVI al XX* (Lima, 1976).
74. Germán Carrera Damas, Preliminary study to *Materiales para el estudio de la cuestión agraria en Venezuela, 1800–1830*, vol. 1 (Caracas, 1964).
75. Lucía Sala de Touron, Julio Carlos Rodríguez, and Nelson de la Torre, *Estructura económico-social de la colonia* (Montevideo, 1967); and, by the same authors, *Evolución económica de la Banda Oriental* (Montevideo, 1967), *La revolución agraria artiguista* (Montevideo, 1969), and *Después de Artigas (1820–1829)* (Montevideo, 1972).
76. Timothy Anna, *The Fall of the Royal Government in Mexico City* (Lincoln, Nebr., 1978); Anna, *The Fall of the Royal Government in Peru* (Lincoln, Nebr., 1979).
77. D. C. M. Platt, *Latin America and British Trade, 1806–1914* (London, 1973).
78. Sergio Villalobos, *El comercio y la crisis colonial: Un mito de la independencia* (Santiago de Chile, 1968).
79. David Bushnell, *The Santander Regime in Gran Colombia* (Newark, Del., 1954).
80. William Lofstrom, *The Promise and Problem of Reform: Attempted Social and Economic Change in the First Years of Bolivian Independence* (Ithaca, N.Y., 1972).
81. Simon Collier, *Ideas and Politics of Chilean Independence, 1808–1833* (Cambridge, England, 1967).

82. Daniel Cosío Villegas, *Historia moderna de México* (Mexico City, 1955–73).
83. It is true that Basadre's virtues as an historian are easier to perceive in the earlier, more manageable editions of his *Historia de la república del Perú* (see, for instance, 3d ed., Lima, 1946).
84. Miron Burgin, *The Economic Aspects of Argentine Federalism, 1820–1852* (Cambridge, Mass., 1946).
85. Charles Bergquist, *Coffee and Conflict in Colombia, 1886–1910* (Durham, N.C, 1978).
86. John Lynch, *Argentine Dictator: Juan Manuel de Rosas, 1829–1852* (Oxford, 1981).
87. Indalecio Liévano Aguirre, *Los grandes conflictos sociales y económicos de nuestra historia*, 4 vols. (Bogotá, 1961).
88. François Bourricaud, *Pouvoir et société dans le Pérou Contemporain* (Paris, 1967).
89. David Rock, *Politics in Argentina, 1890–1930: The Rise and Fall of Radicalism* (Cambridge, England, 1975).
90. Peter H. Smith, *Politics and Beef in Argentina: Patterns of Conflict and Change* (New York, 1969).
91. Peter H. Smith, *Argentina and the Failure of Democracy: Conflict Among Political Elites, 1904–1955* (Madison, Wisc., 1974).
92. Peter H. Smith, *Labyrinths of Power: Political Recruitment in Twentieth-Century Mexico* (Princeton, 1979).
93. James R. Wilkie, *The Mexican Revolution: Federal Expenditure and Social Change Since 1910* (Berkeley, 1966).
94. Herbert S. Klein, *Parties and Political Change in Bolivia, 1880–1952* (Cambridge, England, 1969).
95. Jonathan Kelley and Herbert S. Klein, *Revolution and the Rebirth of Inequality: A Theory Applied to the National Revolution in Bolivia* (Berkeley, 1981).
96. John Coatsworth, *Growth Against Development: The Economic Impact of Railroads in Porfirian Mexico* (De Kalb, Ill., 1981).
97. Carlos Díaz-Alejandro, *Essays on the Economic History of the Argentine Republic* (New Haven, 1970).
98. Roberto Cortés Conde, *El progreso argentino, 1880–1914* (Buenos Aires, 1979).
99. Rosemary Thorp and Geoffrey Bertram, *Peru, 1890–1977: Growth and Policy in an Open Economy* (New York, 1978).
100. Luis Ospina Vázquez, *Industria y protección en Colombia, 1810–1930* (Medellín, Colombia, 1965).
101. Luis Eduardo Nieto Arteta, *Economía y cultura en la historia de Colombia*, 2d ed. (Bogotá, 1962).
102. Marco Palacios, *Coffee in Colombia, 1850–1970: An Economic, Social and Political History* (Cambridge, England, 1980).

103. José Pedro Barrán and Benjamín Nahum, *Batlle, los estancieros y el imperialismo británico*, 5 published vols. (Montevideo, 1979–).

104. James R. Scobie, *Revolution in the Pampas: A Social History of Argentine Wheat, 1860–1910* (Austin, Tex., 1964).

105. E. Bradford Burns, *The Poverty of Progress: Latin America in the Nineteenth Century* (Berkeley, 1980).

106. Richard M. Morse, *From Community to Metropolis: A Biography of Sāa Paulo, Brazil* (Gainesville, Fla., 1958).

107. James R. Scobie, *Buenos Aires: Plaza to Suburb, 1870–1910* (New York, 1978).

108. Arnold J. Bauer, *Chilean Rural Society from the Spanish Conquest to 1930* (Cambridge, England, 1975).

109. José Pedro Barrán and Benjamin Nahum, *Historia rural del Uruguay moderno*, 6 vols. (Montevideo, 1967–77).

110. Ezequiel Gallo, *La pampa gringa: La colonización agrícola en Santa Fe (1870–1895)* (Buenos Aires, 1983).

111. Florencia E. Mallon, *The Defense of Community in Peru's Central Highlands: Peasant Struggle and Capitalist Transition, 1860–1940* (Princeton, 1983).

112. Rodrigo Montoya. *Capitalismo y no-capitalismo en el Perú: Un estudio histórico de su articulación en un eje regional* (Lima, 1980).

113. Charles A. Hale, *Mexican Liberalism in the Age of Mora, 1821–1853* (New Haven, 1968).

114. Frank Safford, *The Ideal of the Practical: Colombia's Struggle to Form a Technical Elite* (Austin, Tex., 1976).

115. Enrique Krauze, *Caudillos culturales en la Revolución Mexicana*, (Mexico City, 1976).

116. Hugo Vezzetti, *La locura en la Argentina* (Buenos Aires, 1983).

117. Friedrich Katz, *The Secret War in Mexico: Europe, the United States and the Mexican Revolution* (Chicago, 1981).

118. Héctor Aguilar Camín, *La frontera nómada: Sonora y la Revolución Mexicana* (Mexico City, 1977).

VALENZUELA: Political Science

I wish to acknowledge the advice provided by Felipe Agüero, Ronald Chilcote, Jonathan Hartlyn, Manuel Antonio Garretón, Terry Karl, Robert Kaufman, Abraham Lowenthal, Christopher Mitchell, and Mitchell Seligson in the preparation of this paper. I am also grateful to Richard Fagen, Daniel Levine, and Barbara Stallings, who provided insightful comments at the "State of the Discipline" panel at the Latin American Studies Association International Congress held in Albuquerque, New Mexico, in April 1985. I owe a special debt of gratitude to Pamela Constable and Ed Lehoucq. The views reflected here, however, are strictly my own.

1. See Jorge I. Dominguez, "Consensus and Divergence: The State of the Literature on Inter-American Relations in the 1970s," *Latin American Research Review*, 13 (1978): 87–126; Dominguez, "Political Relations in the Western Hemisphere," in Viron Vaky, ed., *Governance in the Western Hemisphere* (New York, 1982); Abraham F. Lowenthal, *Partners in Conflict: The United States and Latin America* (Baltimore, 1987). Also see Cole Blasier, *The Hovering Giant: U.S. Responses to Revolutionary Change in Latin America*, 2d ed. (Pittsburgh, 1986); Blasier, *The Giant's Rival: The U.S.S.R. and Latin America* (Pittsburgh, 1985).

2. They are listed in R. A. Gomez, *The Study of Latin American Politics in University Programs in the United States*, Institute of Government, Comparative Government Studies no. 2 (Tucson, 1967).

3. Merle Kling, "The State of Research on Latin America: Political Science," in Charles Wagley, ed., *Social Science Research on Latin America* (New York, 1964).

4. Ibid., p. 189.
5. Ibid., p. 174.
6. Gomez, *Study*, pp. 37–38.
7. Kling, "Research." p. 179.
8. Ibid., pp. 181–90.
9. Ibid., p. 196.

10. See the excellent study by Robert Packenham, *Liberal America and the Third World* (Princeton, 1973). Also see Arturo Valenzuela, "Doctrinas y políticas de desarrollo de Estados Unidos hacia América Latina," in Heraldo Muñoz, ed., *Crisis y desarrollo alternativo en Latinoamérica* (Santiago, 1985).

11. Peter Ranis, "Trends in Research on Latin American Politics, 1961–67," *Latin American Research Review*, 3 (1968): 71–78.

12. A representative collection of articles is Seymour Martin Lipset and Aldo Solari, eds., *Elites in Latin America* (New York, 1967). On the military, see note 15, below.

On the church, see Luigi Einaudi, Richard Maullin, Alfred Stepan, and Michael Fleet, *Latin American Institutional Development: The Changing Catholic Church* (Santa Monica, Calif., 1969); Frederick C. Turner, *Catholicism and Political Development in Latin America* (Chapel Hill, N.C., 1971); Ivan Vallier, *Catholicism, Social Control, and Modernization in Latin America* (Englewood Cliffs, N.J., 1970). The literature on the church blossomed in the late 1970's and early 1980's. See Phillip Berryman, *The Religious Roots of Rebellion: Christians in the Central American Revolutions* (Maryknoll, N.Y., 1984); Thomas Bruneau, *The Political Transformation of the Brazilian Catholic Church* (New York, 1974); Bruneau, *The Church in Brazil: The Politics of Religion* (Austin, Tex., 1982); Daniel H. Levine, ed., *Church and Politics in Latin America* (Beverly Hills, 1979); Levine, *Religion and*

Politics in Latin America: The Catholic Church in Venezuela and Colombia (Princeton, 1981); Scott Mainwaring, *The Catholic Church and Politics in Brazil, 1916–1983* (Stanford, Calif., 1987); Brian Smith, *The Church and Politics in Chile: Challenges to Modern Catholicism* (Princeton, 1982). Useful reviews of the church include Daniel Levine, "Religion and Politics: Dimensions of Renewal," *Thought: A Review of Culture and Ideas*, 59 (June 1984): 117–35; Thomas G. Sanders, "Review Essay: The Politics of Catholicism in Latin America," *Journal of Inter-American Studies and World Affairs*, 2 (May 1982): 241–58; Brian Smith, "Religion and Social Change: Classical Themes and New Developments in the Context of Recent Developments," *Latin American Research Review*, 20 (Summer 1975): 3–34.

On urban dwellers, see Glenn H. Beyer, ed., *The Urban Explosion in Latin America* (Ithaca, N.Y., 1968); William P. Mangin, ed., *Peasants in Cities: Readings in the Anthropology of Urbanization* (Boston, 1970); and the two-part review essay by Richard Morse, "Trends and Issues in Latin American Urban Research, 1965–1970," *Latin American Research Review*, 6 (Spring 1971): 3–52, and 6 (Summer 1971): 19–75. For later studies, see note 29 below.

On peasants, see Henry Landsberger, ed., *Latin American Peasant Movements* (Ithaca, N.Y., 1969); Rodolfo Stavenhagen, ed., *Agrarian Problems and Peasant Movements in Latin America* (Garden City, N.Y., 1970).

13. On Cuba, see R. E. Bonachea and N. P. Valdez, eds. *Cuba in Revolution* (Garden City, N.Y., 1972); Richard R. Fagen, *The Transformation of Political Culture in Cuba* (Stanford, Calif., 1969); Carmelo Mesa-Lago, ed., *Revolutionary Change in Cuba* (Pittsburgh, 1971); Mesa-Lago, ed., *Cuba in the 1970s: Pragmatism and Institutionalization*, 2d ed. (Albuquerque, 1978); Hugh Thomas, *Cuba: The Pursuit of Freedom* (New York, 1971). On Mexico, see William P. Glade and Charles W. Anderson, *The Political Economy of Mexico* (Madison, Wisc., 1963); Pablo González Casanova, *Democracy in Mexico* (New York, 1970); Roger Hansen, *The Politics of Mexican Development* (Baltimore, 1971); Vincent Padgett, *The Mexican Political System*, 2d ed. (Boston, 1976); Robert E. Scott, *Mexican Government in Transition* (Urbana, Ill., 1959). On Chile, see Federico G. Gil, *The Political System of Chile* (Boston, 1966). On Brazil, see Ronald M. Schneider, *The Political System of Brazil: Emergence of a "Modernizing" Authoritarian Regime* (New York, 1971); Thomas L. Skidmore, *Politics in Brazil, 1930–1964: An Experiment in Democracy* (New York, 1967); Philippe Schmitter, *Interest Conflict and Political Change in Brazil* (Stanford, Calif., 1971). Later case studies, drawing on different perspectives, include, for Cuba, Jorge I. Dominguez, *Cuba: Order and Revolution* (Cambridge, Mass., 1978); for Mexico, Susan Kaufman Purcell, *The*

Mexican Profit-Sharing Decision: Politics in an Authoritarian Regime (Berkeley, 1975); for Chile, Barbara Stallings, *Class Conflict and Economic Development in Chile, 1958–1973* (Stanford, Calif., 1978), and Arturo Valenzuela, *The Breakdown of Democratic Regimes: Chile* (Baltimore, 1978).

14. For a comparative study of parties, see Ronald MacDonald, *Party Systems and Elections in Latin America* (Chicago, 1971). For a discussion of recent literature, see Mary Jeanne Reid Martz, "Studying Latin American Political Parties: Dimensions Past and Present," *Journal of Latin American Studies*, 12 (May, 1980): 139–67. The Wilson Center in Washington, D.C., has initiated a major project on political parties in the Southern Cone. See the rapporteurs' report by Felipe Agüero, Charles Gillespie, and Tim Scully, "The Role of Political Parties in the Return to Democracy in the Southern Cone" (Washington, D.C.: Latin American Program, Woodrow Wilson International Center for Scholars, 1985). Also see the following individual country reports: Marcelo Cavarozzi, "The Argentine Parties: Strong Subcultures, Weak System"; Luis E. Gonzalez, "Political Parties and Redemocratization in Uruguay"; Bolivar Lamounier and Rachel Meneguello, "Political Parties and Democratic Consolidation: The Brazilian Case"; Arturo Valenzuela, "Origins and Characteristics of the Chilean Party System: A Proposal for a Parliamentary Form of Government."

15. Abraham Lowenthal, "Armies and Politics in Latin America," *World Politics*, 27 (October 1974): 127. For other treatments of the military in Latin America, see Abraham Lowenthal, ed., *Armies and Politics in Latin America* (New York, 1976), which contains a slightly revised version of his review article first published in *World Politics*. For discussions of this literature, see Mauricio Solaun and Michael A. Quinn, *Sinners and Heretics: The Politics of Military Intervention in Latin America* (Chicago, 1973); Philippe Schmitter, ed., *Military Rule in Latin America: Function, Consequences, and Perspectives* (Beverly Hills, 1973). The best single case study produced during this period remains Alfred Stepan, *The Military in Politics: Changing Patterns in Brazil* (Princeton, 1971).

Among the more noteworthy volumes that have appeared since the early 1970's are John Fitch, *The Military Coup d'Etat as Political Process: Ecuador, 1948–1966* (Baltimore, 1977); Edmundo Campos Coelho, *Em busca de identidade: O exercito e a politica na sociedade brasileira* (Rio de Janeiro, 1976); Maria Helena Moreira Alves, *State and Opposition in Brasil, 1964–1984* (Austin, Tex., forthcoming); Jorge Rodriguez Beruff, *Los militares y el poder: Un ensayo sobre la doctrina militar en el Perú, 1948–68* (Lima, 1983); Alain Rouquié, *Poder militar y sociedad política en la Argentina*, vols. 1 and 2 (Buenos Aires, 1978); Augusto Varas, Felipe Agüero, and Fernando Bustamante, *Chile, democracia y fuerzas armadas* (Santiago, 1980).

More general treatments appearing recently include Mario Esteban

Carranza, *Fuerzas armadas y estado de excepción en América Latina* (Mexico City, 1978); Isaac Sandoval, *Las crisis políticas latinoamericanas y el militarismo*, 4th ed. (Mexico City, 1981); Alain Rouquié, *L'Etat militaire en Amérique Latine* (Paris, 1982). Also, on doctrines of national security, see Roberto Calvo, *La doctrina de seguridad nacional: Autoritarismo político y neoliberalismo económico en el Cono Sur* (Caracas, 1979); Genaro Arriagada H. and Manuel Antonio Garretón M., "Doctrina de seguridad nacional y régimen militar," *Estudios Sociales Centroamericanos*, 20 and 21 (1978). Both works contain extensive bibliographies. Also see Genaro Arriagada, *El pensamiento político de los militares* (Santiago, n.d.). For recent reviews on the armed forces in Latin America, see Mario Carranza, "Golpes de estado y militarización en América Latina," *Desarrollo Económico*, 24 (July–Sept. 1984): 319–27; Arturo Valenzuela, "A Note on the Military and Social Science Theory," *The Third World Quarterly*, 7 (Jan. 1985): 132–43. Finally, see the following bibliographies for additional sources: Nicolle Ball, *The Military in the Development Process: A Guide to Issues* (Claremont, Calif., 1981); Herbert E. Gooch, *The Military and Politics in Latin America* (Los Angeles, 1979).

16. Valenzuela, "A Note."

17. John Martz, "Political Science and Latin American Politics: A Discipline in Search of a Region," *Latin American Research Review*, 6 (Spring 1971): 73–100. Curiously, in his prescriptions Martz called for the application of the same concepts from political development articulated by Kling, citing in fact the same quote from Huntington.

18. Kalman H. Silvert, "Politics and the Study of Latin America," in Lucien Pye, ed., *Political Science and Area Studies: Rivals or Partners?* (Bloomington, Ind., 1975), p. 160.

19. Ibid., p. 165.

20. Ibid.

21. The writings on dependency are vast. Reviews of the literature include Richard R. Fagen, "Studying Latin American Politics: Some Implications of the *Dependencia* Approach," *Latin American Research Review*, no. 2 (1977): 3–26; Instituto de Investigaciones Sociales de la UNAM, *Clases sociales y crisis política en América Latina* (Mexico City, 1977); Gabriel Palma, "Dependency: A Formal Theory of Underdevelopment or a Method for the Analysis of Concrete Situations of Underdevelopment," *World Development*, 6 (July–Aug. 1978): 881–924; J. Samuel Valenzuela and Arturo Valenzuela, "Modernization or Dependency: Alternative Perspectives in the Study of Latin American Underdevelopment," *Comparative Politics*, 10 (July–Aug. 1978): 535–57. Many of the debates in dependency theory, among both Latin and North Americans, have been covered by the journal *Latin American Perspectives*. For insightful discussions of these controversies, see Ronald H. Chilcote, ed., *Dependency and Marxism: Toward a Resolution of the Debate* (Boulder,

Colo., 1982); Ronald H. Chilcote and Joel C. Edelstein, *Latin America: Capitalist and Socialist Perspectives on Development and Underdevelopment* (Boulder, Colo., 1986); Ronald H. Chilcote, ed., *Theories of Development and Underdevelopment* (Boulder, Colo., 1984).

22. An essay that reflects this shift is Fred Riggs, "The Rise and Fall of Political Development," in Samuel L. Long, ed., *The Handbook of Political Behavior* (New York, 1981), vol. 4, pp. 289–348. Also see Joel S. Midgal, "Studying the Politics of Development and Change: The State of the Art," in Ada W. Finifter, ed., *Political Science: The State of the Discipline* (Washington, D.C., 1983).

Recently published works that rely upon the concepts and theories generated by Latin Americanists include Robert Bianchi, *Interest Groups and Political Development in Turkey* (Princeton, 1984); Thomas M. Callaghy, *The State-Society Struggle: Zaire in Comparative Perspective* (New York, 1984); and John Waterbury, *The Egypt of Nasser and Sadat: The Political Economy of Two Regimes* (Princeton, 1983). Also see Bruce Cumings, "Origins and Development of the Asian Political Economy: Industrial Sectors, Product Cycles, and Political Consequences," *International Organization*, 38 (Winter 1984): 1–40; Stephen Haggard and Chung-in Moon, "The South Korean State in the International Economy: Liberal, Dependent or Mercantile," in John Gerard Ruggie, ed., *The Antinomies of Interdependence: National Welfare and the International Division of Labor* (New York, 1983). Gary Gereffi and Donald Wyman jointly are working on a project comparing the East Asian and Latin American development experiences in the twentieth century.

23. Some of these observations are drawn from Valenzuela and Valenzuela, "Modernization or Dependency." The focus on political alliances and structural constraints to individual action anticipated later work in comparative politics in "rational choice" theory.

24. Concern for authoritarianism is not surprising. Only three countries in the region—Costa Rica, Colombia, and Venezuela—maintained democratic continuity without a regime change. See John A. Peeler, *Latin American Democracies: Colombia, Costa Rica, and Venezuela* (Chapel Hill, N.C., 1984).

For works on authoritarianism and the state in Latin America, see William L. Canak, "The Peripheral State Debate: State Capitalist and Bureaucratic-Authoritarian Regimes in Latin America," *Latin American Research Review*, 19 (1984): 3–36; Cesar N. Caviedes, *Southern Cone: Realities of the Authoritarian State* (Totowa, N.J., 1984); Joe Foweraker, *Class Domination and the Authoritarian State: A Political Economy of Latin America* (London, forthcoming); Norbert Lechner, *Estado y política en América Latina* (Mexico City, 1981); James M. Malloy, ed., *Authoritarianism and Corporatism in Latin America* (Pittsburgh, 1977); Marcos Kaplan, *Estado y sociedad en América Latina* (Mexico City, 1984). Also see

José Luis Reyna and Richard S. Weinert, eds., *Authoritarianism in Mexico* (Philadelphia, 1977); Alfred Stepan, ed., *Authoritarian Brazil* (New Haven, 1973); Thomas C. Bruneau and Philippe Faucher, eds., *Authoritarian Capitalism: Brazil's Contemporary Economic and Political Development* (Boulder, Colo., 1981); Fernando Henrique Cardoso, *Autoritarismo e democratizaçao* (Rio de Janeiro, 1975); Alfred Stepan, *The State and Society: Peru in Comparative Perspective* (Princeton, 1978); J. Samuel Valenzuela and Arturo Valenzuela, eds., *Military Rule in Chile: Dictatorships and Oppositions* (Baltimore, 1986); Manuel Antonio Garretón, *El proceso político chileno* (Santiago, 1983). See note 25 below for a listing of the books and articles surrounding the work of Guillermo O'Donnell.

25. Guillermo O'Donnell's work includes the following: *Modernization and Bureaucratic-Authoritarianism: Studies in South American Politics* (Berkeley, 1973); "Modernization and Military Coups: Theory, Comparisons and the Argentine Case," in Abraham F. Lowenthal, ed., *Armies and Politics in Latin America* (New York, 1976); "Reflections on the Patterns of Change in the Bureaucratic-Authoritarian State," *Latin American Research Review*, 13, no. 1 (1978): 3–38; "Corporatism and the Question of the State," in James M. Malloy, ed., *Authoritarianism and Corporatism in Latin America* (Pittsburgh, 1977); "Tensions in the Bureaucratic-Authoritarian State and the Question of Democracy," in David Collier, ed., *The New Authoritarianism in Latin America* (Princeton, 1979); "Las fuerzas armadas y el estado autoritario del Cono Sur de América Latina," in Norbert Lechner, ed., *Estado y política en America Latina* (Mexico City, 1981); "Estado y alianzas en la Argentina, 1956–76," *Desarrollo Económico*, 16 (Jan.–Mar. 1977): 523–54; "Notas para el estudio de la burguesía nacional en sus relaciones con el aparato estatal y el capital internacional," *Estudios CEDES*, 1978; *1966–1973: El estado burocrático autoritario: Triunfos, derrotas y crisis* (Buenos Aires, 1982).

For a symposium and bibliographical essay, see the excellent volume *New Authoritarianism*, ed. Collier. Also see Karen L. Remmer and Gilbert Merkx's very perceptive essay "Bureaucratic-Authoritarianism Revisited," *Latin American Research Review*, 17 (1982): 3–40.

26. For an exhaustive bibliographic essay on the work produced by Latin Americans, see Jorge Graciarena and Rolando Franco, "Social Formations and Power Structures in Latin America," *Current Sociology*, 26 (Spring 1978): 5–275.

27. Glaúcio Soares points to the greater advantages of Latin American scholarship vis-à-vis U.S. scholarship in his "Latin American Studies in the United States: A Critique and a Proposal," *Latin American Research Review*, 11 (1976): 51–69.

28. See the *Boletín CLACSO*, published by the Consejo Latinoamericano de Ciencias Sociales. A particularly helpful issue was the July–December issue of 1979 (vol. 10).

29. On urban politics, see David Collier, *Squatters and Oligarchs: Authoritarian Rule and Policy Change in Peru* (Baltimore, 1976); Wayne Cornelius, *Politics and the Migrant Poor in Mexico City* (Stanford, Calif., 1975); Susan Eckstein, *The Poverty of Revolution: The State and the Ur an Poor in Mexico* (Princeton, 1977); Larissa Adler Lomnitz, *Networks and Marginality: Life in a Mexican Shantytown* (New York, 1977); Janice E. Perlman, *The Myth of Marginality: Urban Poverty and Politics in Rio de Janeiro* (Berkeley, 1976); Joan M. Nelson, *Access to Power: Politics and the Urban Poor in Developing Nations* (Princeton, 1979); Alejandro Portes and John Walton, *Labor, Class, and the International System* (New York, 1981); Bryan Roberts, *Cities of Peasants: The Political Economy of Urbanization in the Third World* (Beverly Hills, 1978).

On international relations, see, most recently, Kevin J. Middlebrook and Carlos Rico, eds., *The United States and Latin America in the 1980s: Contending Perspectives on a Decade of Crisis* (Pittsburgh, 1985); Heraldo Muñoz and Joseph Tulchin, *Entre la autononomía y la subordinación: Política exterior de los países latinoamericanos*, 2 vols. (Buenos Aires, 1984). For an insightful review article, see Jorge I. Dominguez, "Consensus and Divergence: The State of the Literature on Inter-American Relations in the 1970s," *Latin American Research Review*, 13 (1978): 87–126. Also see Abraham F. Lowenthal, "Research in Latin America and the Caribbean on International Relations and Foreign Policy," *Latin American Research Review*, 18 (1983): 154–74; Lowenthal, *Partners in Conflict*, cited in note 1, above. Lastly, consult the following journals: *Foro Internacional, Estudios Internacionales*, and *Journal of Inter-American and World Affairs*. An exhaustive bibliography is Organization of American States, *Bibliografía de artículos sobre las relaciones internacionales de América Latina y el Caribe: 1975–81*, Documento SG/Ser. L/I.2 (Washington, D.C., 1981).

On multinational corporations, see Douglas C. Bennett and Kenneth E. Sharpe, *Transnational Corporations Versus the State: The Political Economy of the Mexican Auto Industry* (Princeton, 1985); Francisco de Oliveira and María Angélica Travolo Popuotchi, *Transnacionales en América Latina: El complejo automotor en Brasil* (Mexico City, 1979); Peter B. Evans, *Dependent Development: The Alliance of Multinational, State, and Local Capital in Brazil* (Princeton, 1979); Peter B. Evans and Gary Gereffi, "Foreign Investment and Dependent Development: Comparing Brazil and Mexico," in Sylvia Hewlett and Richard Weinert, eds., *Brazil and Mexico: Patterns in Late Development* (Philadelphia, 1982); Fernando Fajnzylber and Trinidad Martínez Tarrago, *Las empresas transnacionales: Expansión a nivel mundial y proyección en la industria mexicana* (Mexico City, 1976); Gary Gereffi, *The Pharmaceutical Industry and Dependency in the Third World* (Princeton, 1983); Rhys Jenkins, *Transnational Corporations and Industrial Transformation in Latin America* (London, forthcoming); Theodore H. Moran, *Multinational Corporations and the Politics of Dependence: Copper in Chile* (Princeton, 1974); Moran, "Multinational Corporations and Dependency: A Dialogue for Dependentistas and Non-Dependentistas," *International Organization*, 32 (Winter 1978): 79–199; Richard S. Newfarmer, *Transnational Conglomerates and the Economics of Dependent Development* (Greenwood, Conn., 1980); Newfarmer, ed., *Profits, Progress, and Poverty: Case Studies of International Industries in Latin America* (Notre Dame, Ind., 1985).

On the breakdown of democratic regimes, see Juan Linz and Alfred Stepan, eds., *The Breakdown of Democratic Regimes: Latin America* (Baltimore, 1978); Arturo Valenzuela, *The Breakdown of Democratic Regimes: Chile* (Baltimore, 1978).

30. Bill Warren, "Imperialism and Capitalist Industrialization," *New Left Review*, 81 (Sept.–Oct. 1973): 3–44. This is particularly true of the work of André Gunder Frank. See his *Capitalism and Underdevelopment in Latin America* (New York, 1967). See also Susanne Bodenheimer, "Dependence and Imperialism," *Politics and Society*, 1 (May 1971): 327–57.

31. Fernando Henrique Cardoso, "Associated-Dependent Development: Theoretical and Practical Implications," in Alfred Stepan, ed., *Authoritarian Brazil: Origins, Politics, and Future* (New Haven, 1973). Also see Fernando Henrique Cardoso and Enzo Faletto, *Dependency and Development in Latin America* (Berkeley, 1979).

32. See the work of Immanuel Wallerstein: *The Modern World System, I: Capitalist Agriculture and the Origins of the European World Economy in the Sixteenth Century* (New York, 1974); *The Modern World System, II: Mercantilism and the Consolidation of the European World-Economy, 1600–1750* (New York, 1980). Also see the two collections of his essays: *The Capitalist World Economy* (New York, 1979); *Political Economy of the World Economy: The States, the Movements, and the Civilizations* (New York, 1984). See also articles published in *Latin American Perspectives*.

33. Osvaldo Sunkel attempted such a project out of the University of Sussex, but it never got off the ground.

34. A noteworthy exception is Jonathan Hartlyn, "The Impact of Patterns of Industrialization and of Popular Sector Incorporation on Political Regime Type: A Case Study of Colombia," *Studies in Comparative International Development*, 19 (Spring 1984): 29–60.

35. See Collier, ed., *New Authoritarianism*; Remmer and Merkx, "Bureaucratic-Authoritarianism."

36. One of the very best studies to appear on a single country in Latin America is, in fact, Guillermo O'Donnell's *1966–73: El estado burocrático autoritario* (Buenos Aires, 1984).

37. Robert Kaufman, "Trends and Priorities for Political Science Re-

search on Latin America," in *Trends and Priorities for Research on Latin America in the 1980s*, Woodrow Wilson International Center for Scholars Working Paper No. 111 (Washington, D.C., 1982), p. 42.

38. Articles that missed this point include: David Ray, "The Dependency Model of Latin American Politics: Three Basic Fallacies," *Journal of Inter-American Studies and World Affairs*, 15 (Feb. 1973): 13–18; Tony Smith, "The Underdevelopment of Development Literature: The Case of Dependency," *World Politics*, 31 (Jan. 1979): 247–88. On this issue, see Raymond D. Duvall, "Dependence and *Dependencia* Theory: Notes Toward the Precision of Concept and Argument," *International Organization*, 32 (Winter 1978): 51–78. See also Raymond D. Duvall et al., "A Formal Model of 'Dependencia Theory': Structure and Measurement," in Richard L. Merritt and Bruce M. Russett, eds., *From National Development to Global Community: Essays in Honor of Karl Deutsch* (Boston, 1981). For a skeptical reflection on U.S. efforts to study dependency, see Fernando Henrique Cardoso, "The Consumption of Dependency Theory in the United States," *Latin American Research Review*, 12 (1977): 7–24.

39. Remmer and Merkx, "Bureaucratic Authoritarianism," p. 7.

40. There are several studies describing the state of research in Latin America. See Jeffrey Puryear, "Higher Education, Development, and Repressive Regimes," *Studies in Comparative International Development*, 17 (1982): 3–35. For Chile, see the excellent volume by Manuel Antonio Garretón, *Las ciencias sociales en Chile* (Santiago, 1982), which was prepared as part of a broader CLACSO study. These generalizations are more true for the early stage of authoritarian regimes. A good case can be made that once the informal academic institutes became institutionalized, the quality of their work surpassed what was earlier done in universities.

41. For useful review essays of the burgeoning literature on Central America, see Mark B. Rosenberg, "Central America: Toward a New Research Agenda," *Journal of Inter-American Studies and World Affairs*, 26 (Feb. 1984): 145–54; J. Mark Ruhl, "Understanding Central American Politics," *Latin American Research Review*, 19 (1984): 143–42; James D. Cochrane, "Perspectives on the Central American Crisis," *International Organization*, 39 (Autumn 1985): 755–77. An excellent treatment of the region is Morris J. Blackman. William M. LeoGrande, and Kenneth E. Sharpe, eds., *Confronting Revolution: Security Through Diplomacy in Central America* (New York, 1986). The tremendous vitality of Brazilian political science can be traced in the following journals: *Dados: Revista de Ciencia Socais; Novos Estudos CEBRAP; Revista de Ciencia Politica; Revista Brasileira de Estudos Políticos; Revista de Ciencia Sociales; Revista de Instituto de Estudos Brasileiros*.

42. Kaufman, "Trends and Priorities," p. 43.

43. I am grateful to Jonathan Hartlyn for the way this point is articulated.

44. I am grateful to Manuel Antonio Garretón, with whom I have discussed these points at great length.

45. Fernando Henrique Cardoso, "On the Characterization of Authoritarian Regimes in Latin America," and Guillermo O'Donnell, "Tensions in the Bureaucratic-Authoritarian State and the Question of Democracy," in David Collier, ed., *The New Authoritarianism in Latin America* (Princeton, 1979).

46. I have dealt with the question of parties, in collaboration with Samuel Valenzuela, in "Party Oppositions Under the Chilean Authoritarian Regime," in J. Samuel Valenzuela and Arturo Valenzuela, eds., *Military Rule in Chile: Dictatorship and Oppositions* (Baltimore, 1986). See also Arturo Valenzuela, "Orígenes y características del sistema de partidos en Chile: Proposición para un gobierno parlamentario," *Estudios Públicos*, 18 (Fall 1985): 87–154.

47. For an elaboration of my views on the military, see "A Note on the Military and Social Science Theory."

48. For a sampling, see Christian Anglade and Carlos Fortín, ed., *The State and Capital Accumulation in Latin America* (Pittsburgh, 1985); Esperanza Durán, eds., *Latin America and the World Recession* (New York, 1985); Richard Fagen, ed., *Capitalism and the State in U.S.-Latin American Relations* (Stanford, Calif., 1979); Alejandro Foxley, *Latin American Experiments in Neo-Conservative Economics* (Berkeley, 1983); Ricardo Ffrench-Davis, *Las relaciones financieras externas y su efecto en la economía latinoamericana* (Mexico City, 1983); Jonathan Hartlyn and Samuel A. Morley, eds., *Latin American Political Economy: Financial Crisis and Political Change* (Boulder, Colo., 1986); Antonio Jorge, Jorge Salazar-Carrillo, and Frank Diaz-Pou, eds., *External Debt and Development Strategy in Latin America* (Elmsford, N.Y., 1985); Rosemary Thorp and Lawrence Whitehead, eds., *Inflation and Stabilization in Latin America* (New York, 1979); Barbara Stallings, *Banker to the Third World: U.S. Portfolio Investment in Latin America 1900–1986* (Berkeley, 1987); Miguel Wionczek, ed., *Politics and Economics of Latin American Indebtedness* (Boulder, Colo., 1984).

49. Kaufman, *Trends and Priorities*, p. 40.

50. There is growing attention to public policy studies in Latin America. See Oscar Ozslak and Guillermo O'Donnell, "Estado y políticas estatales en América Latina: Hacia una estrategia de investigación," Doc. CEDES/G.E. CLASCO, No. 4 (Buenos Aires, 1976); Oscar Ozslak, "Public Policies and Political Regimes in Latin America," Woodrow Wilson International Center for Scholars, Latin America Program, Working Paper No. 139 (Washington, D.C., 1984). See also John W. Sloan, *Public Policy in Latin America: A Comparative Survey* (Pittsburgh,

1984). Insightful case studies include William Ascher, *Scheming for the Poor: Income Redistribution in Latin America* (Cambridge, Mass., 1984); Peter S. Cleaves, *Bureaucratic Politics and Administration in Chile* (Berkeley, 1974); Peter S. Cleaves and Martin Scurrah, *Agriculture, Bureaucracy, and Military Government in Peru* (Ithaca, N.Y., 1980); Merilee S. Grindle, *Bureaucrats, Politicians, and Peasants in Mexico: A Case Study in Public Policy* (Berkeley, 1977); James M. Malloy, *The Politics of Social Security in Brazil* (Pittsburgh, 1979); Peter McDonough and Amaury de Souza, *The Politics of Population in Brazil: Elite Ambivalence and Public Demand* (Austin, Tex., 1981); Susan Kaufman Purcell, *The Mexican Profit-Sharing Decision: Politics in an Authoritarian Regime* (Berkeley, 1975); Gary Wynia, *Argentina in the Postwar Era: Politics and Economic Policy-Making in a Divided Society* (Albuquerque, 1978).

51. For discussion of the appropriateness of presidentialism in Latin America, see Juan J. Linz, "Democracy: Presidential or Parliamentary, Does It Make a Difference?" Paper presented at the 83rd Annual Meeting of the American Political Science Association, Sept. 3–6, 1987, Chicago. See also Arturo Valenzuela, "Orígenes y características."

FISHLOW: Economics

1. UN Economic Commission for Latin America, *The Economic Development of Latin America in the Post-War Period* (New York, 1964), p. 1.

2. Since this discussion is necessarily brief, I limit my attention to issues of aggregate performance, to the detriment of the large literature on specific fields like industrial organization, migration and labor markets, financial institutions, and so on. Because my principal concern is the theoretical basis for economic policy rather than the history of thought, I also refrain from referring to the individual contributions of many authors, Latin American and others. For an earlier treatment in a similar vein, see Albert O. Hirschman, "Ideologies of Economic Development in Latin America," in Albert O. Hirschman, ed., *Latin American Issues* (New York, 1961), pp. 3–42.

3. For discussion of Latin American structuralism, see, among others, H. W. Arndt, "The Origins of Structuralism," *World Development*, 13 (Feb. 1985): 151–59; Werner Baer, "Import Substitution and Industrialization in Latin America: Experiences and Interpretations," *Latin American Research Review*, 7 (Spring 1972): 95–121; Carlos F. Diaz-Alejandro, "On the Import Intensity of Import Substitution," *Kyklos*, 18 (1965): 495–511; Aldo Ferrer, *The Argentine Economy* (Berkeley and Los Angeles, 1967); Albert Fishlow, "Origins and Consequences of Import Substitution in Brazil," in Luis E. DiMarco, ed., *International Economics and Development; Essays in Honor of Raúl Prebisch* (New York and London, 1972), pp. 311–65; Fishlow, "Reciprocal Trade Growth: The Latin American Integration Experience," in Moises Syrquin et al., eds., *Economic*

Structure and Performance: Essays in Honor of Hollis B. Chenery (Orlando, Fla., 1984); Celso Furtado, *Diagnosis of the Brazilian Crisis* (Berkeley and Los Angeles, 1965); M. June Flanders, "Prebisch on Protectionism: An Evaluation," *The Economic Journal*, 74 (June 1964): 305-26; Albert O. Hirschman, "The Political Economy of Import-Substituting Industrialization in Latin America," *Quarterly Journal of Economics*, 82 (Feb. 1968): 1-32; Hirschman, ed., *Latin American Issues* (New York, 1961); Nora Lustig, "Characteristics of Mexican Economic Growth: Empirical Testing of Some Latin American Structuralist Hypotheses," *Journal of Development Economics*, 10 (1982): 355-76; Guillermo A. O'Donnell, "Reflections on the Patterns of Change in the Bureaucratic-Authoritarian State," *Latin American Research Review*, 12 (Winter 1978): 3-38; Raúl Prebisch, *The Economic Development of Latin America and Its Principal Problems* (Lake Success, N.Y., 1950); Dudley Seers, "A Theory of Inflation and Growth in Underdeveloped Economies Based on the Experience of Latin America," *Oxford Economic Papers*, 14 (June 1962): 173-95; Hans Singer, "The Distribution of Gains Between Investing and Borrowing Countries," *American Economic Review*, 40 (May 1950): 473-85; Osvaldo Sunkel, "La inflación chilena: un enfoque heterodoxo," *El Trimestre Económico*, 25 (Oct.-Dec. 1958): 570-99; Maria da Conçeicão Tavares, *Da substituição de importaçoēs ao capitalismo financeiro: Ensaios sobre economia brasileira* (Rio de Janeiro, 1972).

4. For a discussion of dependency theory, see, among others, Samir Amin, *Accumulation on a World Scale: A Critique of the Theory of Underdevelopment*, vols. 1 and 2 (New York and London, 1974); Fernando Henrique Cardoso and Enzo Faletto, *Dependency and Development in Latin America* (Berkeley and Los Angeles, 1979); David Collier, ed., *The New Authoritarianism in Latin America* (Princeton, 1979); Theotonio dos Santos, "The Structure of Dependence," *American Economic Review*, 60 (May 1970): 231-36; Arghiri Emmanuel, *Unequal Exchange* (New York and London, 1972); Peter Evans, *Dependent Development: The Alliance of Multinational, State, and Local Capital in Brazil* (Princeton, 1979); Peter Evans, Dietrich Rueschmeyer, and Theda Skocpol, *Bringing the State Back In* (Cambridge, Mass., 1985); Andre Gunder Frank, *Capitalism and Underdevelopment in Latin America: Historical Studies of Chile and Brazil* (New York and London, 1967); Celso Furtado, "The Concept of External Dependence in the Study of Underdevelopment," in Charles K. Wilber, ed., *The Political Economy of Development and Underdevelopment* (New York, 1970); Gary Gereffi and Peter B. Evans, "Transnational Corporations, Dependent Development, and State Policy in the Semiperiphery: A Comparison of Brazil and Mexico," *Latin American Research Review*, 16 (1981): 31-64; Rui M. Marini, *Dialéctica de la dependencia* (Mexico City, 1973); Richard Newfarmer, ed., *Profits, Progress, and Poverty: Case Studies of International Industries in Latin America* (Notre Dame, Ind., 1985);

Gabriel Palma, "Dependency: A Formal Theory of Underdevelopment or a Methodology for the Analysis of Concrete Situations of Underdevelopment?" *World Development*, 6, nos. 7–8 (1978); José Serra and Maria da Conceição Tavares, "Màs allà del estancamiento: Una discusión sobre el estilo del desarrollo reciente en Brasil," in José Serra, ed., *Desarrollo latinoamericano: Ensayos críticos, lecturas del fondo de cultura económica*, No. 6 (Mexico City, 1974), pp. 203–48; Osvaldo Sunkel, "National Development Policy and External Dependence in Latin America," *Journal of Development Studies*, 6 (Oct. 1969): 23–48.

5. D. C. M. Platt, "Dependency in Nineteenth-Century Latin America," *Latin American Research Review*, 15 (1980): 113–50. See also the comment by S. Stein and B. Stein and the reply by Platt in the same issue.

6. See, for example, R. Berry, "Redistribution, Demand Structure, and Factor Requirements: The Case of India," *World Development*, 9 (1981): 621–36; and other case studies cited. For an excellent recent analysis of Brazil, see R. Bonelli and P. Vieira da Cunha, "Distribução de renda e padrões de crescimento: Um modelo dinámico da economia brasileira," *Pesquisa e Planejamento Econômico*, 13 (1983): 91–155.

7. For a discussion of monetarism and international monetarism, see, among others: Werner Baer and Isaac Kerstenetsky, *Inflation and Growth in Latin America* (New Haven, 1964); Nicolas Ardito Barletta, Mario I. Blejer, and Luis Landau, eds., *Economic Liberalization and Stabilization Policies in Argentina, Chile, and Uruguay: Applications of the Monetary Approach to the Balance of Payments* (Washington, D.C., 1984); Roberto de Oliveria Campos, "Two Views on Inflation in Latin America," in Albert Hirschman, ed., *Latin American Issues* (New York, 1961); Sebastian Edwards, "Stabilization with Liberalization: An Evaluation of Ten Years of Chile's Experiment with Free Market Policies," *Economic Development and Cultural Change*, 33 (Jan. 1985): 223–54; Jacob A. Frenkel and Harry G. Johnson, eds., *The Economics of Exchange Rates: Selected Studies* (Reading, Mass., 1978); Arnold C. Harberger, "The Dynamics of Inflation in Chile," in Carl Christ et al., *Measurement in Economics: Studies in Mathematical Economics and Econometrics in Honor of Y. Grenfeld* (Stanford, Calif., 1963); International Monetary Fund, *The Monetary Approach to the Balance of Payments* (Washington, D.C., 1977); A. C. Lemgruber, "Real Output–Inflation Trade-offs: Monetary Growth and Rational Expectations in Brazil, 1950–79," *Brazilian Economic Studies*, 8 (1984): 37–72; Joseph Ramos, "The Economics of Hyperstagflation: Stabilization Policy in Post-1973 Chile," *Journal of Development Economics*, 7 (Dec. 1980): 467–88; Mario Simonsen, "Inflation and Anti-Inflationary Policies in Brazil," *Brazilian Economic Studies*, 8 (1984): 1–36; Susan M. Wachter, *Latin American Inflation* (Lexington, Mass., 1976); M. Whitman,

"Global Monetarism and the Monetary Approach to the Balance of Payments," *Brookings Papers on Economic Activity,* 3 (Washington, D.C., 1975); *World Development,* 13 (Aug. 1985). Special issue: "Liberalization with Stabilization in the Southern Cone of Latin America."

8. Manuel Guitian, in T. Killick, ed., *Adjustment and Financing in the Developing World* (Washington, D.C., 1982), p. 95.

9. For a generally positive and advocatory view on outward-oriented development, see, among others, Bela Balassa, "Exports, Policy Choices, and Economic Growth in Developing Countries After the 1973 Oil Shock," *Journal of Development Economics,* 18 (May–June 1985): 23–35; Balassa, *Change and Challenge in the World Economy* (London, 1985); Balassa, "The Process of Industrial Development and Alternative Development Strategies," *Princeton Essays in International Finance,* no. 141 (Princeton, 1981); Jagdish N. Bhagwati, *Anatomy and Consequences of Exchange Control Regimes,* vol. 11 of *Foreign Trade Regimes and Economic Development* (Cambridge, Mass., 1978); William R. Cline, *Exports of Manufactures from Developing Countries: Performance and Prospects for Market Access* (Washington, D.C., 1984); Anne O. Krueger, "Comparative Advantage Development Policy Twenty Years Later," in Moises Syrquin et al., eds., *Economic Structure and Performance: Essays in Honor of Hollis B. Chenery* (Orlando, Fla., 1984); Krueger, *Liberalization Attempts and Consequences,* vol. 10 of *Foreign Trade Regimes and Economic Development* (Cambridge, Mass., 1978); Anne O. Krueger, Hal B. Lary, Terry Monson, and Narongchai Akrasanee, eds., *Trade and Employment in Developing Countries,* vols. 1–3 (Chicago, 1981–83); Jeffrey Sachs, "External Debt and Macroeconomic Performance in Latin America and East Asia," *Brookings Papers on Economic Activity,* no. 2 (Washington, D.C., 1985): pp. 523–64.

10. Anne O. Krueger, "Import Substitution Versus Export Promotion," *Finance and Development,* 22 (1985): 20.

11. Bela Balassa, "Exports and Economic Growth: Further Evidence," *Journal of Development Economics,* 5 (June 1978): 187.

12. See Anne O. Krueger, *Trade and Employment in Developing Countries,* vol. 3 (Chicago, 1983), pp. 41–46; R. Agarwala, "Price Distortions and Growth in Developing Countries," *World Bank Staff Working Papers,* no. 575 (Baltimore and London, 1983), p. 55.

13. This regression makes use of the Agarwala sample and data (see note 12, above), as do my other subsequent regressions (t-values are in parentheses and $\bar{R}^2$ is adjusted for degrees of freedom):

$$Gy = 2.06 + 0.84Ga + 0.15Gx \qquad \bar{R}^2 = 0.58$$
$$(3.6)\quad(4.8)\quad(3.2)$$

where Gy is growth of income, Ga is growth of agriculture, and Gx is growth of exports.

14. The equation is:
$$Gy = 5.2 + 0.08(Gx - Gy) \qquad \bar{R}^2 = -0.01$$
$$(11.4) \quad (0.8)$$
15. The equations are:
$$Gy = 3.5 + 0.33Gm \qquad \bar{R}^2 = 0.46$$
$$(7.9) \quad (5.1)$$
$$Gy = 3.4 + 0.10Gx + 0.27Gm \qquad \bar{R}^2 = 0.50$$
$$(8.1) \quad (1.8) \qquad (3.8)$$
16. Agarwala, "Price Distortions," pp. 3, 4.
17. *World Development Report* (Washington, D.C., 1983), p. 61.
18. The equation is:
$$Gx = 5.3 - 1.1DXR \qquad \bar{R}^2 = -0.01$$
$$(2.0) \quad (0.8)$$
where DXR is the distortion index of the exchange rate.
19. The equation is:
$$Ga = 3.8 - 0.44DA \qquad \bar{R}^2 = 0.01$$
$$(4.5) \quad (1.1)$$
where DA is the distortion index for agriculture.
20. Agarwala, "Price Distortions," p. 46.
21. For examples of the neostructuralist approach, see, among others, Edmar Bacha and Carlos F. Diaz-Alejandro, "International Financial Intermediation: A Long and Tropical View," *Princeton Essays in International Finance*, no. 147 (Princeton, 1982); Michael Bruno, "Stabilization and Stagflation in a Semi-Industrialized Economy," in Rudiger Dornbusch and Jacob Frenkel, eds., *International Economic Policy: Theory and Evidence* (Baltimore, 1979); Edward Buffie, "Financial Repression, the New Structuralists, and Stabilization Policies in Semi-Industrialized Economies," *Journal of Development Economics*, 14 (1984): 305–22; Adolfo Canitrot, "Orden social y monetarismo," *Estudios CEDES*, 4 (1983): 1–49; Carlos F. Diaz-Alejandro, "Southern Cone Stabilization Plans," in William R. Cline and Sidney Weintraub, eds., *Economic Stabilization in Developing Countries* (Washington, D.C., 1981); Rudiger Dornbusch, "Policy and Performance Links Between LDC Debtors and Industrial Nations," *Brookings Papers on Economic Activity*, no. 2 (Washington, D.C., 1985), pp. 303–56; *Estudios CIEPLAN*, 17 (1985), Numero Especial: "Deuda Externa, Industrializacion y Ahorro en America Latina"; Alejandro Foxley, *Latin American Experiments in Neoconservative Economics* (Berkeley and Los Angeles, 1984); Ricardo Ffrench-Davis, ed., *Relaciones financieras externas* (Mexico City, 1983); Ricardo Ffrench-Davis, "The Monetarist Experiment in Chile: A Critical Survey," *World Development*, 11 (1983): 905–26; Robert Frenkel, "Inflación y salario real: Un enfoque estructuralista," *Estudios CEDES*, 1984; Andre Lara Resende, "A moeda

indexada: Nem magica nem panaceia," and "A moeda indexada: Ume proposta para eliminar a inflação inercial," *Revista de Economia Política*, 5 (Apr.–June 1985): 124–29 and 130–34; Francisco L. Lopes and Edmar L. Bacha, "Inflation, Growth, and Wage Policy: A Brazilian Perspective," *Journal of Development Economics*, 13 (Aug.–Oct. 1983): 1–20; Francisco L. Lopes, "Inflação inercial, hiperinflação e desinflação: Notas e conjecturas," *Revista de Economia Política*, 5 (Apr.–June 1985): 135–51; José Antonio Ocampo, "El sector externo y la política macroeconómica," *Desarrollo y Sociedad*, 10 (Jan. 1983): 121–48 (Centro de Estudios sobre Desarrollo Económico, Facultad de Economía, Universidad de los Andes, Bogotá); PREALC, *Màs allà de la crisis* (Santiago, 1985); Juan Sourruille, "Política económica y processos de desarrollo: La experiencia argentina entre 1976 y 1981," CEPAL, 1983; Lance Taylor, *Structuralist Macroeconomics: Applicable Models for the Third World* (New York, 1983); Rene Villarreal, *La contrarrevolución monetarista* (Mexico City, 1983); Miguel S. Wionczek, ed., *Politics and Economics of External Debt Crisis: The Latin American Experience* (Boulder, Colo., 1985).

22. J. Williamson, ed., *Inflation and Indexation: Argentina, Brazil, and Israel* (Cambridge, Mass., 1985).

PORTES: Sociology

The author wishes to thank Susan Eckstein, Louis W. Goodman, J. Samuel Valenzuela, Elizabeth Jelin, and the editor of this volume for valuable comments on the original version of this chapter. None bears any responsibility for its content.

1. See, for example, my "From Dependency to Redemocratization: New Themes in Latin American Sociology," *Contemporary Sociology*, 13 (1984): 546–49; and Peter Evans, "After Dependency: Recent Studies of Class, State, and Industrialization," *Latin American Research Review*, 20 (1985): 149–60.

2. For an analysis of the impact of the authoritarian experience on intellectual life in the largest country of the region, see Bernardo Sorj and Maria Herminia Tavares de Almeida, eds., *Sociedade e politica no Brasil pos-64* (São Paulo, 1984), especially the chapters by Fernando Henrique Cardoso and Otavio Guilherme Velho. For Argentina, see Marcelo Cavarozzi, *Autoritarismo y democracia (1955–1983)* (Buenos Aires, 1983). For Chile, see Manuel A. Garretón, "Procesos políticos en un regimen autoritario: Dinámicas de institucionalización y oposición en Chile, 1973–1980," Latin American Program Working Paper, the Wilson Center, Washington, D.C., 1980. A comparative overview of the Southern Cone countries during this period is found in the collection published under the title "Sociedad civil y autoritarismo," in *Crítica y Utopía*, 6 (1982).

3. A detailed analysis of events leading to this situation is found in

my "Trends in International Research Cooperation: The Latin American Case," *The American Sociologist*, 10 (1975): 131–40.

4. Representative titles are Dagmar Raczynski and Claudia Serrano, "La cesantía: impacto sobre la mujer y la cultura popular," *Estudios CIEPLAN*, 14 (1984): 61–97; Maria del Carmen Feijoo, "Las luchas de un barrio y la memoria colectiva," *Estudios CEDES*, 4, no. 5 (1981); Clarisa Hardy and Luis Razeto, "Los nuevos actores y prácticas populares: Desafíos a la concertación," Working Paper no. 47, Centro de Estudios del Desarrollo, Santiago de Chile, 1984; Ruth C. L. Cardoso, "Movimentos sociais urbanos," in Sorj and Tavares de Almeida, eds., *Sociedade*, pp. 215–39; José A. Moises and Verena Martinez-Alier, "A revolta dos suburbanos ou 'patrao, o trem atrasou,' " in F. C. Weffort, ed., *Contradicoes urbanas e movimentos sociais* (São Paulo, 1977), pp. 13–63; Suzana Prates, "Cuando el sector formal organiza el trabajo informal: Las trabajadoras domiciliarias en la manufactura del calzado en Uruguay," Working Paper, Centro de Informaciones y Estudios del Uruguay (CIESU), Montevideo, 1983.

5. See Irving L. Horowitz, *The Rise and Fall of Project Camelot* (Cambridge, Mass., 1967); Portes, "Trends."

6. In addition to studies cited above, see Elizabeth Jelin, Juan J. Llovet, and Silvina Ramos, "Un estilo de trabajo: La investigación microsocial," paper presented to the seminar on Problems of Integration of Demographic Analysis into Social Research, Belo Horizonte, Brazil, November 1982. This paper describes the style of research adopted by Argentine sociologists, and in particular those working at CEDES for the analysis of urban popular groups and movements. Examples of research on social stratification and mobility include: Carlos Filgueira, *Expansión educacional y estratificación social in America Latina, 1960–1970* (Buenos Aires, 1977); Carlos Filgueira and Carlo Geneletti, "Estratificación y movilidad ocupacional en America Latina," *Cuadernos de la CEPAL*, 39 (1981); José Pastore and Archibald O. Haller, "The Socioeconomic Status of the Brazilian Labor Force," *Luso-Brazilian Review*, 1 (1977): 1–28; José Pastore, *Inequality and Social Mobility in Brazil* (Madison, Wisc., 1982); Neuma Aguiar, "Divisao do trabalho, tecnologia, e estratificacão social," *Dados*, 3 (1977): 110–39; José Alberto Magno de Carvalho and Charles H. Wood, "Mortality, Income Distribution, and Rural-Urban Residence in Brazil," *Population and Development Review*, 4 (1978): 405–20; Luis A. Beccaría, "Una contribución al estudio de la movilidad social en Argentina: Analisis de los resultados de una encuesta para el Gran Buenos Aires," *Desarrollo Económico*, 17 (1978): 593–618.

7. Latin American reviews of the U.S. research literature include: R. Bayce, *La investigación contemporanea en educación: Una evaluación epistemologica de teoria y metodos* (Montevideo, 1983); Carlos Filgueira, "To

Educate or Not to Educate: Is that the Question?" *CEPAL Review*, 21 (1983): 57–80; special issue of *Revista Mexicana de Sociología*, 4 (1979), dedicated to North American studies of Mexico. For concise statements about the impact of Latin American sociology on North American research, see Evans, "After Dependency"; Gary Gereffi, "A Critical Evaluation of Quantitative, Cross-National Studies of Dependency," paper presented at the panel on Dependency Theory, meetings of the International Studies Association, Toronto, 1979.

8. Susan Eckstein, *The Poverty of Revolution: The State and the Urban Poor in Mexico* (Princeton, 1977); Peter Evans, *Dependent Development* (Princeton, 1979); Gary Gereffi, *The Pharmaceutical Industry and Dependency in the Third World* (Princeton, 1983); Karen L. Remmer and Gilbert W. Merkx, "Bureaucratic Authoritarianism Revisited," *Latin American Research Review*, 17 (1982): 3–40; Stephen G. Bunker, *Underdeveloping the Amazon: Extraction, Unequal Exchange, and the Failure of the Modern State* (Urbana, Ill., 1985); Sherri Grasmuck, "Immigration, Ethnic Stratification, and Native Working-Class Discipline: Comparisons of Documented and Undocumented Dominicans," *International Migration Review*, 67 (1984): 692–713.

9. Susan Eckstein, *Poverty of Revolution*; Eckstein, "Después de la revolución: Una comparación de México y Bolivia," *Estudios Andinos*, 10 (1974–75): 5–38; Gary Gereffi and Peter Evans, "Transnational Corporations, Dependent Development, and State Policy in the Semi-Periphery: A Comparison of Brazil and Mexico," *Latin American Research Review*, 16 (1981): 31–64; Saskia Sassen-Koob, "Direct Foreign Investment: A Migration Push Factor?" *Government and Policy*, 2 (1984): 399–416; William L. Canak, "The Peripheral State Debate: State Capitalist and Bureaucratic-Authoritarian Regimes in Latin America," *Latin American Research Review*, 19 (1984): 3–36.

10. For examples of this recent literature, see Carlos Filgueira, "Mediación política y apertura democrática en el Uruguay," in C. Gillespie, L. Goodman, J. Rial, and P. Winn, eds., *Uruguay y la democracia* (Montevideo, 1985), pp. 53–75; Norbert Lechner, "Especificando la política," *Crítica y Utopía*, 8 (1982): 31–52.

11. See Neil Smelser, *Essays in Sociological Explanation* (Englewood Cliffs, N.J., 1968), p. 138.

12. Kenneth Bollen and Robert W. Jackman, "Political Democracy and the Size Distribution of Income," *American Sociological Review*, 50 (1985): 438–57.

13. Cavarozzi, *Autoritarismo y democracia*.

14. Fernando Henrique Cardoso, "La democracia en las sociedades contemporaneas," *Crítica y Utopía*, 6 (1982): 25–38.

15. Ibid. Also see Portes, "From Dependency."

16. Volker Bornschier and Christopher Chase-Dunn, *Transnational*

Corporations and Underdevelopment (New York, 1985). Also see Volker Bornschier, Christopher Chase-Dunn, and Richard Rubinson, "Cross-national Growth and Inequality," *American Journal of Sociology*, 84 (1978): 651–83.

17. See Gereffi, "Critical Evaluation"; Fernando Henrique Cardoso, "The Consumption of Dependency Theory in the United States," *Latin American Research Review*, 12 (1977): 7–24.

18. Heather Jo Hammer and John Gartrell, "American Penetration and Canadian Development: A Case Study of Mature Dependency," *American Sociological Review*, 51 (1986): 201–13.

19. See Immanuel Wallerstein, *The Modern World-System* (New York, 1974); Terence K. Hopkins and Immanuel Wallerstein, "Patterns of Development of the Modern World-System," *Review*, 1 (1977): 111–45. Also see Andre Gunder Frank, *World Accumulation, 1492–1789* (New York, 1978); Daniel Chirot, *Social Change in the Twentieth Century* (New York, 1977).

20. As examples, see Evans, *Dependent Development*; Bunker, *Underdeveloping the Amazon*; Frederick C. Deyo, "Proletarianization, Community Structure, and Worker Power: The Latin American and Asian Newly-Industrialized Countries," paper presented at the meetings of the Latin American Studies Association, Albuquerque, New Mexico, April 1985. Also see my "Latin American Class Structures: Their Composition and Change During the Last Decades," *Latin American Research Review*, 20 (1985): 7–39.

21. A fine non–Latin American example is a recent case study of offshore electronics production in Hong Kong, which shows how, through creative state policies, a "platform" industry established to take advantage of cheap Chinese labor was gradually transformed into a domestic industry with a rapidly expanding technological base. See Jeff Henderson, "Plant Relocation and Its Aftermath: Off-shore Electronics Production in Hong Kong," Working Paper, Department of Sociology, University of Hong Kong, 1985.

22. See Deyo, "Proletarianization." Also see Frederick C. Deyo, "Export Manufacturing and Labor: The Asian Case," paper presented at the workshop on The Political Economy of Development in Latin America and East Asia, University of California–San Diego, December 1985; and Gary Gereffi, "Power and Dependency in an Interdependent World: A Guide to Understanding the Contemporary Global Crisis," *International Journal of Comparative Sociology*, 25 (1984): 91–113.

23. George M. Thomas and John Mayer, "The Expansion of the State," *Annual Review of Sociology*, 10 (1984): 461–82; John Boli-Bennett, "Global Integration and the Universal Increase of State Dominance," in A. Bergesen, ed., *Studies of the Modern World-System* (New York, 1980), pp. 77–107; Joseph A. Kahl, *Modernization, Exploitation, and Dependency*

in *Latin America* (New Brunswick, N.J., 1976); Janice E. Perlman, *The Myth of Marginality: Urban Poverty and Politics in Rio de Janeiro* (Berkeley, 1976); Eckstein, *Poverty of Revolution*; Guillermo O'Donnell, "Tensions in the Bureaucratic-State and the Question of Democracy," in D. Collier, ed., *The New Authoritarianism in Latin America* (Princeton, 1979), pp. 285–318; Norbert Lechner, "El proyecto neoconservador y la democracia," *Crítica y Utopía*, 6 (1982): 39–78; Fernando Henrique Cardoso, "On the Characterization of Authoritarian Regimes in Latin America," in Collier, ed., *New Authoritarianism*, pp. 33–57; Glaucio A. Soares, "After the Miracle," *Luso-Brazilian Review*, 15 (1978): 278–301.

24. See, for example, Maria Patricia Fernandez-Kelly, "Mexican Border Industrialization, Female Labor Force Participation, and Migration," in J. Nash and M. P. Fernandez-Kelly, eds., *Women, Men, and the International Division of Labor* (Albany, N.Y., 1983), pp. 205–23; Manuel Castells, "Small Business in a World Economy: The Hong Kong Model, Myth and Reality," in Alejandro Portes, ed., *The Urban Informal Sector: Recent Trends in Research and Theory* (Baltimore, 1984), pp. 161–223; Saskia Sassen-Koob, "Labor Migration and the New Industrial Division of Labor," in Nash and Fernandez-Kelly, eds., *Women, Men*, pp. 175–204; Aihura Ong, "Global Industries and Malay Peasants in Peninsular Malaysia," ibid., pp. 407–25; Grasmuck, "Immigration"; Lourdes Beneria, "Industrial Home Work and the Decentralization of Modern Production," in Portes, ed., *Urban Informal Sector*, pp. 1–21.

25. John Walton, *Capital and Labour in the Urbanized World* (London, 1985), p. 4.

26. See Michael J. Piore and Charles Sabel, *The Second Industrial Divide* (New York, 1984), chap. 9.

27. Walton, *Capital and Labour*, p. 4.

28. See Saskia Sassen-Koob, "Growth and Informalization at the Core: The Case of New York City," in Portes, ed., *Urban Informal Sector*, pp. 492–518. Also see my "The Informal Sector: Definition, Controversy, and Relation to National Development," *Review*, 7 (1983): 295–315; Roger Waldinger, "Immigration and Industrial Change in the New York City Apparel Industry," in G. J. Borjas and M. Tienda, eds., *Hispanics in the U.S. Economy* (New York, 1985), pp. 323–49.

29. Jorge Balan, Harley L. Browning, and Elizabeth Jelin, *Men in a Developing Society: Geographic and Social Mobility in Monterrey, Mexico* (Austin, Tex., 1973).

30. The results of these collaborations are apparent in a series of publications in English, Spanish, and Portuguese. See the articles by Magno de Carvalho and Wood and by Pastore and Haller, cited above. Also see A. O. Haller and José Pastore, "Labor Market Segmentation, Sex, and Income in Brazil," Paper presented at the 6th World Congress of the International Industrial Relations Associations, Kyoto, March

1983; Bernardo Sorj, Fernando Henrique Cardoso, and Mauricio Font, eds., *Economía e movimentos sociais na America Latina* (São Paulo, 1985).

31. Recent examples of research from a global comparative perspective include: Deyo, "Proletarianization"; Saskia Sassen-Koob, "Direct Foreign Investment"; John Walton, *Reluctant Rebels: Comparative Studies of Revolution and Underdevelopment* (New York, 1984); and Peter B. Evans, "Transnational Linkages and the Economic Role of the State: An Analysis of Developing and Industrialized Nations in the Post–World War II Period," in P. B. Evans, D. Rueschemeyer, and T. Skocpol, eds., *Bringing the State Back In* (New York, 1985), pp. 192–226.

32. Mark Granovetter, "Economic Action and Social Structure: The Problem of Embeddedness," *American Journal of Sociology*, 91 (1985): 481–510.

ARIZPE: Anthropology

1. Two reviews of such studies can be found in Florestan Fernandes, *Investigação etnológica no Brasil e outros ensaios* (Petrópolis, Brazil, 1975); Julio Cesar Melatti, "A etnólogia das populações indígenas do Brasil: Nas duas últimas décadas," in *Anuario Antropológico, 80* (Rio de Janeiro, 1982).

2. Robert Redfield, *The Little Community and Peasant Society and Culture* (Chicago, 1960); Manuel Gamio, *El valle de Teotihuacán* (Mexico, 1979); Oscar Lewis, *Life in a Mexican Village: Tepoztlán Restudied* (Urbana, Ill., 1951); Bernard Mishkin, "The Contemporary Quechua," in Julian Haynes Steward, ed., *Handbook of South American Indians* (Washington, D.C., 1946), vol. 2, pp. 411–70; George Foster, *Tzintzuntzán* (Boston, 1967).

3. Gonzolo Aguirre Beltrán, *Regiones de refugio* (Mexico, 1981); Eric Wolf, *Peasants* (Englewood Cliffs, N.J., 1966).

4. Rodolfo Stavenhagen, *Las clases sociales en las sociedades agrarias* (Mexico, 1968).

5. José Matos Mar, ed., *Perú problema* (Lima, 1968).

6. Orlando Fals Borda, *Crítica y política en ciencias sociales: El debate sobre la teoría y la práctica*, 2 vols. (Bogotá, 1978). More recently, there is Orlando Fals Borda, *Conocimiento popular* (Mexico, 1986).

7. Paulo Freire, *Pedagogy of the Oppressed* (New York, 1970).

8. Cynthia Hewitt de Alcántara, "Boundaries and Paradigms: The Anthropological Study of Rural Life in Postrevolutionary Mexico," M.A. thesis, Institute of Social Studies, The Hague, 1982, p. 185 (to be published).

9. Darcy Ribeiro, *Os indios e a civilização: A integração das populações indígenas no Brasil moderno* (Rio de Janeiro, 1970).

10. Judy Friedlander, *Being Indian in Hueyapan* (New York, 1975).

11. Lourdes Arizpe, *Migración, etnicismo y cambio económico* (Mexico City, 1978).

12. Salomon Nahmad, "La política indigenista," in *Boletín del Instituto Nacional Indigenista* (Mexico City, 1982).

13. José Matos Mar, *Peru ¿País bilingüe?* (Lima, 1975); Felix Baez-Jorge and A. Rivera Balderas, "La educación bilingüe y bicultural ¿encrucijada de lealtades o conflictos de clase?" in *Educación, etnias y descolonización en América Latina* (Mexico, 1983), pp. 265–80.

14. Matos Mar, *Perú problema*; Rodolfo Stavenhagen, "La sociedad plural en América Latina," *Diálogos*, 55 (1974): 5–8; Lourdes Arizpe, *El reto del pluralismo cultural* (Mexico, 1978).

15. Recent publications: Manuel Ortega Hass, "El conflicto etnianación en Nicaragua," in *Civilización: Configuraciones de la diversidad* (Mexico, 1984), pp. 359–81; Philippe Bourgeois, "Las minorías étnicas en la revolución nicaragüense," ibid., pp. 111–39.

16. Leonel Durán et al., *Cultura popular y políticas culturales* (Mexico, 1983).

17. W. Dostal, ed., *The Situation of the Indian in South America* (Geneva, 1972). The work of Robert Jaulin on ethnocide was also influential in the early seventies. For more recent literature, see Silvia Rivera Cuzicanqui's important book *Oprimidos pero no vencidos* (La Paz, Bolivia, 1986).

18. Among them are the Aymara ethnologist, Mauricio Mamani. See William Carter and Mauricio Mamani, *Irpa Chico: Individuo y comunidad en la cultura aymara* (La Paz, Bolivia, 1982). Also, in Mexico, see Jacinto Arias Sojom, *El mundo numinoso de los Mayas* (Mexico, 1978).

19. For example, the new rendering of the sacred texts of the Mayan "Popol Vuh" by a native ki-che speaker from Guatemala: Adrián Chávez, *Pop Wuj* (Mexico, 1979). Also see the work of Luís Reyes, a Nahua historian.

20. For example, Giorgio Alberti and E. Mayer, *Reciprocidad e intercambio en los Andes peruanos* (Lima, 1974).

21. John Murra, *Formaciones económicas y políticas del mundo andino* (Lima, 1975); Murra, "Current Research and Prospects in Andean Ethnohistory," *Latin American Research Review*, 5 (Spring 1970): 3–36. For more recent literature, see Nathan Wachtel, John Murra, and Jacques Revel, eds., *Historical Anthropology of Andean Polities* (Cambridge, England, 1986). The debates in Andean anthropology can be followed in *Revista Andina*, published in Cuzco.

22. Karen Spalding, *De Indio a campesino* (Lima, 1974). Also see Spalding, *Huarochirí: An Andean Society Under Inca and Spanish Rule* (Stanford, Calif., 1986).

23. See W. P. Mangin, "Thoughts on Twenty-four Years of Work in

Peru: The Vicos Project and Me," in G. C. Foster et al., *Long-Term Field Research in Social Anthropology* (New York, 1979), pp. 65–84.

24. José Matos Mar and José M. Mejía. *Reforma agraria: Logros y contradicciones, 1969–1979* (Lima, 1980); J. M. Caballero, *Agricultura, reforma agraria y pobreza campesina* (Lima, 1980).

25. Rodrigo Montoya et al., *La SAIS Cahuide y sus contradicciones* (Lima, 1974); Montoya, *Capitalismo y no capitalismo en el Perú: Un estudio histórico de su articulación en un eje regional* (Lima, 1980).

26. Among them were Michel Gutman, Alain de Janvry, Carmen Diana Deere, Norman Long, Michael Redclift, David Winder, Olivia Harris, Michael Taussig, Lasse Kranz, Robert Wasserstrom, Verena Stolcke, Kate Young, Ernest Feder, Eugene Havens, Barbara Bradby, and many others.

27. See, for example, A. V. Chayanov, *The Theory of Peasant Economy* (Homewood, Ill., 1966).

28. Ernest Feder, "Campesinistas y descampesinistas: Tres enfoques divergentes (y no incompatibles) sobre la destrucción del campesinado," *Comercio Exterior*, 27 (1977): 1439–46. For a thorough and scholarly analysis of this debate, see Hewitt de Alcántara, "Boundaries and Paradigms."

29. Among others, see Arturo Warman, *Y venimos a contradecir* (Mexico, 1976); Gustavo Esteva, *La batalla del campo* (Mexico, 1979).

30. Roger Bartra, *Estructura agraria y clases sociales en México* (Mexico, 1974); Héctor Díaz Polanco, *Teoría marxista de la economía campesina* (Mexico, 1977).

31. Armando Bartra, *La explotación del trabajo campesino por el capital* (Mexico City, 1979).

32. See Larissa Lomnitz, *Como sobreviven los marginados* (Mexico, 1976). For an excellent overview, see Ruth Cardoso, "O desafio da cidade: Reflexões sobre o trabalho do antropólogo urbano," in *Anuario antropológico 80* (Rio de Janeiro, 1982); Lomnitz, *A aventura antropológica* (São Paulo, 1986). In fact, Brazilian anthropology is flourishing in the eighties, through the work of, among others, Roberto Da Matta, Ruth Cardoso, and Roberto Cardoso de Oliveira. From the latter, see *Tempo y tradição* (Brasilia, 1984); *Lectura de cultura de una prospectiva antropológica* (Brasilia, 1985).

33. See Betty Meggers, *Amazonia: Man and Culture in a Counterfeit Paradise* (Chicago, 1974); Daniel Gross, "Protein Capture and Cultural Development of the Amazon Basin," *American Anthropologist*, 77 (1975): 526–49; Katherine Milton, "Protein and Carbohydrate Resources of the Mahu Indians of Northwest Amazonia," *American Anthropologist*, 86 (1984): 7–27.

34. Andrew Fuchs, "Coca Chewing and High-Altitude Stress: Possi-

ble Effects of Coca Alkaloids on Erythropoiesis," *Current Anthropology*, 19 (1978): 277–93.

35. See Carmen Diana Deere and Magdalena Leon, "Peasant Production: Proletarianization and the Sexual Division of Labor in the Andes," *Signs*, 7 (1981): 338–60.

36. See Magdalena Leon, *Las trabajadoras del agro* (Bogotá, 1982); Kate Young, "Modes of Appropriation and the Sexual Division of Labor: A Case Study from Oaxaca, Mexico," in A. Kuhn and A. Wolpe, eds., *Feminism and Materialism* (London, 1978); Susan Bourque and Kay Warren, *Women of the Andes: Patriarchy and Social Change in Two Peruvian Towns* (Ann Arbor, 1981).

37. As examples of such research, see Helen Safa, "Women, Production, and Reproduction in Industrial Capitalism: A Comparison of Brazilian and U.S. Factory Workers," in June Nash and María Patricia Fernández-Kelly, eds., *Women, Men, and the International Division of Labor* (Albany, N.Y., 1984); Lourdes Arizpe and Josefina Aranda, "Women Workers in the Strawberry Agribusiness in Mexico," in Eleanor Leacock and Helen Safa, eds., *Women's Work: Development and the Division of Labor by Gender* (South Hadley, Mass., 1986); María Patricia Fernández-Kelly, *For We Are Sold, I and My People: Women and Industry in Mexico's Frontier* (Albany, N.Y., 1983).

SOSNOWSKI: Literary Criticism

1. "La crítica literaria hoy" [Literary Criticism Today], *Texto Crítico*, 3, no. 6 (1979): 6–36. Respondents were Enrique Anderson Imbert, Antonio Cornejo Polar, José Pedro Díaz, Roberto Fernández Retamar, Margo Glantz, Domingo Miliani, José Miguel Oviedo, and Saúl Sosnowski.

Hugo Achugar, "Notas para un debate sobre la crítica literaria latinoamericana" [Notes for a Debate on Latin American Literary Criticism], *Casa de las Américas*, 19, no. 110 (1978): 3–18.

Jean Franco, "Trends and Priorities for Research on Latin America in the 1980's (Latin American Literature)," The Wilson Center Working Papers, no. 111 (Washington, D.C., 1981), pp. 25–35. This essay has been published as "Tendencias y prioridades de los estudios literarios latinoamericanos" [Trends and Priorities in Latin American Literary Studies], in *Escritura*, 6, no. 11 (1981): 7–20; also in *Ideologies and Literature*, 4, no. 16 (1983): 107–20, in a special issue devoted to "Problemas para la crítica socio-histórica de la literatura: Un estado de las artes" [Problems for Social-Historical Criticism of Literature: A State of the Art]. Attention should also be paid in that issue to the adjustments presented in alternate views in Hernán Vidal's "Para una redefinición culturalista de la crítica literaria latinoamericana" [For a Culturalist Redefinition of Latin American Literary Criticism], pp. 121–32, and in René Jara's "Crítica de una crisis: Los estudios literarios hispanoamericanos" [Criticism of a Crisis: Spanish-American Literary Studies], pp, 330–52.

Continuing reviews and updates of criticism are regularly offered by the very nature of several literary journals. As was shown by Francine R. Masiello in the case of Argentina, these are useful for recording and measuring the changes in the conception and function of the critical enterprise. See Francine R. Masiello, "Argentine Literary Journalism: The Production of a Critical Discourse," *Latin American Research Review*, 20, no. 1 (1985): 27–60.

Diana Sorensen Goodrich has done an analytic synthesis of the theoretical approaches that have been of interest to U.S. and European criticism. Forcefully, inevitably, and, in the best of cases, fortunately, these approaches are being assimilated into Latin American critical thinking. See Diana Sorensen Goodrich, "La crítica de la lectura: Puesta al día" [Reader Response Criticism: An Update], *Escritura*, 6, no. 11 (1981): 21–74; Goodrich, "Rezeptionaesthetik: Teoría de la recepción alemana" [Reception Aesthetic: German Reception Theory], *Escritura*, 6, no. 12 (1981): 219–46. In this same issue (pp. 247–61), Terry Eagleton reviews and criticizes "El idealismo de la crítica norteamericana" [The Idealism of North American Criticism].

In addition, there exist reviews and bibliographical annuals that list or account for the state of literary criticism in their respective countries.

2. Without any desire to exclude other meritorious publications or to impose dogmatic emphases, within the U.S., and mostly through the contribution of Latin American critics, it is possible to offer as examples of opposing positions the selections and prominence given to Latin American literature by the journals *Diacritics* (Ithaca, N.Y.) and *Ideologies and Literature* (Minneapolis, Minn.). Their respective transparent preference for extraliterary options is evident from the way these journals favor definitions that are radically different from the ample critical coverage that spans practice. Some of the interests of *Diacritics*, of greater breadth in the theoretical debate, can be seen in the issues devoted to Latin American literature (Winter 1974 and Winter 1978), with texts by Rolena Adorno, Roberto González Echeverría, Alicia Borinsky, Lucille Kerr, Emir Rodríguez Monegal, Irlemar Chiampi Cortez, John Deredita, Enrico Mario Santí, and Octavio Paz, and with interviews of Julio Cortázar and Roberto Fernández Retamar.

3. Carlos Fuentes, *La nueva novela hispanoamericana* [The New Spanish-American Novel] (Mexico City, 1969), and José Donoso, *Historia personal del "boom"* [A Personal History of the "Boom"] (Barcelona, 1972), contribute two interpretive levels of the changes that took place in the

1960's. Emir Rodríguez Monegal contributes to the Boom's greater institutionalization through *Mundo Nuevo* and the texts collected in *El boom de la novela hispanoamericana* [The Boom of the Spanish-American Novel] (Caracas, 1972). Jean Franco noted the changes in "Narrador, autor, superestrella: La narrativa latinoamericana en la época de cultura de masas" [Narrator, Author, Superstar: Latin American Literature in the Era of Mass Culture], *Revista Iberoamericana*, 114 and 115 (1981). Also see: Angel Rama, "*El boom* en perspectiva" [*The Boom* in Perspective], *Escritura*, 7 (1979): 3–45; and the broad view of Tulio Halperín Donghi, "Nueva narrativa y ciencias sociales hispanoamericanas en la década del sesenta" [The New Narrative and Spanish-American Social Sciences in the 60's], *Hispamérica*, 9, no. 27 (1980): 3–18.

Fuentes's essay serves as a useful reminder of the work carried out by other Spanish-American prose fiction writers and poets who, through their own essays, have helped close the gap between theoretical thought and the practice of literature. Borges, Paz, and Lezama Lima are prime examples of the bridge that supports the multiple levels of literary production.

4. See Pierre Bourdieu, "Campo intelectual, campo del poder y hábitos de clase" [Intellectual Field, Field of Power, and Class Habitus], in *Campo del poder y campo intelectual* [Field of Power and Intellectual Field] (Buenos Aires, 1983), pp. 9–35. The original version was published in *Scoliès* in 1971. Bourdieu reformulates some questions central to a certain line of criticism in order to analyze the relationship between the intellectual, his production and social relationship, and how the space set aside for him leads the intellectual to adopt a particular aesthetic or ideological position linked to the position he occupies. That which leads to an understanding of the specific properties of a certain grouping of works, for example, can also be very useful for tracing an integral outline of the critical enterprise in varying *habitus* ("the system of unconscious inclinations produced by internalizing objective structures" [p. 35]) identified in this work.

5. Among the very significant contributions are Jaime Rest, *El laberinto del universo: Borges y el pensamiento nominalista* [The Labyrinth of the Universe: Borges and Nominalist Thought] (Buenos Aires, 1976); John Sturrock, *Paper Tigers: The Ideal Fictions of Jorge Luis Borges* (Oxford, 1977); Emir Rodríguez Monegal, *Jorge Luis Borges: A Literary Biography* (New York, 1978); Silvia Molloy, *Las letras de Borges* [Borges's Writing] (Buenos Aires, 1979); Arturo Echevarría, *Lengua y literatura de Borges* [Borges's Language and Literature] (Barcelona, 1983); the enlarged edition of Ana María Barrenechea, *La expresión de la irrealidad en la obra de Borges* [The Expression of Unreality in the Work of Borges] (Buenos Aires, 1984)—the English expanded version of the first edition was titled *Borges, the Labyrinth Maker*. A useful overview of the bibliography

is found in David William Foster, *Jorge Luis Borges: An Annotated Primary and Secondary Bibliography* (New York and London, 1984).

6. Proofs abound in the annual bibliographical entries of *Publications of the Modern Language Association of America (PMLA)*, in *Hispanic American Periodical Index (HAPI)*, and in the biannual annotated selections in *The Handbook of Latin American Studies*. These sources render unnecessary the repetition here of excessive bibliographical lists.

7. A significant contribution on this issue is Irlemar Chiampi, *O realismo maravilhoso: Forma e ideología no romance hispano-americano* [Magical Realism: Form and Ideology in the Spanish-American Novel] (São Paulo, 1980). Of importance is the reading that Alexis Márquez Rodríguez proposes in *Lo barroco y lo real–maravilloso en la obra de Alejo Carpentier* [The Baroque and the Real-Marvelous in the Work of Alejo Carpentier] (Mexico City, 1982).

8. Three singular examples that document the well-assimilated and integrated readings of three *fundamentally* different approaches are Germán Leopoldo García, *Macedonio Fernández: La escritura en objeto* [Macedonio Fernández: Writing into Object] (Buenos Aires, 1975); Josefina Ludmer, *Onetti: Los procesos de construcción del relato* [Onetti: The Process of Constructing Fiction] (Buenos Aires, 1977)—unique for its excellence in Onetti criticism; George Yúdice, *Vicente Huidobro y la motivación del lenguaje* [Vicente Huidobro and the Motivation of Language] (Buenos Aires, 1978). There are, of course, excellent articles that develop every one of these lines; I am only citing three of the books to avoid an overabundance of citations.

9. Hugo Verani's recent publication, *Octavio Paz: Bibliografía crítica* [Octavio Paz: A Critical Bibliography] (Mexico City, 1983), with over two thousand entries, is a clear indication of this tendency.

10. High levels of narrative experimentation have stirred the interest of numerous critics who cut out and tailor the literary page to their measure. See, for example, the lists of works on José Lezama Lima, to cite a highly demanding and challenging literary accomplishment. This line of analysis is unrestrained as it also affects texts that suggest additional readings; this is confirmed, for example, by the occasional reductions of Roberto Arlt to synthetic formulaic combinations. An example of solid criticism that draws together, joins, suggests, and sums up the different stages of literary production, while also dispensing with obvious pigeonholes, is found in Saúl Yurkievich, *A través de la trama* [Through the Plot] (Barcelona, 1984).

11. Two different approaches appear in Carlos Rincón, *El cambio en la noción de literatura* [The Change in the Notion of Literature] (Bogotá, 1978); Angel Rama, "La tecnificación narrativa" [Narrative Technification], *Hispamérica*, 10, no. 30 (1981): 29–82. The growing interest in

Hans Robert Jauss, Wolfgang Iser, and reception theory is another sign of multiple needs.

12. The discussion of the "Padilla Affair" was published in the first issue (1971) of the journal *Libre* (Paris), edited by Juan Goytisolo, pp. 95–145.

13. A recent text establishes a map of Chicano literature, setting the first use of the term in 1848, and fixing the renewal of its literary tradition in the mid-1960's. See Julio A. Martínez and Francisco A. Lomelí, eds., *Chicano Literature: A Reference Guide* (Westport, Conn., 1985).

14. See Pedro Henríquez Ureña, *Literary Currents in Hispanic America* (Cambridge, Mass., 1945) [Las corrientes literarias en la América Hispánica (Mexico City, 1949)]. On another level, he had already expressed a well-defined intellectual coherence in *Seis ensayos en busca de nuestra expresión* [Six Essays in Search of Our Expression] (Buenos Aires, 1928). Also see José Juan Arrom, *Esquema generacional de las letras hispanoamericanas* [A Generational Outline of Spanish-American Literature], 2d ed. (Bogotá, 1977); and Cedomil Goić, *Historia de la novela hispanoamericana* [History of the Spanish-American Novel] (Valparaíso, 1972). In "Crítica hispanoamericana: La cuestión del método generacional" [Spanish-American Criticism: The Question of the Generational Method], M. A. Giella, P. Roster, and L. Urbina obtained comments and criticism from Goić, Arrom, Enrique Anderson Imbert, Luis Leal, José Olivio Jiménez, Luis Mario Shneider, and Jaime Concha (*Hispamérica*, 9, no. 27 [1980]: 47–67 [includes bibliographies]). Another attempt at a concise presentation is by John Brushwood, *The Spanish-American Novel: A Twentieth-Century Survey* (Austin, Tex., 1975) [*La novela hispanoamericana del siglo XX: Una vista panorámica* (Mexico City, 1984)]. Different observations characterize Carlos Monsiváis, "Proyecto de periodización de la historia cultural de México" [A periodization plan for Mexico's cultural history], *Texto Crítico*, 1, no. 2 (1975): 91–102.

15. Alejandro Losada, "Bases para un proyecto de una historia social de la literatura en América Latina, 1780–1970" [Bases for a Plan for a Social History of Latin American Literature, 1780–1970], *Revista Iberoamericana*, 114–115 (1980): 167–88; Losada, "Articulación, periodización, y diferenciación de los procesos literarios en América Latina" [Articulation, Periodization, and Differentiation of Literary Processes in Latin America], *Revista de crítica literaria latinoamericana*, 9, no. 17 (1983): 7–37 (includes bibliographies). This monographic issue on "Sociedad y literatura en América Latina" [Society and Literature in Latin America] was guest-edited by Losada.

16. See, by Angel Rama: "Indagación de la ideología en la poesía: Los dípticos seriados de *Versos sencillos* de José Martí [Inquiry into

Ideology in Poetry: The Serial Diptychs of *Versos sencillos* by José Martí], *Revista Iberoamericana* 112–113 (1980): 353–400; *Rubén Darío y el modernismo: Circunstancia socio-económica de un arte americano* [Rubén Darío and Modernism: The Socio-economic Circumstance of an American Art] (Caracas, 1970); prologue to *Poesías* (Caracas, 1977); and, most especially, *Transculturación narrativa en América Latina* [Narrative Transculturation in Latin America] (Mexico City, 1982). In a dialogue that was cut short tragically, Alejandro Losada pointed out areas of disagreement with some of Rama's interpretations in his "La contribución de Angel Rama a la historia social de la literatura latinoamericana" [Angel Rama's Contribution to the Social History of Latin American Literature], *Casa de las Américas*, 150 (1985): 44–57.

17. See Roberto Fernández Retamar, *Para una teoría de la literatura hispanoamericana y otras aproximaciones* [For a Theory of Spanish-American Literature and Other Approaches] (La Habana, 1975), especially pp. 53–93; Françoise Pérus, *Literatura y sociedad en América Latina: El modernismo* [Literature and Society in Latin America: Modernism] (La Habana, 1976); Hernán Vidal, *Literatura hispanoamericana e ideología liberal: Surgimiento y crisis (Una problemática sobre la dependencia en torno a la narrativa del boom* [Spanish-American Literature and Liberal Ideology: Emergence and Crisis (Problems of Dependence with Regard to the Narrative of the Boom)] (Buenos Aires, 1976); Vidal, *Sentido y práctica de la crítica literaria socio-histórica: Panfleto para la proposición de una arqueología acotada* [Meaning and Practice of Socio-Historical Literary Criticism: Pamphlet for the Proposal of a Select Archaeology] (Minneapolis, 1984). On these issues, Rafael Gutiérrez Girardot's considerations are noteworthy. See his "Literatura y sociedad" [Literature and Society], *Texto Crítico*, 3, no. 8 (1977): 3–26.

18. Starting points are found in, among others, Walter Mignolo, "Semantización de la ficción literaria" [Semanticization of Literary Fiction], *Dispositio*, 5–6, nos. 15–16 (1980–81): 85–127; Enrique Ballón Aguirre, "La escritura poetológica: César Vallejo, cronista" [Poetological Writing: César Vallejo, Chronicler], *Lexis*, 6, no. 1 (1982): 57–98—more than in his *Vallejo como paradigma: Un caso especial de escritura* [Vallejo as Paradigm: A Special Case of Writing] (Lima, 1974); in the varied readings of Ana María Barrenechea, *Textos hispanoamericanos: De Sarmiento a Sarduy* [Spanish-American Texts: From Sarmiento to Sarduy] (Caracas, 1978); and in the useful manual by Desiderio Blanco and Raúl Bueno, *Metodología de análisis semiótico* [Methodology of Semiotic Analysis] (Lima, 1980). A solid display of the confluence of artificially divergent approaches is found in Nelson Osorio T., "Lenguaje narrativo y estructura significativa de *El señor presidente* de Asturias" [Narrative Language and Significant Structure in Asturias's *Mr. President*] *Escritura*, 5–6 (1978): 99–156. Also see Josefina Ludmer, "*Tres tristes tigres*: Ordenes

literarios y jerarquías sociales" [*Three Trapped Tigers*: Literary Orders and Social Hierarchies], *Revista Iberoamericana*, 108–9 (1979): 493–512.

19. Given his multiple essays, it may be appropriate to situate Noé Jitrik in this context. See, for example: *El fuego de la especie* [The Fire of the Species] (Buenos Aires, 1971); *El no existente caballero: La idea del personaje y su evolución en la narrativa latinoamericana* [The Nonexistent Gentleman: The Notion of the Character and His Evolution in Latin American Prose Fiction] (Buenos Aires, 1975); "Entre el dinero y el ser: Lectura de *El juguete rabioso* de Roberto Arlt" [Between Money and Being: A Reading of *El juguete rabioso* by Roberto Arlt], *Escritura*, 1, no. 1 (1976): 3–39, incorporated into the valuable *La memoria compartida* [Shared Memory] (Xalapa, Mexico, 1982). The heterodoxy that characterizes the critical enterprise of David Viñas is of another kind, as is that which is seen in the criticism of Carlos Altamirano and Beatriz Sarlo in the highly didactic *Literatura/Sociedad* [Literature/Society] (Buenos Aires, 1983).

20. Antonio Cornejo Polar has published essential texts on this issue. See, for example, "El indigenismo y las literaturas heterogéneas: Su doble estatuto socio-cultural" [Indigenism and Heterogeneous Literatures: Their Double Sociocultural Statute], in his *Sobre literatura y crítica latinoamericanas* [On Latin American Literature and Criticism] (Caracas, 1982). The very useful first part of this collection attempts to outline the corpus that should be accounted for by the integral criticism of Latin American literature. The other works on indigenism collected here complement Cornejo Polar's *La novela peruana: Siete ensayos* [The Peruvian Novel: Seven Essays] (Lima, 1977). Another national review is found in Agustín Cueva, "En pos de la historicidad perdida: Contribución al debate sobre la literatura indigenista del Ecuador" [In Search of Lost Historicity: A Contribution to the Debate on Indigenist Literature in Ecuador], *Revista de Crítica Literaria Latinoamericana*, 7–8 (1978): 23–38.

21. The dimensions of this process can be noted in the abundant information and analysis found in Lynn Cortina, *Spanish-American Women Writers: A Bibliographical Research Checklist* (New York and London, 1983), an abundance that has certainly grown since its publication.

22. The index of *Latin American Theatre Review* (Lawrence, Kansas) permits us to confirm these efforts. The publications of Girol Books (Ottawa, Ont., Canada) have begun to respond to academic demands. *Conjunto* (La Habana) continues to provide a wealth of informative material connected to Cuba's cultural politics.

23. The interest in Sor Juana is endless. In addition to the many articles that analyze partial segments of her work, one should add the bibliographical accomplishment of Francisco de la Maza, comp., *Sor Juana Inés de la Cruz ante la historia: Biografías antiguas; La fama de 1700*;

noticias de 1667 a 1892 [Sor Juana Inés de la Cruz Facing History: Old Biographies; The Fame of 1700; News from 1667 to 1892] (Mexico City, 1980); and the monumental and highly debated reading offered by Octavio Paz, *Sor Juana Inés de la Cruz o las trampas de la fe* [Sor Juana Inés de la Cruz or the Pitfalls of Faith] (Barcelona, 1982).

Guamán Poma de Ayala has generated sustained interest and has yielded excellent scholarly results in, among others, Mercedes López-Baralt, "Guamán Poma de Ayala y el arte de la memoria en una crónica ilustrada del siglo XVII" ["Guamán Poma de Ayala and the Art of Memory in an Illustrated Chronicle of the Seventeenth Century], *Cuadernos Americanos*, 224 (1979): 119–51. Collective volumes and special issues of journals have contributed to the dissemination of texts that still await additional analysis and the outline of a provisional jurisdictional map. See, for example, Rolena Adorno, ed., *From Oral to Written Expression: Native Andean Chronicles of the Early Colonial Period* (Syracuse, N.Y., 1982); Raquel Chang-Rodríguez et al., *Prosa hispanoamericana virreinal* [Spanish-American Prose of the Viceroyalty] (Barcelona, 1978); the essays of the *Congreso Internacional de Literatura Iberoamericana*, 3 vols. (Madrid, 1978), devoted to the American Baroque; issues 104–5 (1978) of the *Revista Iberoamericana*, dedicated to Irving A. Leonard. The publication of the meticulous critical edition of Felipe Guamán Poma de Ayala's *El primer Nueva Corónica y Buen Gobierno* (Mexico City, 1980), edited by John V. Murra and Rolena Adorno, is a particularly praiseworthy scholarly contribution.

Well-deserved recognition and praise for its contributions to the knowledge of this area of Latin American culture are due to the Biblioteca Ayacucho for its publication of volumes devoted to, in order of publication: the Inca Garcilaso de la Vega (by Aurelio Miró Quesada); the literature of Old Mexico (by Miguel León-Portilla); Juan Miramontes y Zuazola (by Rodrigo Miró); Mayan literature (by Mercedes de la Garza); Francisco López de Gómara (by Jorge Gurria Lacroix); Guaraní literature (by Rubén Bareiro Saguier); an edition by Franklin Pease of *Nueva Corónica y Buen Gobierno*; Quechua literature (by Edmundo Bendezú Aybar); Fray Bernardino de Sahagún (by José Luis Martínez); Juan de Velasco (by Alfredo Pareja Diezcanseco); Juan Ruiz de Alarcón (by Margit Frenk); Juan de Espinosa Medrano (by Augusto Tamayo Vargas); Carlos Sigüenza y Góngora (by Irving A. Leonard); Juan del Valle y Caviedes (by Daniel R. Reedy); and Fray Bartolomé de las Casas (by André Saint-Lu).

24. In the first three issues (1982–84), one notes a marked emphasis, within the breadth of material included, on "the popular" (photonovels and other magazines, films, posters, comic strips, popular music and dances, etc.) and the role filled by these materials within, and as an interpretation of, their respective societies.

25. It is evident that political reasons have increased recent attention on Central American literature. Within the region, however—as can be seen through the proliferation of anthologies and critical works—there had been for some time a deep interest in extending the knowledge of local culture as a definition of what is at once national and Latin American. Two dissimilar examples (also insofar as their motivations and goals are concerned) are Jorge Eduardo Arellano, *Panorama de la literatura nicaragüense* [Panorama of Nicaraguan Literature] (Managua, 1982; 1st ed., 1966); Ramón Luis Acevedo, *La novela centroamericana: Desde el Popol-Vuh hasta los umbrales de la novela actual* [The Central American Novel: From the Popol-Vuh to the Beginnings of the Contemporary Novel] (Río Piedras, Puerto Rico, 1982).

26. *El aleph* (Buenos Aires, 1968), p. 45.

Index

Index

In this index an "f" after a number indicates a separate reference on the next page, and an "ff" indicates separate references on the next two pages. A continuous discussion over two or more pages is indicated by a span of page numbers, e.g., "pp. 57–58." *Passim* is used for a cluster of references in close but not consecutive sequence.

Abolitionism, 20, 30
Administration, national, *see* specific countries, organizations, types
Agriculture: agrarian reforms, 5–6, 93, 150, 155ff; plantation society, 18–19, 32; history of, 31, 46; coffee crops, 31, 56; Indians and, 38; peasant society and, 41, 44, 59, 68, 151–57; Mexican society and, 46; revolution and, 50–51; structuralism and, 90–91; taxation and, 93; growth effects, 107–10 *passim*; exploitation of, 157. *See also* specific countries, regions
Aguilar Camín, Héctor, 61, 125
Aguirre Beltrán, Gonzalo, 145
Alamán, Lucas, 48, 50
Alden, Dauril, 23

Alliance for Progress, 68, 88, 96, 123
Almond, Gabriel, 67
Alonso, Amado, 167
Amazon Basin, 126, 158
American Sociological Review, 134
American Sociology Association, 126
Andean zone, 37, 42–45, 50, 155, 176
Anna, Timothy, 51
Anthropology, 5, 29, 143–61; agrarian reform and, 5–6, 93, 150, 155f; cultural, 29, 151f, 156–57; evolution of, 143–44; social anthropology, 144, 147, 152, 185; ethnology, 144f, 149–54 *passim*; themes in, 144–47 *passim*, 158; research in, 146–60 *passim*; regional boundaries,

147–49; debates in, 148, 152–57 *passim*; Indians and, 149–54; medical, 158; structuralism and, 160–61. See also Indians; Sociology
Argentina: history of, 53–85 *passim*, 97, 132; economy of, 56, 97, 112–13; education in, 73, 139; administration of, 76, 88, 132; international monetarism and, 88–89, 102
Arguedas, José María, 172
Arizpe, Lourdes, 143
Arlt, Roberto, 165, 169
Arrom, José Juan, 174
Arteta, Nieto, 56
Asad, Talal, 147
Authoritarian regimes, see Bureaucratic-authoritarianism
Aztecs, 39, 41

Bahia, 23, 27
Bajío, 47, 50
Balan, Jorge, 140
Balance-of-payments problems, 88–94 *passim*, 100, 102–5, 112–15 *passim*
Balassa, Bela, 107
Baquero-González, García, 35
Barnet, Miguel, 177
Barrán, José Pedro, 56, 58
Basadre, Jorge, 53
Bastos, Roa, 176
Bauer, Arnold, 57f
Bergquist, Charles, 53
Bertram, Geoffrey, 56
Betéille, André, 147
Biblioteca Ayacucho project, 175
Biogenetics, 136
Black Legend, 39–40
Blacks, in Brazil, 29ff
Blanksten, George, 67
Boas, Franz, 29
Bolívar, Simon, 9, 49, 52
Bolivia, 52f, 112
Bollen, Kenneth, 132
Bonilla, Heraclio, 49f
Borah, Woodrow, 38–39, 46

Borges, Jorge Luis, 165, 169, 172, 182
Bornschier, Volker, 133
Bourbon era, 35, 37, 46f, 60
Bourricaud, François, 54
Brading, David, 46ff
Brazil: education in, 4, 24, 27–28, 34, 73, 139, 163; history of, 21–25 *passim*, 32–34; homogeneity of, 22; slave trade, 22–25 *passim*; administration of, 22–31 *passim*, 68, 126; Bahia, 23, 27; regimes of, 24, 97; Pernambuco uprising (1817), 25; bureaucratic-authoritarianism in, 28; patriarchal society, 29; African presence in, 29ff; agriculture in, 31f; economy of, 32–33, 57, 88f, 97–102 *pasim*, 111–13; military in, 88, 97; industrial production of, 99; Amazonians, 144; literature of, 163
Browning, Harley L., 140
Buenos Aires, regional studies, 37
Bunker, Stephen, 126
Bureaucratic-authoritarianism, 4, 8, 71f, 82, 85; model for, 28, 75, 97, 126; military regimes and, 37, 68f, 83, 118, 123ff, 196; state administration and, 72, 78–82 *passim*; studies of, 78, 129; literature on, 186, 198, 209
Burga, Manuel, 50
Burgin, Miron, 53
Burkholder, Mark A., 36
Burns, E. Bradford, 57
Bushnell, David, 52
Business associations, 82
Byars, Robert S., 2

Caballero y Góngora, Mario, 37
Cabrera Infante, Guillermo, 171
Camelot project, 74
Canak, William, 128
Cândido, Antônio, 29
Capital (Marx), 44
Capitalism, 135, 159

Index   231

Capital markets, 104, 115
Cardenal, Ernesto, 180
Cardoso, Fernando Henrique, 16, 30, 75, 77, 81, 130–33, 137
Cardoso, Ruth, 125
Caribbean region, 17–22, 65, 121, 137, 187
Carmagnani, Marcello, 16, 48
Carpentier, Alejo, 171, 176
Carrera Damas, Germán, 49f
Carvalho Franco, Maria Silvia de, 31
Caso, Alfonso, 150
Catholic Church, 27, 64, 68, 194
Cavarozzi, Marcelo, 132
Censorship, 9–10
Center for the Study of Economic and Social Reality (CERES), 125
Center for the Study of State and Society (CEDES), 73, 125
Central America, 45, 65, 80f, 180
Cepero Bonilla, Raul, 19
Chase-Dunn, Christopher, 133
Chayanov, A. V., 156
Chevalier, François, 47
Chile: administration of, 11, 64, 68, 82–83; local scholars of, 73; military regimes, 76, 85; economy of, 88–89, 99, 102, 107, 116; research centers in, 139; Camelot project, 148
Cicero, Father, 27
Civil rights movement, 147
Class structures, 129
Cline, Howard, 2
Coatsworth, John, 33, 46, 48, 56
Coffee agriculture, 31, 56
Colegio de México, 14
Collier, Simon, 52
Colombia, 52–56 *passim*, 64, 68, 145
Colonial society, 15, 41, 146, 155, 178; administration in, 8, 23; history of, 17, 34–48 *passim*, 51; economy of, 45, 57
Comparative advantage theory, 105
Comparative development, U.S. and, 126, 128
Consejo Latinoamericano de Ciencias Sociales (CLACSO), 73
Coronelismo, Brazilian, 27
Cortázar, Julio, 165–72 *passim*
Cortés Conde, Roberto, 56
Cosío Villegas, Daniel, 53
Costa, Emilia Viotti da, 30f
Costa Rica, 64
Cotler, Julio, 74, 146
Creoles, 36, 40, 44, 48
Cuadra, Pablo Antonio, 180
Cuba, 18–21, 64, 180, 188; revolution in, 63, 123, 171
Cultural anthropology, 29, 151f, 156–57
Cultural forms, 5, 136–37, 142
Cultural relativism, 145

Dandler, Jorge, 140
Darío, Rubén, 173
Dean, Warren, 31, 33
De Baquijano y Carrillo, José, 36–37
Debt crisis, 99, 104, 106, 111–12, 140
Deconstruction, 167f, 179
Degler, Carl, 30
De la Fuente, Julio, 145
Della Cava, Ralph, 27
Democracy, 64–86 *passim*, 119, 129, 132–33; transition to, 74f, 80ff; regimes, 85, 201
Demographic history, 38
Dependency theory, 3ff, 70–76 *passim*, 97, 99, 126, 205; model for, 76–77; historical analysis, 88; economy of, 98, 134; studies of, 131–34 *passim*, 141
De Sanctis, Francesco, 29
Devaluation, 92, 104, 111–12
Development, *see* Economic development
Díaz-Alejandro, Carlos, 56
Diégues, Manuel, 2
Direct investment, 98, 107ff
Discrimination, ethnic, 147
Doherty Foundation, 7

Domínguez, Jorge, 51
Dominican Republic, 126
Droguett, Carlos, 169
Drug use, 158

East Asia, export-led growth in, 105–8 *passim*
Eckstein, Susan, 126, 128, 137
Ecology, 156
Economic anthropology, 157–58
Economic Commission for Latin America, 87
Economic development, 90, 96, 109, 113f; theories of, 5, 8, 207; sociology in, 9, 130–39; political economy and, 33, 56–57, 84–85, 115–19; dependency theory and, 71–72, 97–100; business associations, 82; industrial sector and, 84, 90–91; structuralism and, 87–97; foreign investment administration and, 94, 98, 101, 107–10 *passim*, 136; administration and, 95, 111, 114–15; direct investment, 98, 107ff; global monetarism and, 100–109, 134–35; export-led growth and, 105–10; private sector role, 116–17; studies of, 125, 141; causes of, 133. See also Economics, national; specific countries, organizations, policies
Economics, national, 5, 99f, 136, 157; history and, 5, 32, 46, 55–56; income distribution and, 8, 46, 95, 99–100, 104, 110–14; models in, 8, 89, 92–93; state of, 35, 87–119, 134–36; market economy, 58–59, 90–91, 96, 98; import substitution and, 75, 87–88, 93–98, 137, 144; exchange rates, 89–90, 94, 96, 101–10 *passim*; devaluation, 92, 104, 111–12; inflation, 92–96, 100–102, 111–12, 117; international financial markets, 94, 96, 101–10 *passim*, 115; debt crisis, 99, 104, 106, 111–12, 140; sociological effects, 140–41. See also Economic development; specific countries
Educational policies, 125, 150
Electronics, 136
Elitism: political, 6, 55; colonial, 19, 50–51, 92–93; landowning and, 31; Indians and, 41f
Esquenazi-Mayo, Roberto, 2
Ethnology, 144f, 149–54 *passim*
Evans, Peter, 126, 128, 136
Exchange rates, 94, 96, 101–10 *passim*
Exports, 94, 105–10

Facultad Latinoamericana de Ciencias Sociales (FLACSO), 73
Fagen, Richard, 74
Faletto, Enzo, 16, 75, 77
Fals Borda, Orlando, 145f
Family structures, 27, 123–26 *passim*
Faoro, Raimundo, 24
Farriss, Nancy, 39–42 *passim*
Fausto, Boris, 28, 33
Feder, Ernest, 157
Feminist criticism, 177
Fernandes, Florestan, 6–7, 30
Fernandez, Macedonio, 165
Fernandez-Kelly, Maria Patricia, 213
Field research, 125, 131
Filgueira, Carlos, 125
Financial markets, international, 94, 96, 101–10 *passim*, 115
Fisher, John, 37
Fishlow, Albert, 87–119, 144, 159
Fitzgibbon, Russell Humke, 64, 67
Florescano, Enrique, 14, 46
Flory, Thomas, 26
Ford Foundation, 7, 74
Foreign Assistance Act, 10, 68
Foreign exchange, 89–90, 94, 96, 101–10 *passim*, 115
Foreign investment, 94, 98, 101, 107–10 *passim*, 136

Foster, George, 145
Foucault, Michel, 60, 179
Franco, Jean, 181
Frank, André Gunder, 16
Free trade reforms (1780), 35
Freire, Paulo, 146
Freyre, Gilberto, 29f
Fuentes, Carlos, 165, 169
Fulbright program, 7
Functionalism, 145
Furtado, Celso, 32

Gallo, Ezequiel, 58
Gamio, Manuel, 145
Gaos, José, 59
García Márquez, Gabriel, 176
Gereffi, Gary, 126, 128, 136
Gibson, Charles, 39–41 *passim*
Godelier, Maurice, 147
Goić, Cedomil, 174
Gold standard, 101
Gomez, R. A., 66, 74
Góngora, Mario, 48
Granovetter, Mark, 141
Grasmuck, Sherri, 126
Grassroots movements, 124f, 138–39
Great Depression, U.S., 92, 110
Great Latin American Depression, 88–89, 92
Guatemala, 44
Guerra y Sánchez, Ramiro, 18f
Guevara, Ernesto "Che," 64

Hale, Charles, 60
Haller, A. O., 140
Halperín Donghi, Tulio, 3, 7, 9, 154f, 159
Hamill, Hugh, 50
Handbook of Latin American Studies, 17
Havens, A. Eugene, 140
Henríquez Ureña, Pedro, 174
Hernandez, Felisberto, 165–69 *passim*
Hewitt de Alcántara, Cynthia, 146
Historiography: Latin American, 2, 13–62 *passim*; trends in, 6, 15–17, 20–21, 34, 56–59; political, 15, 29, 49, 56; new methods of, 60–61
History, Latin American, 8, 15, 30–38 *passim*, 59; nationalistic orientation in, 7, 15; research methods in, 13, 55, 61, 126; Latin American, 14–15; Caribbean, 17–21; Marxist, 19, 32; social history, 33–34, 40, 57–58; of ideas, 34, 59f; Colonial Spanish America era, 34–48; foreign perspectives, 35, 53; literature and, 35, 179; peasants and, 41, 44, 57; economic, 55f. *See also* Historiography; specific countries, events, persons
Holloway, Thomas, 31
Holmberg, Allan, 155
Huamanga Indians, 43
Huidobro, Vicente, 173
Human Area Files, 149
Hume, David, 100
Hunefeldt, Christine, 50
Huntington, Samuel, 67

Ianni, Octavio, 30
Iberian empire, 21–24 *passim. See also* Spanish America
Ideology, 34, 59f, 136–37
Immigration, 31, 138–41 *passim*
Imperialism, 18, 23–26 *passim*, 127
Import substitution, 75, 87–88, 93–98, 137, 144
Inca Empire, 35, 42f, 155
Income distribution, 8, 95, 99–100, 104, 110–14
Independence era, 49, 51
India, exports from, 107
Indians: militancy of, 37, 152, 160; agriculture and, 38; culture of, 38, 44, 144–52 *passim*, 159; society of, 39–43; transition to peasants, 41–44, 58, 152, 155; land control and, 47; anthropological issues, 145, 153–54; as subordinate communities, 149–

50; women and, 159. *See also* specific groups
Indigenismo participativo, 150
Industrial sector, 87, 94–95, 103, 111, 137–39
Inflation, 92–96, 100–102, 111–12
Instituto de Estudios Peruanos, 73, 155
Instituto Latinoamericano de Planificación Económica y Social, 73
Instituto Sanmartiniano, Argentina, 49
Inter-American Development Bank, 88, 96
Inter-American Foundation, 7, 10, 74
Interest rates, exports and, 105, 110
International monetarism, 89, 100–105, 111–13
International Monetary Fund (IMF), 89, 104–5, 111–13
International trade strategy, 89
International Work Group for Indigenous Affairs (IWGIA), 154

Jackman, Robert, 132
Japan, exports from, 107
Jaruzelski, General, 38
Jelin, Elizabeth, 125, 140
Jews, Cuban, 188
Judicial systems, 26, 36, 38, 85

Kahl, Joseph, 137
Katz, Friedrich, 61
Kaufman, Robert, 77, 80, 84
Kelly, Jonathan, 55
Kicza, John, 48
Klein, Herbert, 35, 55
Kling, Merle, 66f, 74
Knight, Franklin, 18, 20
Korea, 99, 107–10 *passim*
Korean War, 92ff, 110
Krauze, Enrique, 60

Labor force: peasants in, 41, 44, 59, 145, 151, 155–57, 195; studies of, 57, 74; international division of, 82, 137–38; wage disparities, 98, 105, 114–15; migrant, 125, 157, 159; underground economies and, 137–41 *passim*
Ladurie, Emmanuel Leroy, 14
Laissez-faire theory, 105
Land tenure, 47, 50, 91, 93, 159
Larson, Brooke, 44
Las Casas, Fray Bartolomé de, 153
Latin-American Social Science Council (CLACSO), 125
Latin American Studies Association (LASA), 6f, 121, 148, 187
Law of one price, 100, 102
Leadership, 83
Lechner, Norbert, 74, 137
Lenin (Ulyanov, Vladimir Ilyich), 54
León-Portilla, Miguel, 38
Le Riverend, Julio, 19
Lewin, Linda, 27
Lewis, Oscar, 145
Lezama Lima, José, 166, 171
Lievano Aguirre, Indalecio, 54
Linguistics, 154, 179
Linowitz Commission, 187
Literature, 4, 163–82, 219; society and, 6, 167, 177; nationalization and, 7, 172; history, 29, 174; modernization and, 67–68, 72, 173, 175; Latin America, 70; Cuban Revolution and, 164; ideological markings, 164; trends in, 164; boom, 164f, 169; resources for, 165; effect of publish or perish policy, 166; universal codes, 168; poetry, 168, 174; periodicals, 168–69; critical journals, 168–69, 173, 175; reception in the West, 171; of exile, 171–72; internationalization of, 172; cult figures, 172–73; generational studies in, 174; periodization of, 174; research in, 174; struc-

turalism and, 175; dictatorial regimes in, 176; thematic analyses, 176; non-Spanish speaking countries and, 176–77; testimonial, 177; women writers, 177; theater and, 177–78; colonial, 178, 181; definition of, 179; traditional genres, 179; Central American, 180; critical expansion, 180; church and, 194; dependency writings and, 197; authoritarianism in, 198; narrative experimentation, 220; Chicano, 221. See also specific authors, works
Lockhart, James, 45
Lofstrom, William, 52
Lombardi, John, 48
Losada, Alejandro, 174
Love, Joseph L., 2, 26
Lowenthal, Abraham F., 65, 69
Low-income groups, 123, 125, 151
Luxemburg, Rosa, 134
Lynch, John, 35, 37, 49, 53

McAlister, Lyle, 37
McLeod, Murdo, 45
Magno de Carvalho, 125
Mallon, Florencia, 50, 58f
Mandel, Ernest, 134
Market economy, 58–59, 90–91, 96, 98
Marrero, Levi, 19
Marshall Plan, 92
Martí, José, 173
Martínez Peláez, Severo, 40, 44
Martz, John, 69f
Marx, Karl Heinrich, 44
Marxism, 19, 32, 147, 151, 157, 160, 167
Matos Mar, José, 145f, 155
Maurras, Charles, 54
Maxwell, Kenneth, 22
Maya Indians, 39–43 passim, 47
Mayer, John, 136
Medical anthropology, 158
Meillassoux, Claude, 147

Merkx, Gilbert, 77f, 126
Messianism, 27
Mexico: revolution, 3–4; silver age in, 14; history of, 33, 41, 46, 47–48, 60ff, 154; economy of, 33, 47–48, 104, 107, 111, 113; Indian groups of, 38–40, 145; Aztec, 39, 41; administration of, 46, 137, 150; Bajío, 47, 50; local scholars, 73; industry in, 126, 137; cultural pluralism, 151; ethnolinguistics, 154
Meyer, Michael C., 2
Miceli, Sergio, 34
Migrant labor, 57, 74, 82, 128, 137, 147, 158–60
Military organizations, 26, 37, 68f, 83, 118, 123ff, 196
Mining, 45
Mishkin, Bernard, 145
Misquito Indians, 151
Mobility, 140
Modernization, 67–72 passim, 98, 141, 173, 175. See also specific programs
Monetarism, international, 100–109, 206
Money supply, inflation and, 117
Montoya, Rodrigo, 58, 155
Moreno Fraginals, Manuel, 19ff
Morin, Claude, 47
Morse, Richard, 16, 57
Mota, Carlos Guilherme, 25ff
Multinational corporations, 5, 74f, 98, 126ff, 142, 200
Murra, John, 44

Nabuco, Joaquim, 24
Nahum, Benjamin, 56, 58
Native populations, see Indians
Neostructuralism, 111–15, 208
Neruda, Pablo, 173
Nicaragua, 64, 99, 180
Notary records, 45
Novaes, Fernando, 22–25 passim

O'Donnell, Guillermo, 72, 81, 137
Oil economy, 88, 106

Open economy, 118
Ortíz, Fernando, 18
Ospina Vázquez, Luis, 56

Palacios, Marco, 56
Paraiba, Brazil, 27
Parliamentary regimes, 86
Pastore, José, 125, 140
Paz, Octavio, 169
Peasants: history of, 41, 44; culture of, 59, 145, 151, 155–57; studies of, 68, 128, 195
Pereira de Queiroz, Maria Isaura, 27
Pérez de la Riva, Juan, 20
Perlman, Janice, 137
Perón, Juan, 117
Perroux, François, 44
Peru: regional studies, 36–37; history of, 37, 43–44, 50–56 *passim*; economy of, 56, 112; local scholars in, 73; Indian groups of, 145; migrants, 158. See also Andean zone
Peru-Cornell Vicos Project, 155
Pérus, Françoise, 175
Phelan, John L., 23f, 36f
Pinochet regime, 11
Plantation society, 18–19, 32
Platt, Christopher, 51
Pluralism, 40
Poetry, 168, 174
Poitiers Seminars, 169
Political conflicts, 53
Political history, Spanish American, 5–6, 48–55
Political parties, 68, 74, 82–83
Political science, 5–7, 63–86
Poma, Guaman, 43
Poniatowska, Elena, 177
Popular culture, 8, 179
Population growth, 46, 73–74
Populism, 28, 31, 75, 124
Portes, Alejandro, 10
Portugal, 21–34 *passim*
Positivism, 60
Post-structuralists, 165, 175
Prado, Caio, Jr., 32

Presidentialism, 86
Price controls, 92, 109f, 114
Project Camelot, 74
Protectionism, 90, 101, 106
Psychoanalysis, 167
Public-sector planning, 112, 117
Puerto Rico, 18
Puig, Manuel, 172

Raczinsky, Dagmar, 125
Railways, 56
Rama, Angel, 175
Rama Indians, 151
Ramirez, Sergio, 180
Ranis, Peter, 68
Reagan, Ronald, 117
Reception, theory of, 179
Redemocratization, 129
Redfield, Robert, 145
Reformism, inadequacy of, 88
Religious history, 27, 64, 68, 194
Remmer, Karen, 77f, 126
Research methods, 68, 73, 78–83 *passim*, 202
Retamar, Fernández, 175
Rey, Phillipe, 147
Ribeiro, Darcy, 150, 155
Ricard, Robert, 39
Roa Bastos, Augusto, 169
Rock, David, 55
Rostow, W. W., 32f
Rubinson, Richard, 133
Rural society, 47

Saco, José Antonio, 20
Safford, Frank, 60
Salazar Bondy, Augusto, 146
Salvador de Madariaga, 49
Salvucci, Richard, 48
Sarduy, Severo, 171f
Sassen-Koob, Saskia, 128
Schwartz, Stuart B., 23, 31
Schwartzman, Simon, 26
Scobie, James, 57
Scott, Robert, 67
Semiotics, 167, 179
Sempat Assadourian, Carlos, 44–45

Service industry, 103–4
Sierra, Justo, 40
Silver age, in Mexico, 14
Silvert, Kalman, 69f
Simonsen, Roberto, 32
Skidmore, Thomas, 27–28
Slavery, 18–25 *passim*, 29–31
Smelser, Neil, 131
Smith, Adam, 52, 91
Smith, Peter, 55
Soares, Glaucio, 137, 140
Social anthropology, 144, 147, 152, 185
Social Science Program of Central American Universities, 73
Social Science Research Council, 7, 74
Sociology, 33–34, 40, 57–58, 149; institutional survival, 5, 123, 129, 161; dependency theory in, 5, 133–35; literature and, 6; elitism, 6, 19, 31, 41f, 50–51, 55, 92–93; inter-American cooperation, 7; Latin American perspectives, 8–11, 121–47 *passim*; future of, 9, 12, 73–74, 139–42; theory of, 77; state of, 121; in U.S., 122, 134; trends in, 122–39 *passim*; military regimes, 123; research in, 123–31 *passim*, 136, 139; social mobility, 125; stratification, 125, 140; geographical specialization in, 128; political research orientation, 128–29; non-specialized nature of, 129–30; redemocratization, 129–33 *passim*; modernization studies, 131–34 *passim*; professional training programs, 139; economics effects on, 140–41. *See also* specific social groups, institutions
Soo Pang, Eul, 27
Sorj, Bernardo, 140
Sosnowski, Saúl, 4, 7, 163–82
Southern Cone: research agendas, 65; role of state in, 102, 114, 123, 196; monetarism approach, 103; fascism in, 171
Spalding, Karen, 41, 43, 47, 49, 155
Spanish America, 17–22; history of, 34, 48–62; political process in, 37, 48–55; literature of, 163
Spanish Atlantic, trade and, 35
Stabilization programs, 89, 105, 112f, 118
State administration, 25–26, 80–85, 114–15, 129, 145
Stavenhagen, Rodolfo, 145, 147
Stein, Barbara, 16
Stein, Stanley, 16, 31, 33
Stern, Steve, 43
Steward, Julian, 145
Structuralism, 88–97, 156, 167; theory of, 91–92; neostructuralism, 111–15; anthropology and, 160–61; literary criticism on, 175, 204
Students, political roles, 82
Sugar production, 19
Suma Indians, 151
Sunkel, Osvaldo, 75
Supply-side economics, 117
Survival International, 154

Taiwan, 99, 107–10 *passim*, 136
Tariffs, 90, 101
Tax, Sol, 145
Taylor, William, 41, 47
Textile industry, 33
Thorp, Rosemary, 56
Tinbergen, Jan, 116f
Tinker Foundation, 7
Transnational corporations, 5, 74f, 98, 126ff, 142, 200
Tutino, John, 47, 50

Underdevelopment, causes of, 133
United Nations Economic Commission for Latin America (ECLA), 145
United States: foreign policy of, 67, 74, 80; sociology of, 121–42 *passim*; immigrants in, 126, 178

Urbanization, 5; poverty and, 8, 126, 128; history of, 57; development and, 74, 124f, 195; politics and, 126, 200; economy and, 138–41 *passim*; anthropology and, 158
Uricochea, Fernando, 26
Uruguay, 50, 56f, 64, 76

Valenzuela, Arturo, 6, 9, 12, 63–86, 159
Vallejo, César, 173
Van Young, Eric, 47, 50
Vargas Llosa, Mario, 165
Vázquez, Mario, 155
Velasco government, 156
Véliz, Claudio, 16
Venezuela, 49, 64
Vezzetti, Hugo, 60
Vidal, Hernán, 175
Vietnam War, 147
Villa, Pancho, 61
Villalobos, Sergio, 51
Villoro, Luis, 49
La Vision des vaincus (Wachtel), 43

Voluntary associations, 158

Wachtel, Nathan, 38, 43
Wage disparities, 98, 105, 114–15
Wagley, Charles, 2
Wallerstein, Immanuel, 134
Walsh, Rodolfo, 177
Walton, John, 138
Wilkie, James, 55
Wolf, Eric, 145
Womack, John, 61
Women, role of, 6, 124–25, 158–59
Wood, Bryce, 2
Wood, Charles, 140
Woodrow Wilson International Center for Scholars, 7, 74
World Bank, 108, 110
World economy, 137
World-system theory, 134–35, 141
Worseley, Claude Peter, 147
Writers, 165, 171–77 *passim*. See *also* Literature

Zapata, Emiliano, 61